D1621201

The Nature of Trout

by
Nick Giles

Illustrated by
Trevor Harrop

Foreword by
Brian Clarke

Perca Press

First Published in 2005 by
Perca Press
50 Lake Road
Verwood, Dorset
BH31 6BX
Tel: 01202 824245
E-mail gilesassociates@btinternet.com

ISBN 0-9543239-1-2

Illustration credits
Trevor Harrop
Ray White
Edward Fahy

The Nature of Trout was printed in the UK by:
Dayfold Ltd, Verwood, Dorset, BH31 6BE.

Contents

Thanks

Thanks to Brian Clarke for his foreword, to John Williams and Fred Scourse (Wild Trout Trust), Dr Dick Shelton (Atlantic Salmon Trust), Paul Knight (Salmon and Trout Association) and to Beth Duris (editor of Trout Unlimited's TROUT magazine) for providing reference material. Thanks to Peter Gathercole for the cover image and to Dr Guy Mawle for his photograph of a River Usk brown trout and to Trevor Harrop for drawing it and the other fine illustrations. Dr Edward Fahy provided the detailed sea trout scale drawing, first published in 'Child of the Tides' and Dr Ray White kindly allowed us to use his excellent stream habitat drawings, first published in 1967. Ray White, Pat O'Reilly, Dr Brian Shields, Shaun Leonard, Trevor Harrop, Ian Watson and Helen Giles provided constructive criticism of early text drafts. Will Giles wrote an Excel macro to calculate trout length for weight comparisons. Tom Giles supplied moral support when various tasks seemed formidable. Special thanks to Helen Giles for expert proof reading, innumerable improvements in the final text and patience over late night returns from fishing trips!

The text for this book proved to be so long that we decided to split it into this volume and a second book on fishery habitat problems and their solutions which is in preparation for publication by Perca Press.

Dedication

To all those good folk who help to conserve aquatic habitats and their wildlife.

Foreword

Salmo trutta is under pressure everywhere. Just as black industrial pollution is on the wane, so new threats, sinister and often invisible, are looming. They arise from our perfectly natural, everyday human ambitions: from our wish for cheap and plentiful food and energy, for comfortable homes, for fast and convenient transport, for a myriad labour-saving devices and all else. And they are taking a dreadful toll.

Diffuse pollution from intensive farming (including the use of insecticides which kill fly life, fertilisers which promote algal growth and the introduction of hormone-mimicking chemicals that can feminise male fish) is a pervasive threat.

Locally, abstraction (which not only reduces living space directly but kills off valuable plant life and causes silts to choke spawning beds) is not far behind. General habitat degradation – from historical neglect, from cattle encroachment, from land drainage schemes and all else – is a widespread problem. There are plenty more.

Most anglers know little about any of this. Indeed, anglers as a group are oblivious to anything that is not under their rod-tops and will be the first to be surprised when fish show their lack of enthusiasm for it all by turning belly-up, dead.

With The Nature of Trout Nick Giles has left his readers with no bolt-hole or excuse for not grasping the manifold pressures on his vibrant subject – and for not doing all they can to alleviate them. The bone and sinew of his book – the biology and behaviour of trout, the status of different trout stocks, the threats to wild fish populations, the measures that might be taken to counter such threats and to improve existing habitats – draws on his background as a biologist and his personal experience as a fisheries consultant. He fleshes it all out in an unconventional way, leavening the technical content with stories of his own angling experiences and the conclusions he draws from them. He communicates it all in simple, clear, lay language.

The Nature of Trout is an unusual book, part technical treatise, part reminiscence; part primer on trout for anglers and part primer on angling for those already in the trout business. It is packed with information and I commend it.

Brian Clarke.

CHAPTER 1
IN THE BEGINNING

DURING their varied natural life cycles, wild trout migrate to reach better habitats within river systems and to and from the sea. People do similar things. In 1960, my father moved jobs from maritime Plymouth, Devon to inland Bath, Somerset, transporting me at a tender age from a marine to a freshwater environment and from a city to the countryside. The Mendip climate was noticeably cooler, especially during the arctic winter of 1962/63 when we had snow half-way up the front door, but it was great for sledging. To my mother's irritation, washing hung out to dry in summer was speckled with dust carried on the wind from the working coal mines but, despite industrial impacts, the nature of the north Somerset countryside held a magnetic attraction for a small boy keen to learn its ways. Scrambling over coal mine spoil heaps my new-found friends and I discovered fossil ferns and fragments of tree bark. Digging in local limestone quarries, we unearthed perfectly-preserved fossil clams, ammonites and squid beaks. Perhaps most tantalising of all, the little River Somer at the bottom of our new garden contained a healthy population of wild brown trout. These and other, smaller, fish could be seen flitting over the gravel and rising for flies on summer evenings. As I gradually ventured out into this little haven, I soon learned to recognise the varied fish and the kingfishers that hunted them, the dragonflies and the water voles, grass snakes, slow worms and frogs. I entered a new watery world which enveloped me with its fascination. Over the next decade, armed with a small, green, solid fibreglass spinning rod (a Milbro Spinwell, kindly given to me by my Uncle Danny), a terribly tangle-prone Intrepid Tru Spin fixed spool reel and a can of worms, I wandered stretches of this stream, sheep dog at heel, peering through vegetation to glimpse wary trout. The brook was cluttered with hazel and bramble thickets, alder and willow beds, littered with dead wood, fallen branches and other assorted natural debris – little room to cast a fly, even if I had had the tackle. Clear water upstream-worming proved absorbing, required a fair degree of skill from a youngster and was, occasionally, successful. I learned how to fish by trial and error and through reading epic angling adventures in second-hand copies of Creel magazine, edited by Bernard Venables. What a great publication that was. My trout fishing became, in my mind's eye, akin to salmon fishing on the mighty River Tay or drifting around on a Norfolk Broad after huge primeval pike: such is the active imagination of a small boy who loves fishing.

Sometimes, using my standard free-lining tackle, I drifted big bushy dry flies down under bushes, waiting for a swirl or splash to indicate a take. The trout were all wild, a big one weighing a pound although 'pound and a halfers' weren't unknown. We put back anything weighing less than about 12 ounces – natural catch-and-release behaviour. This form of conservation was really enlightened self-interest – if you wanted to catch big fish next season, you didn't kill the small ones. Larger fish were ceremoniously carried home, wrapped in wet dock leaves, for parental approval and consumption. Even after all these years, I still have my willow creel, bought in Crudgington's of Bath, and it still smells faintly of trout.

When you are young, time expands to fill the exploration available and I spent many happy hours wandering in the Somerset countryside. During the course of all this fishing I noticed that individual trout were seen in the same feeding places time and again. They chased away interlopers and were extremely wary, bolting for cover at the first sign of danger. Favourite lies always had good cover close by – usually the underwater roots of willows or alders or a waterlogged deadwood snag. Big fish were hard to approach without scaring, let alone catching them, teaching me the value of stealth in fishing. If a big trout was caught and taken for the pot, a new one, usually a bit smaller, would move swiftly in to take its place. Good lies seemed to be at a premium.

The sparkling gravel shallows thronged with small trout and minnows, thriving in a clean environment. Once I saw brook lampreys spawning – I had previously unearthed lamprey larvae in silty stream edges, but failed to recognise them, thinking that they were small eels. In late May each year there was a prolific hatch of mayflies, eagerly gobbled down by trout, mallards, wagtails and flycatchers. Through the long summers the meadows buzzed with grasshoppers and bobbed with butterflies; in the evenings the air hummed with caddis flies and moths which were harried by pipistrelles and other bats. The few cattle that grazed the damp meadows watched lazily as hares browsed the sward, green woodpeckers probed for ants, kestrels and barn owls hunted voles. Foxes, badgers and water voles were abundant and, if you were quiet and kept your eyes open, you could watch them for ages. While off on my bike one morning I overtook a badger padding quietly along the lane – I wished him 'good morning' and he grunted a reply before scarpering through a hole in the hedge. How much more valuable are experiences like that to a child than hours spent looking at a television or computer screen? I didn't realise at the time how lucky I was to live in rural Somerset where farming was less intensive than it is now; the fields weren't drenched in pesticides and not too many people lived close by 'our' stream.

Gradually, I learned the fundamentals of how habitat availability determines how many wild trout a stream can hold. Lots of good lies with plenty of cover meant lots of decent-sized trout. Long, open or densely-shaded uniform stretches – not many trout. Deep corner pools with undercut banks and alder roots – one or two big trout. Gravel shallows with lots of big stones or weed for cover – lots of young trout and young crayfish amongst the weeds. Not rocket science but valid and useful. By the time I was in my early teens my fellow brook fishers, Jeff King, Chris Yeats and I had graduated into trying to improve 'our' brook by making better habitat. This entailed rolling boulders around to form little weirs which created depth and scour, forming new trout lies. Adult crayfish also appreciated the nooks and crannies in and around these boulder weirs. I kept a crayfish in a tank in my bedroom for a couple of years; he hid under a plant pot and ate worms. Eventually I put him back in the stream, but not before I learned how he grew by reversing out of his old shell and then expanding into his new one before it hardened-off. Amazing!

On hot summer days, weir building was much more fun than fishing, especially as the boulders were plastered with invertebrates of differing shapes, sizes and behaviour. Flattened mayfly nymphs gripped the underside of stones in fast water and caddis larvae built amazing cases of sand, gravel, tiny snail shells, twigs and leaves – more fascination for a boy with an in-built love of Nature. Once, whilst lying on my stomach in the long grass, I watched a water shrew clad in an envelope of silver bubbles swim down and turn stones over, foraging for caddis larvae and shrimps. Underwater holes in the bank had crayfish antennae poking out whilst those above water harboured voles, mice, shrews, wasp nests and bumble bee colonies.

Whilst wandering in this paradise we watched kestrels, sparrowhawks, herons, kingfishers, flycatchers, wagtails and wrens going about their everyday business. Butterflies of many species were common, as were damsel and dragonflies. Water voles (which we mistakenly called water rats) scuttled busily amongst reed and rush beds, paddling across the stream carrying mouthfuls of reed back to their burrows. If you remained still, a myopic vole might come and sit right next to your boots while it munched reed stems. These bumbling small mammals must have made easy meals for stalking herons. Sadly, in recent years, they have often made meals for mink and are now an endangered species as a consequence. In the 1960s grass snakes swam across pools and along stream margins in search of the abundant frogs and minnows. In the drier sandy hollows, slow worms were a common sight, as were lizards and warty old toads. Wherever you looked there was something fascinating to watch: ecology grabbed me so securely that I remain hooked, never to be released.

Disaster and re-birth

One summer, our beloved brook was devastated by a mystery pollution that killed many of the trout and much of the invertebrate life. We were both heart-broken and enraged. A major lesson was the realisation that some whopping trout (two pounders!) had been there all the time and we hadn't even seen them, let alone caught them. To count them now, belly-up and stinking, was a hard lesson in the fragility of Nature. Slowly, the trout stock recovered, but the writing was on the wall and, gradually, the water lost its sparkle, the crayfish dwindled, the trout became scarce and dense algal growths blanketed the bed. Fewer nymphs lived under the stones, fewer flies hatched and the flycatchers and wagtails departed. The brook and the Wilderness (as we called it) were succumbing to 'progress'. In my lifetime the world human population has more than doubled and the impact on our environment shows. I had forgotten how deeply the Brook's decline had saddened me until I read Brian Clarke's 'The Stream' (2000); a fine evocation of how a trout stream can suffer at the hands of developers. It is worth reading.

As I sit writing this (summer 2004) I have in front of me a copy of Salmo trutta volume 7 – the annual magazine of the Wild Trout Trust, edited by John Williams. On page 59 there is an article by John de Cesare on the upper Wellow Brook, near Bath, Somerset, close to my old stamping ground, but further downstream. John recounts his long experience of this brook and its trials and tribulations. The old management of alder coppicing had been neglected for fifty years, leaving an over-shaded stream, tunnelled by foliage in summer. Until as recently as twenty years ago, poorly treated sewage effluent still polluted the stream and water was abstracted in summer reducing flows and the ability of the brook to dilute pollution. Even in the early 1990s, a stinking summer sludge coated the bed of the pools. This hideous onslaught thinned out both the wild trout and the anglers. The Wellow Brook Fly Fishing Syndicate, decided to stock the water annually with Loch Leven strain hatchery-raised brown trout. Between sixty and one hundred of them from one to two pounds were introduced, plus occasional bigger fish. Despite the presence of these predatory whoppers, the dear old Wellow Brook still produced annual returns of several hundred brownies, mostly wild fish, caught and released. Despite the obvious habitat degradation, the tenacious yellow-bellied wild trout with their beautiful red and black spotted flanks were still hanging-on in there. Most were the nine to twelve inch fish that I remember so well and occasional lunkers still reached a foot and a half, just as they did when I was a lad.

The Syndicate wanted very much to conserve their wild trout and to manage the brook so as to improve its overall quality. In common with so many trout fishers and, indeed, anglers the world over, they have the best interests of their fishery very much at heart. A habitat improvement programme was launched with the help of the Environment Agency. As fortune would have it, in 2000, John came along to an evening lecture that I gave on trout stream management and he went home with the firm intention of adding further impetus and ideas to the Wellow Brook rehabilitation programme. During a day's fishing on the brook with John Williams, John de Cesare learnt of the Wild Trout Trust advisory visit service and I was duly invited along on a well-attended river walk during which I surveyed the habitat quality, imparted information to the keen trouters present and followed this up a few days later with a formal Advisory Report. Now, the syndicate really had the bit between their collective teeth and the roar of a chainsaw could be heard along the Wellow Valley. Alders were carefully coppiced to let light into specific stream reaches and newly-jetted (de-silted) gravel riffles lay ready to incubate wild trout eggs over winter. Habitat quality was on the up.

The aim of this programme is to create a mixed-mosaic of well-lit, dappled shade and deeply shaded areas, each harbouring its characteristic wildlife. The Syndicate has stopped stocking large trout, the stream is fished with renewed enthusiasm, wild trout are caught and released and, with more diverse habitats available, the conservation value of the brook has increased, for the wildlife, for anglers and for the general public who enjoy walking the valley. All of this has happened through the enthusiasm and hard work of a band of interested fishermen and women. The Somerset brooks that I wandered as a teenager still have their wild trout and I hope they always will. With good management to optimise habitat quality, they can become better than ever!

The state of British trout fisheries

As a freelance fisheries consultant, I get to see a lot of water and to meet lots of visionary folk who want to improve things. One volunteer is worth at least ten conscripts and a lot can be done when you combine sound advice with enthusiastic endeavour. Many of the problems surrounding trout fisheries revolve around maintaining or improving habitat quality. Superficially, this may seem easy, but adverse influences on wild trout are often subtle and insidious, creeping up and taking the fish unawares. Assessing the health of the trout stock and the key factors likely to be limiting trout abundance are of prime importance and, because trout fisheries vary enormously, each requires a tailor-made assessment. Some wild trout waters are still seen to be doing well whilst others have clearly declined in recent decades. How can we get an overview of the current health of trout stocks in the British Isles?

In 1972 the Freshwater Biological Association published an identification key to freshwater fishes, written by Dr Peter Maitland. On page 88 there was a preliminary map showing brown trout distribution in the British Isles. Brown trout were amongst the most widely distributed fish species throughout England, Wales, Scotland and Ireland. In 2004 the Centre for Ecology & Hydrology, Environment Agency and Joint Nature Conservation Committee published a distribution atlas of fishes in England, Wales and Scotland, showing that, 30 years after Maitland's original maps, the distribution of brown and sea trout remained largely unchanged. Earlier, in 2002 the Environment Agency published research on an inventory of trout stocks and fisheries in England and

Wales, noting that brown trout fry and parr densities are generally higher in rivers of the north and west than in the rest of the country. Of 291 sub-catchments surveyed, 41% were classified as supporting 'excellent' or 'good' densities of trout fry, but only 25% held comparable densities of trout parr. Trout fry were, however, present in 78% and trout parr in 90% of the sub-catchments sampled. Trout fry appear to be more abundant in rivers supporting large sea trout fisheries, for example, the Tywi and Teifi in Wales. River catchments in the south east of England generally have low or zero wild trout production and often rely, therefore, completely on stocking to sustain angling interest.

In their 'Our Nations' Fisheries' (2004), the Environment Agency states that brown trout are found in half of our river catchments and that the overall habitat quality at breeding sites is improving. Around 70% of total river length in England and Wales has brown or sea trout present and trout streams tend to be concentrated in north and south-west England and in Wales. Trout are to be found almost everywhere in Welsh rivers. However, distribution maps tell us little about actual trout abundance and it is stated that, in England and Wales, only 'up to a quarter' of rivers contain wild brown trout stocks. Much of the observed trout distribution must, therefore, be comprised of stocked fish - what a sorry state of affairs! Where have so many of the wild trout gone?

There are moves afoot to improve the understanding of wild trout abundance through better designed and analysed fisheries surveys and through the analysis of fishing log books. Factors such as low-flows from excessive water abstraction, siltation, acidification and other forms of pollution, arterial river dredging and flood defence schemes, a lack of skilful habitat management and declining fly life have seriously impacted river trout fisheries. These factors must be addressed effectively, and the sooner the better, if we are to improve the lot of our wild trout.

The detailed ecology of natural British still water trout fisheries remains largely a mystery in terms of both fish abundance and population biology. Natural lake systems have, however, undoubtedly suffered from extensive wetland drainage, water abstraction, damage to inflowing spawning streams and increased nutrient inputs from both agriculture and treated sewage effluent sources. The over-enrichment (eutrophication) of freshwaters, both flowing and still, with nutrients such as phosphorus and nitrogen is a widespread and serious problem. What were once clear-watered, insect-rich trout havens are often now algae-clogged, turbid, silty carp-stocked lakes and pools. I have nothing against carp fisheries, but I think that they are best located in natural coarse fish zones, leaving the cooler, cleaner, usually less productive waters to be the natural domain of salmonid fishes. As with rivers, trout lakes need looking after and it is so easy to lose them to the pressures of development. Once degraded, they are not easy to restore.

The EU Water Framework Directive will require the British Government to instigate better monitoring of our large natural lakes and of our rivers and streams. This should, in turn, improve our understanding of their wild trout and other fish stocks. By the year 2015, all rivers in Europe should be of 'good' ecological and chemical quality. What constitutes good quality is an important question. The preliminary view of the Environment Agency is that only five per cent of rivers and eighteen per cent of lakes are likely to make the grade and that it may cost £12 billion to meet Water Framework Directive standards across England and Wales alone. Twelve billion pounds is a lot of money, but our aquatic environment is priceless. Much scientific effort will be required to assess habitat quality and the health of fish stocks and other wildlife and then much more to implement necessary improvements.

Whilst we have an incomplete knowledge of wild trout distribution and abundance in the British Isles, there is no doubt that this valuable and popular fish declined very substantially during the last Century, especially in southeast England (Giles, 1989, 1992). The challenge is to reverse that change. I'm pleased to say that the Environment Agency's National Trout and Grayling Strategy (2004) should help progress salmonid conservation and sustainable management. Despite generating substantial fishing licence income, trout have been an under-funded fisheries 'Cinderella' for far too long. Widespread stocking of hatchery-produced brown trout occurs in many areas of the UK to compensate for dwindling wild trout populations. Stocked fisheries play a vital role in providing recreational pleasure for many thousands of anglers and it is important that further research is carried out to find ways to improve stocking practices to maximise cost-effectiveness and minimise potential ecological impacts. I will return to this important topic later.

Compared with brown trout, British sea trout appear to be holding their own in those rivers where they still exist. This may be due in part to the fact that sea trout do not seem to undergo long oceanic migrations, perhaps preferring to forage inshore relatively close to their natal rivers. Contrast this with salmon from British rivers which typically migrate far north to feed off the Faroes or West Greenland. Salmon survival at sea has been very poor in recent decades, but sea trout marine survival would appear to have been rather better. Perhaps oceanic habitats have been markedly less supportive of maturing salmon whilst inshore areas have remained more suitable for sea trout. W. R. Turrell (1993) notes that warm phases of climate tend to be related to poor European salmon catches. He warns, however, that sea trout may also be vulnerable to the vagaries of the British climate and that variable weather could have an important bearing on sea trout smolt survival and marine growth. There is some evidence of British migratory trout returning earlier and at smaller sizes than in previous seasons and this needs monitoring. Sea trout smolts in some areas have had terrible problems with sea lice infestations, probably associated with marine salmon farms (Gargan et al, 2002); this, too requires continuing research. A first international symposium on sea trout biology, held in Cardiff in July 2004, led to the following preliminary conclusions (IFM FISH magazine, autumn 2004):

- Sea trout stocks appear healthy in some regions but have collapsed in others.
- Sea trout stocks need better protection and conservation throughout their varied range of natural habitats. Catches need better monitoring, management regulations may require tightening and potential impacts from trout stocking require consideration.
- The economic and social values of sea trout fisheries require further research.
- Better funding for important long-term research on sea trout biology is needed.

The 2002 Fisheries Statistics Review from the Environment Agency states that the (declared) sea trout rod catch for England and Wales was just under 50,000, the highest recorded since 1987 and 20% above the five-year average. This is good news. The conservation ethic amongst sea trout anglers is growing: in 2002, some 51% of rod-caught sea trout were released. Rivers in England and Wales producing more than 1000 sea trout to rods in 2002 included the Tyne, Wear, Ribble, Lune, Eden, Border Esk, Fowey, Camel, Tywi (Towy), Teifi, Dyfi (Dovey), Mawddach, Glaslyn and Dwyfawr. Of these, the famous Welsh rivers Teifi and Tywi were head-and-shoulders above the rest in terms of numbers of sea trout (sewin) caught. The heaviest rod-caught sea trout, on average, in England and Wales came from the Sussex Adur and the Dorset Stour (both 2kg, or more - well over four pounds). Amongst the commercial sea trout net fisheries, the following produced fish which averaged over 2kg weight in 2002: the North East coastal drift nets, Christchurch Harbour

(Hampshire Avon & Dorset Stour), Poole Harbour (Rivers Frome & Piddle), the Tywi, Taf, Dyfi, Glaslyn, Welsh Dee, Ribble & Lune (drift nets), Leven (Lave nets) and the Eden (Coop nets).

The 2003 Fisheries Statistics Report (the most recent available at the time of writing) includes the following information:

- The total sea trout rod catch was just over 45,000 (weighing 38 tonnes) of which 54% were released. This catch was lower than the 2002 catch but equal to the previous five year average.
- Over 29,000 sea trout (52 tonnes) were netted; around 25% fewer than the previous five year average.
- Since 1985 the number of net licences issued had decreased by 54%.
- The rod fishing effort in 2003 was 6% down on 2002, probably due to the low late summer flows prevailing in many rivers.
- The most productive sea trout rivers for angling were the Teifi, Lune, Tyne, Camel and Dyfi with July generally being the best month on most of these rivers.
- In 2003, 60% of angled sea trout were caught on fly, 20% on spinner, 18% on bait and 2% on undefined methods.

UK rod-caught record game fish

As of December 2003, the following UK rod-caught records were accepted by the British Record (rod caught) Committee:

Wild brown trout, 31 pounds 12 ounces (14.4kg) by Brian Rutland from Loch Awe, Argyll, Scotland.
Cultivated brown trout, 28 pounds 1 ounce (12.73kg) by D. Taylor from Dever Springs trout fishery, Hampshire.
Cultivated rainbow trout, 36 pounds 14 ounces (16.7kg), by

C.White from Dever Springs trout fishery, Hampshire.
Sea trout, 28 pounds five ounces (12.85kg) by J. Farrent, from Calshot Spit, River Test, Hampshire.
American brook trout (cultivated), 8 pounds 3 ounces by E. Holland from Fontburn Reservoir, Northumberland.
Arctic char, 9 pounds 8 ounces (4.3kg) by W. Fairburn from Loch Arkaig, Inverness, Scotland.
Atlantic salmon, 64 pounds (29.3kg) by Miss G. Ballantyne, River Tay, Scotland.
Grayling, 4 pounds 3 ounces (1.9kg) by S. Lanigan, River Frome, Dorset.

Larger specimens of some of these species are known to have been caught, but have failed to comply with the regulations for acceptance by the rod-caught record fish committee. It is worth noting, for instance, that Dr Tom Sanctuary caught grayling from the Wiltshire River Nadder of 4lb 9oz on a red quill in 1883 and 4lb 8oz on a dark olive in 1884 and a 4lb 12oz fish from the Hampshire Avon at Britford in 1885, but he cheated with the last one, catching it whilst netting for coarse fish! The fish was returned alive, see Hayter, 2002. With the notable exception of the salmon, all of the current official record fish were captured relatively recently, indicating continuing opportunities for anglers to write their names into the record books. It is, however, a sign of the times that cultivated categories have been included in these famous lists. Fishing is a popular fresh air pastime and long may it remain so. With an increasing interest in wild trout fishing, how can we make the sport accessible to the maximum number of anglers whilst still conserving this valuable natural resource?

Exploitation: how should we harvest wild trout?

The management of exploitation of salmon and trout stocks requires an understanding of what makes the populations tick; how current stocks relate to future recruitment into the fishery. We need to know how abundant fish are at the moment and what proportion of the stock it is safe to harvest, leaving a population that is resilient and sustainable in the long-term. These various parameters can be estimated, given adequate information, but good quality information on fish stocks is generally lacking. This leads to the need for computer modelled scenarios, using the meagre data available from all too few rivers. This is an imprecise art and, as a direct consequence, results generally carry a health warning. It is often necessary to invoke the precautionary principle in order to conserve important natural resources that might otherwise be damaged or lost through bad management. Readers interested in the technical background to these important topics are referred to the recent paper by Ted Potter & colleagues (2003), listed in the bibliography.

There is a great ongoing debate over whether commercial netting of sea trout represents the best use of the resource. Many argue that the economic value of rod-caught fish far exceeds that of commercially netted fish, but much depends upon local circumstances. Netsmen may be willing to forego netting if fairly compensated. There will, however, be cases where nets actually exploit components of a fish stock that anglers hardly ever fish for. An example would be the late-running sea trout found on some river systems. All assessments of the relative merits of rod versus net fisheries must be done on a case-by-case basis: local conditions and circumstances are of critical importance. Current Environment Agency Policy (2004) in England and Wales is to optimise the economic and social value of the sustainable exploitation of fish stocks. The Agency will assist rod and net fishers to reach mutually acceptable agreements in those circumstances where rod fishing interests are willing to compensate netsmen for ceasing to fish. Where rod and / or net exploitation of sea trout is believed to be responsible for preventing a stock from meeting its conservation target (the estimated sustainable population level), the Environment Agency will introduce appropriate measures to restrict catches in an attempt to facilitate a stock recovery.

Economics

Trout angling is not the preserve of the rich and can often be an inexpensive sport, especially where wild stocks abound and where fishing pressure is modest. In the west of Ireland where, arguably, the best brown trout fishing in the British Isles is to be had, the fishing is free! Trout fisheries are, nevertheless, economically important and of considerable capital value. In England and Wales the value of fishing rights on trout fisheries exceeds an estimated £500 million - about five times the value of salmon fisheries (Environment Agency, 2004). I don't have a comparable figure for North American waters, but Christopher Hunter, writing in 1991, estimated that there may have been ten million trout anglers in North America by the turn of the twenty first century. Even if he was optimistic, there are still a fair few trouty fisher folk out there, world-wide. Trout fisheries are, therefore, worth conserving, not only for their utility and natural beauty, but for the rural jobs and small businesses they support. In this light it is perhaps surprising just how many wild trout fisheries have been allowed to become polluted, wrecked by various forms of physical habitat damage, over-exploited or tarnished by intensive stocking or a lack of suitable management. Poaching can also be a big problem.

Sometimes it is only 'one for the pot', but all too often it is wholesale, with monofilament gill nets or, even worse, cyanide compounds that asphyxiate fish in their choking deadly cloud. How can mankind (or unkind) do this to such a precious natural resource?

Everything starts with habitat quality

Whilst trout fisheries often suffer from extensive damage, wild trout are tough survivors and, given adequate habitat quality, can hang in there even when conditions seem pretty dire, re-building numbers if and when conditions improve. Usually, it is we anglers who care enough to ensure that such improvements take place. Habitat restoration on trout streams is of growing interest and importance. Very good results can be achieved with well designed projects. Trout thrive in even the smallest of streams and these can sometimes be restored at very modest cost. Larger rivers usually need proportionately bigger, often collaborative projects.

Wild trout stocks rely on good habitat which in turn supports a wealth of other wetland wildlife - from the humble mayfly and bumbling water vole to the sleek, secretive otter. No true angler is happy to see fisheries brought to their knees by exploitative greed, pollution or a lack of positive management. For Man to have a future, we must learn to live sustainably. The Brundtland Report of 1987 defined sustainable development as:

"development which meets the needs of the present without compromising the ability of future generations to meet their own needs"

Putting it more simply, when it comes to the environment, don't cheat on your children.

Sustainable trout fisheries are within our grasp, we just have to decide that this is what we want as a society and then go for it. For many fisheries, cost-effective habitat restoration will be out of the question and here artificial stocking will continue to be the norm. Also, of course, on most man-made waters there is little or no potential for spawning and so, once more, stocking is the key. Stocked trout fisheries can offer excellent quality fly fishing and many waters have good stocks of fully-finned fish in fine condition which are by no means easy to catch (or so I find!) Stocking is here to stay on many trout fisheries and we are none the worse for that. However, on many more waters than is often realised, the prospect of self-sustaining wild trout fishing is achievable. To be involved in such projects is very rewarding. The first steps are to understand what trout need from their environment, how to sustain these requirements and then how to fish your stock on a long-term sustainable basis. This book aims to help you on this road.

Trout fishing provides a strong economic argument for looking after freshwaters of many types. Trout streams, rivers and lakes may otherwise be drained or deep-dredged for agriculture, polluted, over-abstracted, or filled-in for development. Anglers pay to fish, they look after fisheries and, sometimes, they are able to prosecute and win damages from polluters. In the British Isles, The Anglers Conservation Association (ACA, www.a-c-a.org) helps its members with legal advice and, where polluters can be identified, often takes on cases in the civil court on their behalf. For instance, in the first quarter of 2004 nearly £200,000 was recovered from polluters of fisheries in England and many other cases were under consideration. The ACA has a long successful history of winning compensation for anglers. For a modest annual fee, membership gives you access to their considerable expertise and advice. I recommend that you support them; you never know when disaster may strike your fishery.

Riparian owners can derive substantial long-term incomes from letting their fishing and so have a considerable interest in making sure that their waters remain in good order. Anglers, and those interested in wider conservation matters, often co-operate with owners, Government Agencies and others to develop large scale river restoration projects. In the British Isles, the Irish Central Fisheries Board, the West Galloway Fisheries Trust, the Tweed Foundation, Wye and Usk Foundation, Westcountry Rivers Trust, Wild Trout Trust, Game Conservancy Trust and many fishing clubs and associations spring to mind. These organisations deserve support and encouragement. Some River Trusts are developing fishing passport schemes which help visitors to find affordable day ticket waters and the internet is a fine way of accessing this information. Examples include the Upper Wye Passport Scheme in Wales (www.wyeuskfoundation.org.uk), the Eden Rivers Trust (www.eden-riverstrust.org.uk) of Cumbria and the Westcountry Rivers Trust who operate the similar 'Angling 2000' scheme (www.angling2000.org.uk). The Association of Rivers Trusts (www.associationofriverstrusts.org.uk) is a useful contact point for general enquiries. By encouraging farmers to open up fishing, income is generated and the worth of the river is underlined. This can lead to an increased understanding of problems, reduced habitat impacts and, in some cases, habitat improvement projects (see Environment Agency Reel Life, 2004). For example, one Devon farmer reinvested angling ticket income to instigate habitat improvements on his river. Rod catches improved from around four trout per visit in 2001 to over 14 per visit in 2003. The biggest brown trout caught rose from 12 inches in the season before the improvement work to 16 inches in the season afterwards – great! Improved habitat quality was the key to success. In the next chapter we consider some important aspects of trout ecology and what trout need in their habitats.

CHAPTER 2

HABITATS AND BIOLOGY

As WE have seen, *Salmo trutta* has one of the widest natural distributions of any freshwater fish in the British Isles and has now been introduced to new waters throughout much of the world. This is, indeed, an adaptable species. The natural range of the brown / sea trout lies primarily within Europe (Elliott, 1989), from Iceland, northern Scandinavia and Russia south to the northern Mediterranean and Atlas Mountains of North Africa and east to the Caspian Sea and Ural Mountains. The Mediterranean has no sea trout, but they occur in the Black and Caspian Seas and all along the western European seaboard from northern Spain, France, all around the British Isles, Baltic and Scandinavian coasts up into Barents and Kara Seas of the Arctic Ocean. Brown trout are readily farmed and fertile eggs are easy to transport so their spread around the globe has been rapid to over twenty five countries during the last two centuries. The late 19th Century saw eastern Russia, Australia, Tasmania, both New Zealand Islands, USA, Canada, Sri Lanka, South Africa and Kashmir receive *Salmo trutta*. Early in the 20th century brown trout were imported into several other African and South American countries including Chile and Argentina. Fisheries such as the fabulous Falkland Islands sea trout rivers were founded on artificial stockings of brown trout. Many well known North American trout waters now rely on naturalised brown trout stocks to support much of their fishing. This adaptable species has flourished in its new American homes, for instance, the Flaming Gorge Reservoir, Wyoming has produced fish in excess of 30 pounds – that's a pretty big brown trout!

Habitats

Despite this undoubted adaptability, brown trout are primarily small stream fish, preferring to spawn and live in waters where undercut banks and safe bolt-holes amongst tree roots are never far away. These small trout streams are vulnerable to a wide range of habitat damage. Whilst most people notice when there are fewer house sparrows on the back lawn or butterflies, grasshoppers and wild flowers in the hedgerows, few folk are aware of dwindling fish stocks. Fish are underwater, largely unseen and, consequently, out of mind. Even anglers can't always be sure that our suspicions of declining fish stocks are real or imagined. This is especially true when stocked trout complicate the picture. There is absolutely no doubt, however, that wild trout declined mightily in the British Isles during the last century and that many population declines and local extinctions were habitat-related. This is also true over much of their European range and in many other countries, such as the USA. Americans picked up on the need for habitat restoration a long time before the British and so much of the literature, examples and experience cited in this book and in our forthcoming book on habitat improvement are North American.

Christopher Hunter (1991) commented that, as the USA population grew, interest in trout fishing also grew, but wild trout habitat declined. By 1984 around 54 million hatchery-produced trout were stocked into the waters of 43 States at a (then) cost of $36 million. By 1988 The U.S. General Accounting Office estimated that on public rangeland in some states as many as 90% of federally-managed streams had degraded habitat quality. Since then there has been a growing movement back towards better trout habitat management, more wild trout waters, less stocking, more catch-and-release and a greater appreciation of good quality stream systems. Trout Unlimited (www.tu.org) carries the banner for much of this work in the United States and Canada. In the 2003 financial year, Trout Unlimited volunteers raised just under $6 million and donated an estimated $7 million worth of their time for North American coldwater fisheries conservation projects. That just shows the power of harnessing good will in the angling community. TU's mission statement is 'to conserve, protect and restore North America's coldwater fisheries and their watersheds'. I hope that readers of this book will consider joining (www.tu.org) as they are worth supporting. Their web site gives an impressive list of current projects.

Here in the British Isles, the successful Wild Trout Trust (www.wildtrout.org) are doing a range of positive things for brown and sea trout fisheries. Funded by membership subscriptions and sponsored by English Nature and others, the Trust provides an Advisory Service which I am pleased to help with. As I write this, a total of over a hundred and fifty of such visits have been carried out and reports written up. Some of these projects develop into full-scale fishery restoration schemes. Each year there is a competition for the best wild trout restoration projects which is something to aim for. Membership of the Trust costs a modest sum and gives you potential access to the Advisory Service.

In Scotland, The Atlantic Salmon Trust (www.atlanticsalmontrust.org) provides advice and produces valuable research work on both salmon and sea trout, published in their well known Blue Books. The Salmon and Trout Association (www.salmon-trout.org), based appropriately at Fishmonger's Hall next to London Bridge, work mainly on political lobbying to influence government policy relating to fisheries, freshwater and marine conservation issues. The Association is also actively involved in youth training programmes and in fisheries research projects.

While much of our trout fishing is, of necessity, supported by stocking, many anglers enjoy restoring habitat so their fisheries become more sustainable. Where habitat allows, rather than just stocking expensive hatchery fish every few weeks for the rest of their trout fishing lives, these anglers would rather let nature do it for them. Wild fish are the real thing and, once established, are free! Better trout habitats also provide homes for a wealth of other wildlife, enhancing the conservation values of fisheries and the pleasures derived from a day out at the waterside. The sight of a kingfisher can be as much fun as stalking a rising trout. As we know, there is more to fishing than simply catching fish.

The topics of habitat damage, fishery habitat management, stream and lake restoration are too long to include here and we are currently producing a Perca Press book on this subject. As an illustration of the power of well-targeted management, I will, however, describe the impact of livestock grazing on a trout stream and the effectiveness of a simple fencing program for trout habitat improvement.

The following diagrams were drawn by Dr Ray White for his groundbreaking publication co-authored with Dr Oscar Brynildson: Guidelines for Management of Trout Stream Habitat in Wisconsin (1967) and are used with his kind permission. The text is based largely on the captions to these illustrations in that publication. Firstly, in Figure 1, the stream is seen in heavily over-grazed condition by cattle in summer. Bare soil predominates along the broken down banks, the bed of the stream is silted with little cover and most plants are grazed to soil level. Trout have no spawning habitat, virtually no cover and very little invertebrate food. With so little shade, summer water temperatures may often be too high for trout comfort.

Figure 1.

Now, in Figure 2, the stream has been protected from heavy grazing for around three years. Cress has grown down the edges and trapped silt around its roots, grass turf covers the banks and an emergent fringe of rushes and sedges has grown further back up the bank. Water depths in the narrowed channel have increased, much of the silt has been swept away and there is abundant cover and food for trout. Spawning gravels are now uncovered amongst submerged weed beds. Whilst there is good summer cover, the stream is still bare in winter and trout egg survival is likely to be poor in the silty gravel.

Figure 2.

Figure 3 shows the stream after two more years. Gravels on the bed are now thoroughly scoured, mobile, de-silted and ideal for spawning. Grass and herbs have invaded the turf and are tying together the banks with strong root and runner systems.

Figure 3.

The resulting stabilisation of the silt means that trout egg survival will be improving. Submerged weed beds are prolific and invertebrate food for trout is abundant. Much of the channel is now shaded from the sun and vegetation provides plenty of summer cover. The stream is cool, relatively deep, swiftly-flowing and provides ample spawning habitat, shelter and food for wild trout. Self-restoration of the stream to this stage sometimes proceeds even faster than the five years indicated here.

In Figure 4, a few years later, the silt bars along the stream edge are now fully stabilized by turf root systems and the channel width has halved compared with the original diagram. The water is relatively deep and swift: year-round cover and food for trout are abundant. Submerged weeds and cress are now shaded-out to some degree by the overhanging bank side vegetation. Woody shrubs are starting to invade and dominate banks. This is excellent wild trout habitat.

Figure 4.

Ten to twenty years later, in Figure 5, woody shrubs such as hazel and goat willow, have grown up and invaded much of the channel. Saplings including alder, ash, oak and sycamore are also well established.

Figure 5.

The bankside turf is completely shaded-out, as are submerged weed beds and marginal cress, rushes and sedges. Woody debris is abundant, providing ample year-round cover and impounding flows, leading to deep water. Undercut banks are everywhere, but are vulnerable to trees falling over as they mature. Over-shading has destroyed much of the habitat quality for wild trout although large adults will seek out undisturbed sheltered areas of this type. A mixture of this type of habitat plus the preceding two stages will provide good wild trout fishing and excellent habitat diversity for wildlife in general.

Figure 6, the final stage in this natural developmental sequence ('ecological succession') is mature wet woodland. In many ways, the stream channel characteristics are similar to the initial diagram: over-wide, shallow, silty and with low biological productivity, no spawning or trout fry habitat. Letting light back in with a sky-lighting programme of tree surgery transforms this type of water back to conditions in previous diagrams.

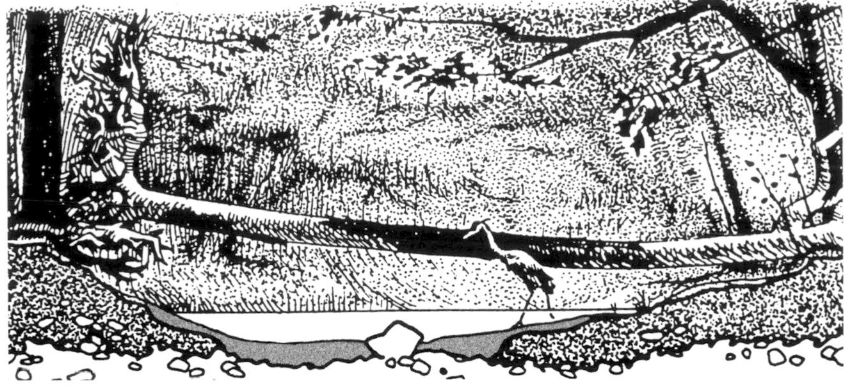

Figure 6.

Clearly, what's needed on a trout stream is to manage streamside vegetation to form habitat-mosaics of the middle stages of the above succession. This need not involve permanent fencing as stock can be moved around and excluded from differing areas at different times of year; local prescriptions for local problems. Varied habitats make for good, interesting fishing and support varied wildlife communities. Who could wish for more?

Moving between habitats

Whilst most trout parr and sub-adults live in small streams, these fish often drop back into main rivers, lakes or to the sea in order to grow to maturity. Trout grow slowly in cold, upland, low-nutrient, acid systems and more rapidly in warmer, more productive (calcium-rich) lowland habitats. Some lowland rivers are, however, too sluggish, warm and enriched for wild trout survival. Variations in growth rates and population densities of trout parr probably have an important bearing on their likelihood of migrating between differing habitats. Crowding and slow growth early in life may be a key trigger, making parr move within the river system or turn into smolts and migrate to sea. Trout are complicated creatures and we don't yet fully understand their biology.

Small stream life enables juvenile brown trout to avoid the difficulties of swimming perpetually against the strong currents found in main river channels. When they are large enough, often at an age of around two years, they drop downstream to find and defend sheltered main channel lies. It follows, of course, that if you wish to look after a wild brown trout fishery on a river or lake, you must conserve the peripheral spawning and nursery habitats which are generally too small to fish, but which are the heart of the system, pumping out young wild trout each year. The example of fencing cattle out of a small stream is a case in point. Without healthy breeding and nursery grounds, a wild trout fishery will inevitably decline. This fact is too often overlooked and the restoration of spawning streams should be a priority when trout habitat improvement projects are contemplated.

Where good quality side streams occur substantial adult brown trout populations can develop in the main rivers; the upper Wye, Severn, Teifi and Usk in the UK, provide good examples. Such rivers can also provide suitable habitats for salmon and sea trout which may spawn in the lowland main channel or in upland tributaries. Sea trout, in particular, will penetrate the smallest of headwaters in their quest for good breeding habitat. River systems such as the Scottish Tweed, Tay and Spey, Welsh Towy, Teifi and Dee and the English Dart, Lune and Tyne spring to mind as lowland corridors for successful sea trout migration to their favoured moorland streams. Good quality breeding tributaries also allow brown and sea trout stocks to flourish in natural still waters such as Lake Windermere, Loch Lomond, Loch Tay, Lough Corrib and Lough Currane. Here, young trout filter downstream from nursery stream habitats and out into the vastness of an unfamiliar lake. Once again, the adaptability of the species becomes apparent.

Homing to breed

In all cases, wherever they go to grow to maturity, all indications lead us to conclude that brown / sea trout, like Atlantic salmon, generally home faithfully back to their natal areas to spawn. This may often mean finding their way back to the same tributary and even to the same gravel shallow where they hatched. The primary sense involved in this accurate homing behaviour appears to be olfactory: salmonids follow the characteristic smell of their home waters. Much of this knowledge is imprinted in the salmon or trout's memory early on when the fish is a small parr. Some straying between river systems occurs amongst returning salmonids, but this seems minor in extent. In a world where good habitat is scarce, homing back to the area where you were born and survived successfully must be a good bet when choosing where to risk placing your own fertilised eggs. Accurate homing behaviour is, therefore, highly adaptive.

Life cycle

A few definitions of salmonid life cycle stages may help at this point.

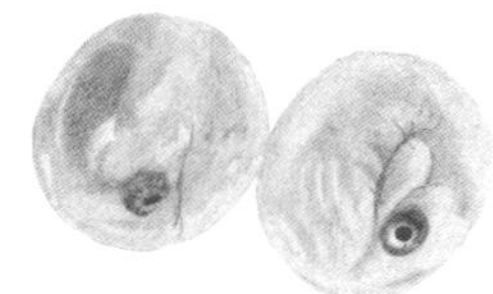

Egg: a fertilised ovum requiring 444 degree days to hatch (eg 88.8 days at 5 degrees C).

Alevin: a hatchling, living within the gravel redd (nest) for five or six weeks and still feeding entirely from the yolk sac.

Fry: a free-swimming trout which is still absorbing the last of the yolk sac, but is also starting to eat tiny invertebrates and to establish a feeding territory. Big (but not too big) wild trout fry have a distinct advantage over smaller ones during this intensely territorial phase of the life cycle.

Parr: a 'fingerling' trout, characteristically having a series of dark 'fingermarks' or 'parr' marks along the flanks which disappear as the fish becomes a sub-adult.

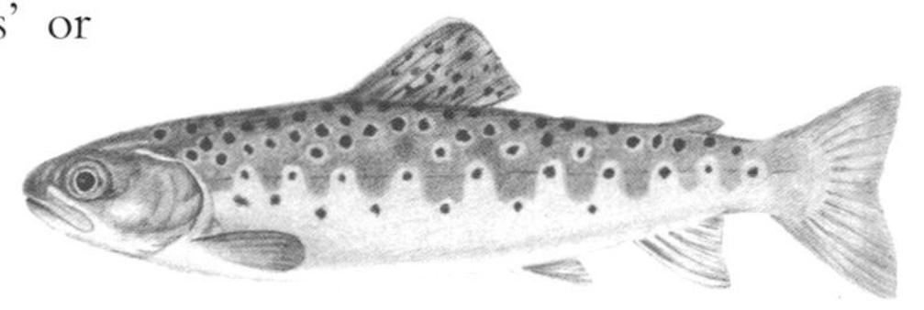

Smolt: a parr which transforms in spring (usually at age two), migrating downstream, becoming silvery in colour and changing in physiology to withstand the very different chemical conditions in the marine environment. Young (one or two year-old) smolts come from relatively warm productive rivers where growth rates are rapid. Older smolts tend to be produced in cold water habitats such as mountain becks where the growing season for trout is relatively short and fish can take several years to reach smolting size.

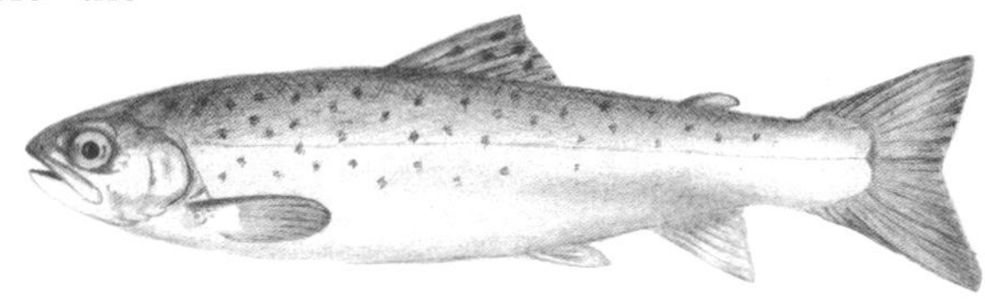

Finnock (Whitling, Peal): sea trout returning to freshwater as post-smolts in summer or autumn after just a few weeks at sea. These fish may or may not spawn the following winter.
Maiden sea trout: sea trout (female or male) returning from the sea for the first time as sexually mature fish which will spawn that winter.
Adult: a fully grown trout capable of breeding.
Kelt: – a spawned-out fish of either sex which may die but may recover condition and survive to spawn again in future. Sea trout kelts generally have a much better chance of survival than salmon kelts. Why this is so is not understood.

Spawning

Any discussion of life cycles involves a chicken-and-egg decision on where to start so I've gone for the egg. Female trout have a big decision to make when choosing both where to spawn and which male fish to spawn with. Her stake in future generations hinges on such decisions. A hen fish may only dig one redd in a given year, placing all of her eggs into that single gravely basket so her choices are critical. Males need to look impressive and to be able to defend prime spawning sites and ripe females from competitors. Males can spare milt (sperm) for many potential matings and so their choice of which female to pair with on a given occasion is less critical. Males also tend to arrive on spawning grounds before females and to leave later, trying to father as many potential offspring as possible. Females, on the other hand, arrive, pair-up, spawn and leave. We have a situation of female choice and male competitiveness based on aggression and size – some things never change!

Prior to spawning, male trout develop larger jaws than females. The lower jaw may form a hooked 'kype' used for sparring between competing males or for nipping small trout on the spawning shallows. Northern Hemisphere brown trout can spawn as early as October or as late as February, depending on environmental conditions, but most spawn from November to December. Gravel shallows in running water are the usual location, but wave-washed lake shores (eg in Lough Corrib) may also be used. These lake-spawning trout may or may not have access to suitable spawning streams. Why some fish stay within lakes to spawn, rather than migrating up side streams is not understood. Brown trout in all types of water are, however, likely to undertake some form of spawning migration. The distances involved may be tens, hundreds or thousands of metres depending on local circumstances. Females choose the redd site and use unknown combinations of environmental cues such as current speed and turbulence, gravel size, hardness of the river bed, current-flow into and/or out of the gravel, suitable dissolved oxygen concentrations, etc to determine where to spawn their eggs.

Redds under the bed

Small hen trout may deposit their eggs only 4-6cm down in pea gravel in a redd the size of a hand basin, whilst a large hen sea trout can shift large potato-sized shingle to a depth of 15-20cm, creating a redd the overall size of a bath tub. As has been stressed, high quality spawning habitats are vital to thriving trout stocks. In many modern day fisheries gravel cleanliness is poor either through siltation or organic pollution. The removal of gravel due to land drainage, flood defence works or the winning of aggregates for local farm track-laying further reduces the availability of potential trout spawning habitat. On some European rivers so many gravel shallows have been removed for flood alleviation projects that there are virtually no suitable fish spawning sites left. Those few gravel riffles which survive become intensely used for spawning and the future of the fish stocks then depends critically on these precious areas of remaining habitat.

During the digging of a redd the hen fish lies on her side, rapidly flapping her tail to lift gravel and to create a pit in the stream bed. The redd-digging behaviour effectively breaks up the bed, partially de-silts the gravel, buries a batch of eggs out of reach of most predators below a layer of cleaner gravel and leaves a hump-backed ridge which helps to 'pull' well-oxygenated water down past the incubating eggs. This water flow sustains egg respiration and takes away waste products such as carbon dioxide and ammonia which could otherwise build up in the redd and damage the eggs. A redd-digging hen trout tests the depth of the spawning pit by crouching over it with her anal fin extended. When she is satisfied that all is well and has been suitably impressed by the males displaying beside her and nuzzling her flanks, she releases a batch of eggs which are fertilised by one or more of the competing cock fish and then moves a little way upstream to dig the next pit. The renewed digging activity cascades relatively silt-free gravel gently down onto the eggs just spawned which then lie in a pocket of loose gravel several centimetres below the surface. Each redd can, therefore, contain several pockets of eggs.

On sea trout systems, small adult male brown trout often reach sexual maturity without the need to migrate to sea. These fish are called precocious parr and they sometimes manage to sneak in amongst larger spawning trout and successfully fertilise eggs. Such a strategy is risky as larger mature male sea trout vying for females often snap at and injure or kill small competitors. Despite this fact, some Norwegian streams, for instance, have more than half of their male trout maturing as large parr. For this to happen in Nature on a widespread basis, it must be a successful strategy. Genetic studies on salmon eggs have shown that half can be fathered by these sneaky little interlopers (Shelton, 2002) and, in many rivers, this may be true for trout, too.

After the fertilised eggs have developed into yolk-sac fry the young fish wriggle around in the spaces between the stones for many more days or weeks, remaining below the surface and avoiding light until most of the yolk sac has been absorbed. They then swim-up towards the light, emerging in early spring, pushing their way through the stream bed to become free-swimming fry. This is a key phase in the population biology of the species. Once a young trout has successfully hatched and wriggled out of its gravely bed, the fish is in for a tough time surviving both the physical and chemical rigours of its environment and strong competition from siblings. There is a lot to learn in trout society if our fish is eventually to produce offspring of its own.

Social behaviour

Trout fry and parr are aggressively territorial, fighting for prime lies in their stream bed micro-habitats. As they grow into their second year of age the territorial imperative seems to slacken-off and sub-adults and adult brown trout may often live in loosely associated groups. Here, social behaviour is still aggression-based, but overt fighting and biting is minimised and the fish often adopt a dominance hierarchy ('pecking order'), based primarily on size. The biggest trout gets the best lie. Where up-and-coming individuals vie for position, posturing and gaping occur. Posturing involves spreading all fins to look as large and menacing as possible sideways-on. Gaping involves opening the mouth wide, lowering the floor of the mouth to flare the gills and advancing towards the opponent. This means 'Buzz off or get bitten'. Body colouration often deepens and darkens at these times of stress. These behaviours develop in parr soon after they have established well-marked feeding territories. Submissive fish close their mouth, contract their fins, go pallid and drop down towards the stream bed. This means 'OK, you win'. If this doesn't work, dominant fish will attack and bite whilst submissive trout turn around and flee, taking up a new, less favoured lie well away from the dominant individual. Actual physical contact and potential damage is minimised by these social rules.

There are very good reasons why such behaviour has evolved. Fighting uses up lots of hard-won energy, makes the fish very conspicuous (perhaps increasing the risk of being seen and caught by a predator) and carries with it the risk of getting hurt. Trout teeth are sharp and tears inflicted on skin may get infected, leading to further problems. In the extreme instance, you could actually get eaten by a really big trout! A social system which minimises stress and injury whilst maintaining the natural order of things makes good sense and this is what you find in wild trout populations. If you peer carefully into a clear pool or glide occupied by a shoal of wild brown trout, you will typically see the biggest fish at the front, close to cover. Here it gets the pick of the food drifting by on the current, but is able to dash to safety at the least sign of danger. The smaller trout in its wake must survive on whatever flies and nymphs the top trout misses. Where two or three fairly evenly-matched trout occupy a pool or glide, they seldom get into fights, preferring instead to circle the available habitat, effectively taking it in turns to be the 'biggest fish in the small pool'.

Where food is abundant, aggression is minimal but when conditions worsen, competition increases and the strongest trout win out in the battle for survival. Often, brown trout will have a safe daytime 'bolt hole' very close to dense cover where they seldom, if ever, feed. Nearby, in shallower water, often close to base of a riffle, is their feeding lie where insects can readily be picked off during daytime or evening hatches. Trout only spend the time in their feeding lie required to maintain health and growth. Being out in the open in relatively shallow water may be good for feeding, but it is potentially dangerous and trout are very wary when in vulnerable locations.

In lakes, where food supplies may be mostly comprised of midge pupae drifting in open water, clouds of water fleas, or shoals of small fish, pelagic (open water) brown trout may hardly be aggressive at all as there is no localised food patch to defend. Equally, whilst migrating or at sea, smolts, post-smolts and sea trout have nothing to gain by defending marine food resources and may have plenty to gain from the 'safety in numbers' provided by a shoal. This helps to explain the fact that a trout which was ruthlessly aggressive and territorial as a parr may be an equable, shoaling fish as a migrant sea trout, but then fiercely aggressive once more when competing for spawning habitats and females. Trout (and other animals) are only aggressive when they really need to be; such is the economy of Nature. Selective breeding of trout over several generations on the fish farm can, however, change all that.

Naïve stockies

Artificial selection for particular characteristics during captive breeding programmes, for instance fish farming, will lead to animals with exaggerated desired features, but such individuals will seldom thrive under natural conditions. Compared with their wild, naturally-selected counterparts, animals selectively-bred over several generations can lack important attributes for survival in the wild. These may include unnaturally high aggression, poor reactions to predators, poor hunting ability and lack of physical fitness, etc. Survival in the wild is neither straightforward nor easy. This is an important fact to bear in mind when considering the wisdom of stocking a fishery. Hatchery trout have often been selectively bred for fast growth and other desirable farming characteristics, such as spawning relatively early in the autumn. Such fish can be far-removed from their wild counterparts, both genetically and behaviourally. Hatchery trout are hand-fed (or hopper-fed) throughout their lives in captivity, living at relatively very high densities, usually in concrete raceways or earth ponds and competing constantly and aggressively for food. Fin-nipping is commonplace, as is fin abrasion from contact with concrete raceways. Stocked fish, especially those grown at the highest densities, tend, therefore, to look a bit ragged around the edges. Even when the fins have healed, it is still usually possible to see bends and twists in the damaged fin rays. These are signs to look out for when distinguishing wild from stocked trout. But it isn't just physical differences which make stocked and wild trout such different beasts; behavioural differences are also of critical importance.

As we have seen, wild stream-dwelling brown trout live in an ordered society, based upon dominance of big fish which defend the best feeding positions. Overt aggression and actual fighting is minimised through posturing. When you introduce socially naïve stocked fish, however, this settled system can be turned on its head. The excellent behavioural studies of Bob Bachman (1984) demonstrate this perfectly. He watched wild and stocked brown trout in an American stream, seeing the natural posturing and energetic economy of the wild fish upset by the constant bickering, biting and fighting by the introduced trout. The stocked trout repeatedly fought with near neighbours, causing endless hassle, energy use, damage and risk of being caught and eaten by predators. This upset affected both the wild trout and the introduced fish. Often, after all this jostling for position, the stocked trout ended up living in ridiculous lies where they had to struggle to maintain position in the main current. The outcome of the stocking was, therefore, to cause strife, energy wastage, increased risk of damage and chaos to the natural order. Whilst wild trout live with social order and energy efficiency, stocked trout are the upstarts, still spoiling for a fight after the hurly-burly life of the trout farm. Stocking can, therefore, potentially upset the natural behavioural system for wild trout populations and is an important component of the negative impact which stocking can have on wild fish.

Water currents- avoiding life in the fast lane

A critically important aspect of life for stream-living animals is their ability to avoid living directly in energy-sapping fast currents. Fish are streamlined for good reasons. Imagine a false March Brown (*Ecdyonurus*) mayfly nymph, the length of your thumb nail, sitting on a stone in a fast riffle in the River Teifi, Wales. Life for this nymph is testing. It has to graze algae from the surface of stones, clinging on tightly whilst the swift current races over it. To lose its foothold would mean being swept away to trout and salmon parr waiting downstream. The nymph is beautifully adapted to this fast water life, being flattened, streamlined and wide with six strong clinging legs. Another key factor weighs in the nymph's favour: friction. As the current passes over the stone it is slowed by friction across a thin layer of turbulent flow; the boundary layer. This is a zone of shelter for stone-clinging invertebrates. Above this thin layer the current rages past. A good analogy is the wind screen on a car – it's a pretty draughty ride without one!

The nymph lives, therefore, in relative calm, scurrying around in search of algal pastures new in its narrow envelope of comfort. As well as a good food supply, the nymph has few potential predators to bother it as long as it clings securely to its stone. What has this got to do with the life of a brown trout? Well, the trout has a similar set of biological problems to solve if it is to survive to maturity and breed. Like the March Brown nymph, trout are streamlined, they also prefer to live in niches out of the main force of the current where they can feed economically and they, too, must evade predators in order to survive. Fortunately for the trout the boundary layer gets thicker as the bed of the stream gets rougher. The 2-3mm thick boundary layer which shelters the nymph on its little stone could be several centimetres deep over a cobble or boulder bed – ample shelter for an adult trout. Small trout swim close to the bed in the sheltered micro-habitats of shingle and cobble zones whilst bigger trout have a wide range of lies between boulders or around dead wood snags. This is why freestone streams (spate rivers) often make such good trout fisheries. The carrying capacity of the habitat is high with many potential lies.

A boulder stemming the flow shows as a boil on the surface. This is worth noting as a feature when you are 'reading' a stream during a fishing trip. The 'dead spot' behind the rock where current speeds are slow and variable and where food items tend to be deposited is an easy feeding lie. Just upstream is an area where the current pushes hard against the rock and is held back, forming a 'cushion'. This, too, is a good efficient lie for trout to occupy. Like the March Brown nymph, trout occupying rocky glides have a wealth of potential shelter offering productive feeding areas. Ideal lies also have safe cover close by; a waterlogged log along a margin or a rock ledge is cover heaven for our wary brown trout.

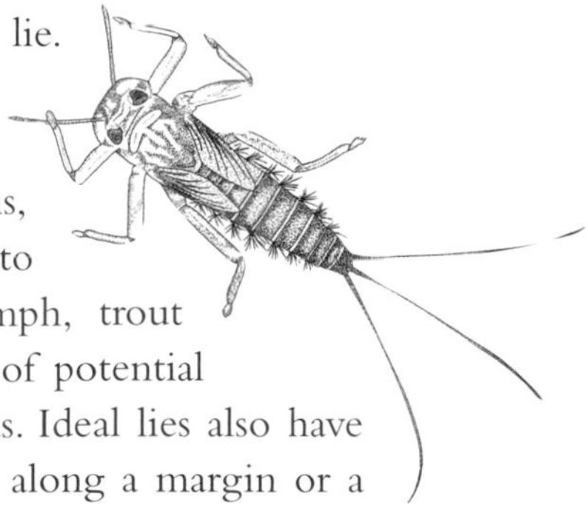

Whilst deeper glides with large boulders shelter big fish, cobbles on shallows are the realm of parr and young sub-adult trout. Here, young brown trout occupy both cushion and dead spot lies. Where stream beds lack many larger stones (eg chalk streams) weed beds can become important spring and summer cover features and dead wood snags are vital all year-round, especially in winter after the weed has died-back. Most of our over-manicured lowland streams benefit from additional securely-staked dead wood cover along their slack water margins. Such management can greatly increase the effective carrying capacity of a fishery and reduce winter losses of trout and grayling to predators such as herons.

Well managed trout streams tend to have sequences of shallow broken water parr habitat, deeper glide sections with good cover for sub-adults and frequent pools for adult trout. Parr may find adequate habitat along the slow current edges of inner bends whilst adult trout will be tucked in underneath any undercut banks close to deeper, faster water. Tree roots here may well offer that perfect combination of shelter from potential predators and from the main thrust of the current. Within the corner pool, the fastest current is at the surface - perhaps 60cm per second, a speed which no self-respecting wild trout would try to swim against, although a stocked trout might, for a while. Around the pool banks and bed friction slows the current to below 30cm per second, the preferred current speed for sensible adult trout. This is primarily why those big browns or rainbows hug banks and stream beds. A second important factor is the overhead cover which they provide. Consider the fact that the current is cork-screwing around the bend, carrying eroded sediments from the fast water on the outer bend across to deposit them on the sandy shallows of the inner bank. The outer bank is scoured and undercut producing great cover. In this way, over many years, rivers cut their way across their valley floors, eroding and depositing sediments as they go. This dynamic process is trout habitat in the making and trout have evolved to thrive in these natural habitats by letting the current bring their food to them. A natural stretch of trout stream has everything a trout needs for spawning, juvenile and adult habitats. Let's now consider an actual example to see how social behaviour and territoriality combine with habitat limitations to make a trout population tick.

The territorial young trout of Black Brows Beck, Cumbria

Malcolm Elliott (1994) provides a review of his twenty five year study of the Black Brows Beck, a headwater of the Cumbrian River Leven which drains Lake Windermere, England's largest lake. The beck is a tiny gravel-bedded stream, less than a metre wide on average and less than half a metre deep in the pools. Despite its small size it supports a sea trout population which has been very amenable to long-term study. Field ecology really needs study over considerable periods of time as only then will large variations in natural conditions be encountered (ideally, on several occasions), revealing their impacts on plants and animals. Determination is required of researchers who stick to their task for a quarter of a century or more. The results, however, can be very illuminating, making the effort worthwhile and indispensable for an understanding of ecology.

Black Brows Beck runs from rough grassland, through coniferous and oak woodland down to lowland grazing, having few dissolved nutrients and is weakly acidic. Trout living as adults in the Leven estuary ('slob trout') and adjacent Irish Sea run the beck to spawn each year in November or December. Most of these breeding adults spent two years as parr in freshwater, smolted, went to sea for a year and then returned as four-year-old maiden sea trout. Males of only three years of age also frequently spawned, returning as whitling (peal, finnock) after spending only one summer at sea. Very few fish appear to survive to spawn a second time. A fisheries study on the River Leven conducted in the 1930s found the same basic age structure of sea trout in the river, indicating that it has been stable over a considerable period of time (in human terms). The Windermere system as a whole runs larger/older sea trout than those found in the little Black Brows Beck. Some of these big sea trout weigh over 5kg and are older than 5 years, presumably spawning in the larger streams and rivers around the lake. These big fish were also present in the 1930s.

Whilst Elliott's recent study found that most of the beck's sea trout smolt after two years of freshwater growth, in the 1930s, many smolted at three years of age. This may indicate better growing conditions (warmer climate, more nutrients in the streams) and, hence, earlier smolting in recent decades. This phenomenon of earlier smolting may be widespread amongst British sea trout populations. Black Brows female trout typically lay 500-1800 eggs in a series of batches in their redds. Larger females spawn before smaller fish and produce more and larger eggs which hatch into larger fry which have a competitive advantage over small fry. This may be the key evolutionary advantage of migrating to sea: the ability to invest more energy in reproduction of sturdy offspring. Egg quality may, therefore, dictate the need for migration. Eggs hatch in February / March and young fry emerge from the gravel in April / May. Then comes a period of fundamental importance; the establishment of feeding territories.

Because the gravel in the stream is relatively silt-free, egg survival is high and many alevins hatch. As the young fry disperse from the redd and settle into lies on the stream bed, a relatively short and critical phase of intense competition for space occurs. When these tiny trout compete at high densities for available space a high proportion die as they are excluded from the relatively few suitable niches on the stream bed. At lower population densities, however, the long-term study showed that a higher proportion of fry survive. This phenomenon is termed density-dependent mortality: the proportion of individuals dying being related to the density of the population. Elliott found that this critical phase for survival occurs over about 30-70 days in Black Brows Beck. The larger, more aggressive fry tend usually to win out, filling up the best available habitat. It seems, however, that it is possible to be too big, as well as too small in this early battle for survival, as the largest of fry as well as the smallest had lower survival rates than the middling individuals (Elliott, 1994).

Carrying capacity

Carrying capacity (the number of trout a stream can support), varies with habitat quality, food availability, water flows and other climatic influences. A very interesting finding from Malcolm Elliott's research is that, when the areas of all the tiny trout parr territories in Black Brows Beck are added up, they account for only a small percentage of the habitat which seems, at a glance, suitable for them. How can this be when the annual battle for space is such a life-and-death affair? The answer seems to lie in the fact that a suitable lie for a trout must have the correct balance of shelter from the flow, shelter from attacks by predators and other trout and a sufficient supply of invertebrate food arriving on the current. Such ideal homes must, despite appearances, be relatively few and far between. Better small parr habitat can sometimes be created by adding cobbles and boulders to relatively bare stretches downstream of riffles, creating many new hiding places and potential sheltered lies. In this way the overall number of trout territories can be increased and the population increased. This type of positive habitat management increases the 'carrying capacity' of the fishery and can be applied to various types of habitat needed by trout of differing sizes and ages. Where habitats are degraded, an understanding of this type of management is vital to the success of wild trout conservation.

As the years of the Black Brows Beck study progressed, it became obvious that the densities of trout parr present varied from year to year. Elliott became fascinated to discover what drives trout population dynamics. He found that, in Black Brows Beck, territoriality limits production when fry densities are high by killing a high proportion of juvenile trout. Severe droughts such as those of 1983 and 1984 reduced the overall trout stock for a number of years until it recovered with the return of more usual rainfall patterns. Drought is a classic example of a climatic extreme decimating a trout stock, irrespective of the numbers of fish present. This phenomenon is termed density-independent mortality: the numbers or proportion dying bear no relation to the density of fish present. After the droughts, stock densities were low and so losses to territorial aggression were also low: the population therefore bounced-back to re-fill the available habitat. At such critical times, individuals best adapted to survive low-flows tend to proliferate in the stock. Natural selection is hard at work weeding-out frail individuals and leaving the strong survivors. As Charles Darwin spotted, without some form of natural population regulation, animal numbers would soon get out of hand. He proposed, rather sensibly, that life under natural conditions is a struggle and that only the best adapted individuals are likely to survive to adulthood. For most species, the vast majority of individuals never get a chance to breed, having been weeded out by natural selection earlier on in life.

Density-dependent factors tend, naturally, to lead to relatively similar numbers of adults being produced at the end of each cohort. They are a series of natural checks and balances, having the ability to regulate numbers. If there are a number of density-dependent factors operating on a population, they can compensate for each other to varying degrees, depending on the strengths and direction of their effects. For instance, if a high proportion of young trout die from territorial competition in a given stream, fry eaten by fish-eating birds over this phase of the life cycle may not matter in population terms as their loss can be compensated for through better survival of remaining individuals. This fact can make the interpretation of factors such as predation pressure on trout parr difficult to assess.

Density-independent factors such as severe pollution, siltation of spawning gravels or chronic drought don't impose this smooth natural damping of numbers and can lead to wildly fluctuating populations. High numbers survive in equable environments, but far fewer when conditions are harsh. Density independent factors thus determine numbers in a population, but do not have the capacity for fine-tuned regulation. The ultimate density-independent type of factor would be, for instance, in Yellowstone Park where whole populations could be exterminated by a violent volcanic eruption. In fact, such an event is reckoned to be due at Yellowstone sometime in the next few thousand years: it has happened before, potentially with major consequences for global weather patterns.

Cycles of abundance

The famous biologist J.B.S. Haldane noted that animal populations are likely to be regulated by density-dependent factors where environmental conditions are favourable and thus where the population could potentially run wild. Density-independent factors tend to act in unfavourable environments, where populations might be more liable to exhibit 'boom and bust' cycles of abundance. In reality, of course, there will be a complex mix of mortality effects acting upon individuals within populations which will vary with population size and with fluctuating environmental conditions. Localised density-dependent effects may be important on a small stream, but lose their actual importance for the main river which the stream drains into because of wider-scale variations in habitat availability and quality. Also, fish excluded from the best habitat available locally may be able to survive by migrating to pastures new where there may be suitable un-occupied habitat. This sort of migration is termed 'functional redistribution' and may be very important in some river systems. Reduced numbers of trout in a given stream stretch may not, therefore, mean that the 'missing' fish have actually died; they may be alive and well and living just around the corner!

The brown trout of Wilfin Beck

Malcolm Elliott also studied the wild trout of Wilfin Beck, a small Cumbrian stream only 3km from Black Brows Beck. Whilst Black Brows trout always migrate to sea before spawning, Wilfin Beck trout do not – they remain in freshwater throughout their life cycle as brown trout. Why? Wilfin Beck, about 4km long, has a similar chemistry to Black Brows and tends to have a steeper gradient, higher current speeds and an unstable bed. There is an impassable waterfall towards the bottom of the stream, close to Lake Windermere so trout can migrate downstream, but no sea trout can get back up. Here lies the explanation for the obligate brown trout life cycle. These brown trout mature and produce eggs at the same age as Black Brows fish, but tend to survive longer. Mature females can be of several different year classes. In contrast to the density-dependent mortality amongst fry seen on Black Brows Beck, Wilfin Beck trout had a relatively even chance of survival, irrespective of stock size. This may have been because the overall density of trout fry and parr was low and competition for resources was less intense than at Black Brows. At low densities the number of juveniles produced tended to be more directly proportional to the number of eggs laid.

The importance of egg size

Wilfin Beck female brown trout were smaller and produced fewer and smaller eggs than Black Brows sea trout. These small eggs produced small fry and the resulting trout remained relatively small throughout the life cycle, never catching up in size with Black Brows fish. Neither Black Brows Beck nor Wilfin Beck trout seemed limited in their parr growth by food availability. In both, initial fry size and subsequent water temperatures seem to account for the observed growth rates which were close to maximum for both populations. Older Wilfin Beck brown trout seemed food-limited, but all Black Brows adults grew principally at sea where food availability was greater.

Black Brows Beck is much more productive of trout than Wilfin Beck where the breeding adult brown trout stock takes up food and space, but adds little growth of trout flesh each year. These mature brown trout have stopped growing in size and diverted their excess energy into reproduction. Black Brows hen sea trout invested about twice as much of their body reserves in the production of eggs than equivalent-sized Wilfin Beck brown trout. The energy supply enabling this egg production comes from rich marine food resources. In a world where survival as a fry necessitates being large, hatching from a large egg gives a fish a good start in life.

Scale reading

A trout first grows scales as a fry, when it is an inch or two long. From that point, as it grows in length, the scales grow larger, adding new bands of hard tissue around the edges, just like the growth rings in a tree trunk. Fish scales are, effectively, a suit of armour, keeping out too much water (in freshwater) or too much salt (in the sea), protecting the underlying muscles from physical knocks and making it more difficult for predators or parasites to gain a hold on the slimy body. If a scale is dislodged, it will soon re-grow, but earlier growth bands are lost in this process and the scale is termed a replacement and is useless for ageing purposes.

Trout are usually considered to have their birthday in February in the year when the eggs hatch so that an '0+ fish' is in its first year and a '3+ fish' is between three and four years of age. Where food supplies are reasonable, growth tends to be governed primarily by water temperature and so varies through the year. Linear growth produces a pattern of concentric rings on the scales and, with experience, scales can be read to produce quite reliable age estimates for a given fish. It helps if you have a large sample of scales from differing-sized fish to help 'get your eye in'. In most fisheries, trout grow rapidly in summer provided that the water does not get too warm, slowing down in the autumn before ceasing growth in winter. Summer growth is typified by a band of widely-spaced rings on the scale, the rings being closer together as the growth slows in autumn. This area of changing ring spacing is known as a 'growth check' and it is the number of annual growth checks which are used to determine the probable age of the fish. The annual growth check can occur at different times in differing habitats, for instance between August and November in Lyn Tegid (Wales) which is probably typical for British trout (see Frost & Brown, 1967).

Care is needed in the interpretation of fish scales as growth checks can also occur during phases of injury and healing (perhaps after electric-fishing or a close encounter with a predator, monofilament net or after being caught-and-released), during adverse weather conditions (prolonged floods or droughts, for instance) or during bouts of pollution. Also, mature fish which have stopped growing in length may live-on for a number of years whilst adding very few additional growth rings at the edge of their scales. This can lead to under-estimates of the true age of old fish, a well-known fact in fisheries circles.

G.H. Nall (1930) wrote the early definitive book on sea trout biology in the British Isles and his work remains a fine reference text, even after 75 years. Nall's ageing system works as follows. Freshwater parr growth is given as a figure in years with a plus sign for significant growth after the last freshwater growth check. Then there is a decimal point followed by the subsequent life history. A scale reading of 2+. relates to a two year old smolt. A scale reading of 2+.1+ would be for a similar fish returning to spawn after one winter at sea. A reading of 2+.1+2SM+ would be for a similar fish which had survived to spawn twice – SM denoting a spawning mark on the scales. The total age of this fish would be 5+ years. Spawning marks occur as erosions of recent growth rings, probably due to the re-absorption of protein and calcium during the physiologically demanding migratory and sexual maturation phases of the life cycle. A hen trout maturing eggs mobilises much of her reserves of oils, proteins, carbohydrates and minerals, losing body condition and eroding her scales in the process.

Scales taken from a mature sea trout can, therefore, potentially reveal the rate and duration of freshwater growth as a parr, the age at smolting, the subsequent time spent at sea, marine growth rates and the number of times the fish has spawned. There is more to a trout scale than meets the eye! However, scale reading is far from infallible and is best done as part of a large-scale study (pardon the pun), during which a 'feel' can be gained by the researcher of typical growth and longevity of the fish in a given population. Great care is needed in interpretation as growth checks can often be indistinct and, as mentioned above, 'false' checks can occur for various reasons. Spawning marks are often much more distinct in some populations, perhaps those with arduous migration routes, but may go un-noticed in others. Much of the scientific information available on sea trout stocks originates from high quality scale reading studies.

The diagram on the facing page shows a detailed drawing made by Dr Edward Fahy (1985), of a scale taken from a specimen Irish sea trout. This scale was obtained from a seven pound Irish sea trout of 9+ years of age. Its life history, revealed by the scale is two years parr life (1 & 2), then further growth and a winter at sea (I), followed by a maiden spawning as a one sea-winter fish (S.M.1) then five further years of spawning (S.Ms 2-6). The fish was caught before its seventh attempt at spawning. The formula for this scale is, therefore: 2.1+ 6 S.M.+

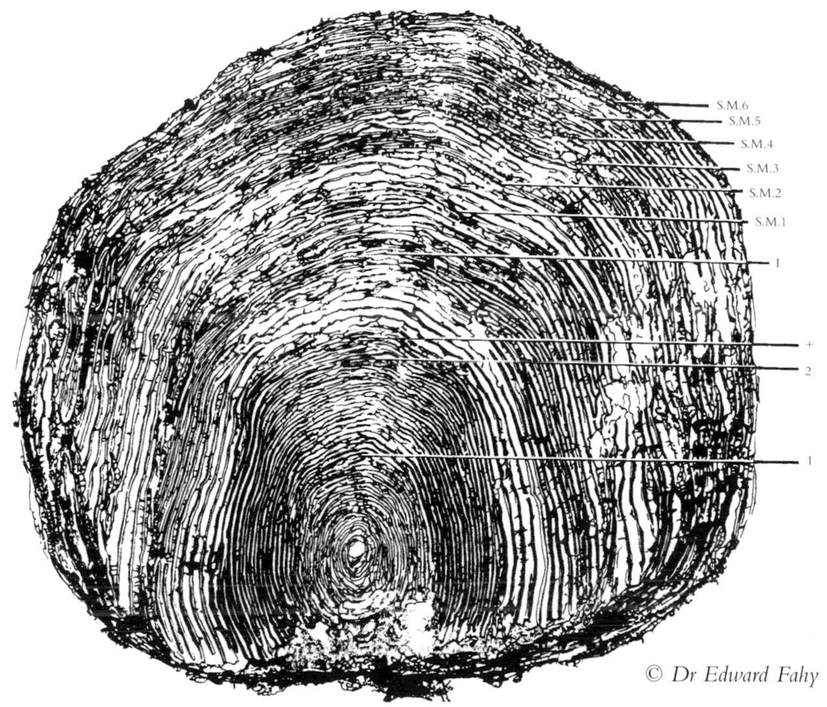

© Dr Edward Fahy

In order to manage fish populations effectively, it is important for us to be able to understand the principal factors likely to be determining growth and abundance on a given fishery. Large river stocks are unlikely to be as readily understood (or as amenable to research) as those in small streams. Much more scientific research is required before trout population regulation is understood across the full natural range of the species. Readers particularly interested in this aspect of biology are recommended to read Malcolm Elliott's excellent book – 'Quantitative Ecology and the Brown Trout' (Oxford University Press, 1994) and / or the journal Fisheries Management (volume 62(2), 2003). These are both readily available through the UK inter-library loan system. By reading widely, the tremendous variability found in natural trout populations will become apparent. Where do all these differences between trout stocks come from?

Nature and Nurture

Some of the observed differences between trout stocks will be genetic and others environmental. This mix of influences, often termed the balance between 'Nature and Nurture', produces the variety of individuals which characterise natural populations. In isolated populations, the genetic constitution of brown trout can drift through random processes, leading to differentiated stocks which may not necessarily be particularly specially adapted to their environment. In general, however, genetic differences between populations are likely to be based on important characteristics which help trout to survive in their particular local environments.

Dr Andy Walker of the Freshwater Fisheries Laboratory, Pitlochry, Scotland carried out stocking experiments with young trout taken from two tributaries of the River Tay, one noted for its sea trout (the Findhu Glen burn, River Earn) and the other for its brown trout (the Moulin Burn, River Tummel). By transferring fish between streams, he found indications of both inherited tendencies to migrate and modified behaviour in response to environment. Sea trout tend to produce parr which migrate, but the availability of richer feeding increases the tendency to remain at home as brown trout. As food supply seems to be a vital influence on trout population ecology, let's now consider the range of natural feeding opportunities available to trout stocks.

The productivity of natural waters: moorland lakes and upland rivers

Trout fisheries, both running and still water, naturally come in a range of productivities. Least productive tend to be cold upland streams and moorland lakes, often with acid water and peaty soils. The bed rock is likely to be hard and impervious, leading to few dissolved nutrients in the water, poor light penetration owing to the naturally turbid, peat-stained (dystrophic) waters and, consequently, modest algal and weed growth. Low levels of plant growth support few invertebrates and small, slow-growing brown trout. As we have just seen, sea trout are often produced by such impoverished habitats. Often, within such a trout population, more sea trout are female and resident brown trout male. You have to be big to produce lots of large eggs but even a small male trout can produce lots of viable milt (sperm).

Typical aquatic plants of oligotrophic waters include filamentous algae, mosses, shore weed, some pond weeds, bog bean, rushes and reeds. Aquatic invertebrates include midge larvae, beetles, water boatmen, stoneflies, black flies, some mayflies and caddis flies, snails and leeches. In large, cold northern European lakes and streams, brown trout may live with Arctic char, grayling, pike, burbot and whitefishes. In North America, brown trout may share cold, oligotrophic lake and stream habitats with rainbow trout, brook trout, lake trout and arctic grayling. Both brook and lake 'trout' are actually species of char in the genus Salvelinus.

The Connemara white trout loughs (Fahy, 1985)

Edward Fahy's excellent 'Child of the Tides' (Glendale Press, 1985) describes the biology of sea trout (white trout) in Ireland. The Western Fisheries Region includes a wide range of magnificent Connemara and Mayo loughs extending over the limestone catchments of the north and central areas which have the famous brown trout fisheries of Loughs Carra, Mask and Corrib and the extensive granite-based peat bog moor land of the south and west. The wet, peaty habitats produce hoards of tiny biting midges (Ceratopogonids or 'no-see-ums') which can drive you absolutely crazy on warm, muggy summer evenings. If ever midge repellent is a necessary part of your fishing kit, it is here!

The peaty loughs, linked by little rivers, streams and extensive ditch systems, allow access from the Atlantic for many localised sea trout stocks which characterise the small catchments of this maritime zone. Water chemistries of peaty waters have perhaps a tenth of bone-growing calcium compared with limestone systems. A typical Connemara sea trout system will be upland in character with small streams running down from mountain or hill sides, through peaty moorland providing sparse sheep grazing of purple moor and cotton grasses. Farm incomes are modest. Mosses and algae provide the bulk of the in-stream plant growth although there may be a few beds of various pond weed species. Dead grasses falling or blowing into the streams provide important additional inputs of decaying organic matter, eaten by invertebrates. Flies and beetles blown off the moor are eagerly snatched by hungry trout parr. Stream invertebrates are represented by low densities of stone flies, caddis flies, more numerous olive mayfly nymphs and chironomid (non-biting) midge larvae. Shrimps occur in patches. Trout fry and parr mostly eat tiny drifting midge larvae, pupae and olive mayfly nymphs but where loughs outflow to streams, they also eat tiny water fleas and copepods drifting in the water column.

Trout parr normally take two or three years to grow large enough to become silvery smolts which migrate in April or May or 'brown parr' which migrate in autumn. Parr which aren't quite big enough to smolt in spring wait, growing a little larger (so-called 'B-growth'), then migrate later in the season. In colder, higher altitude streams, parr may take four or even five years to become smolts or to drop downstream as large parr (Fahy, 1985). Smolt size in a given catchment tends to be quite constant; trout migrate when they have reached a critical size threshold. Warmer phases of climate tend to generate faster parr growth and earlier smolting. Enrichment of the catchment through fertilising farmland may increase in-stream productivity and boost parr growth rates. Some male parr remain in freshwater, maturing at a small body size and awaiting the return of mature hen sea trout.

After dropping downstream, smolts remain in estuaries for a while, gradually adjusting to marine conditions. At sea, smolts and post-smolts must run the gauntlet of many predators and of parasites such as larval and adult sea lice (parasitic copepods) which can be lethal where they occur at high densities. (This problem is discussed further in a later section on west coast Irish and Scottish sea trout populations). Those post-smolts which survive these rigours find themselves in a habitat rich in copepods, shrimps, young sand eels and small sprats. For fish used to getting by on occasional passing insect larvae, this must seem like a feast and growth at sea is rapid. By the end of the summer, post-smolts have developed into small sea trout. These little summer sea trout, called finnock, whitling or peal, depending upon where you live, often push back into estuaries or the lower reaches of rivers in their roaming search for food. Such fish may often visit estuaries far from their natal rivers and fisheries for finnock can be composed of mixed stocks from various river systems.

West coast Connemara sea trout tend to remain in the Atlantic for one or more years, typical growth attained being around 30cm after one year, 40cm after two years, 48cm after three years and 53cm after a fourth year. Over the other side of the country, east coast Irish Sea-feeding sea trout grow more rapidly, typically attaining lengths of 33cm after one year, 51cm after two years, 63cm after three years and 70cm after a fourth year (Fahy, 1985). The Irish Sea-feeding trout of South Welsh rivers also show this rapid growth pattern. Sea trout body condition can vary widely between years; poor feeding leading to thin (low 'condition factor') fish and rich feeding to sleek, fat individuals.

In Connemara, most sea trout return to spawn either after a single summer (as finnock) or after one year at sea. Many finnock return to freshwater in winter but do not appear to spawn. The average age of sea trout at first spawning is between 1.5 and 2.5 sea years (Fahy, 1985).

In County Kerry the longer lived sea trout of Lough Currane often stay at sea for two or more years before first returning to spawn. These older maiden spawners may then live on for several more years, returning to spawn again over two, three or even four subsequent winters. Long-lived sea trout stocks occur only in a very few Irish fisheries, but are more common along the west coasts of Scotland and Wales. These fisheries are the ones which produce specimen-sized fish. On all sea trout fisheries it seems that the largest fish returning to spawn tend to do so early in the season, from March onwards. This is a parallel with salmon where large 'springers' run early in the year. Some rivers also run large 'back-end' sea trout and salmon, these fish often escaping the rods by migrating after the end of the fishing season. To maximise benefits, it would be sensible to re-assess the timing of the close season on such waters.

The River Scorff, Brittany (see Bagliniere & Maisse, 1999)

The River Scorff is a coastal river in Brittany where the bedrocks are granites and schists, the water is slightly acidic (pH 6.5) and low in calcium (5 mg/l), but generally of good quality and the flows are often high in winter, low in summer. Trout, salmon, eels, pike, bullheads and stone loach are present amongst other fish species. Electric-fishing surveys show the normal pattern of most trout streams with fry occurring in the tributaries, parr on the stony riffles and rapids and adults in the deeper pools. In the main river, during fisheries surveys 80% of brown trout were caught close to cover. Within the Scorff system trout parr migrate downstream from small sheltered tributaries at an age of around one year, but salmon parr live in fast water habitats on the main river straight after hatching. Salmon can cope with faster current speeds than trout at all stages of the life cycle.

The main channel of the Scorff also holds resident adult brown trout which only venture into the smaller side streams around spawning time. These brown trout can live for five years or more and most mature after two. Spawning occurs from November to January. Trout migrate up the main river until they reach their target spawning tributary where they wait until spates trigger a further upstream migration to the spawning riffles. Males migrate first, possibly to establish territorial dominance in pools close to spawning areas, females wait until ovulation is imminent, run up, spawn and then vacate the tributary. As appears to be the case in all trout populations studied, male mortality is higher than that of females throughout life. Average survival of trout in their first year in the Kernec stream, a tributary of the Scorff, was estimated at around 5%, in the second and third years 40%, in the fourth and fifth years 50% and zero in the sixth year (Bagliniere & Maisse, 1999).

Mesotrophic lakes and rivers

Next up in the food stakes are upland rivers and lakes based upon more soluble rocks which yield more nutrients to their waters (mesotrophic waters) and have around pH-neutral soils. Such lakes tend to be clear-watered, growing a wide range of submerged aquatic plants, having moderately abundant and diverse invertebrate communities and plenty of trout growing to medium sizes. Sea and brown trout often form mixed stocks in these waters. Mesotrophic lakes are often prone to agricultural intensification in their catchments and artificial nutrient-enrichment (eutrophication) leads to algal blooms, cloudy water and the progressive loss of sensitive plant and invertebrate species. At extreme levels, the trout themselves will be threatened with extinction from factors such as low dissolved oxygen concentrations, high ammonia levels and / or physical damage to side stream spawning and nursery areas.

Typical aquatic plants found in clean lakes include reeds, rushes, mosses, water crowfoots, starworts, pond weeds, water celery, water parsnip, arrowhead and water lilies. Typical river invertebrates include diverse mayflies, stoneflies, caddis flies, midges, black flies, snails, water limpets, shrimps, worms, dragonflies and damselflies and, sometimes, pearl mussels and native crayfish.

Loch Lomond and the River Endrick (Slack, 1957, Maitland, 1966)

This section is based on the books of Harry Slack (1957) and Peter Maitland (1966). When these books were written, the Loch was considered to be oligo/mesotrophic. Loch Lomond straddles Scotland's Highland Boundary Fault with the lowlands to the south and the uplands to the north. It is shaped like a long narrow triangle with the apex reaching up into the mountainous highlands at Ardlui where the River Falloch flows in, the loch here being very deep and steep-sided. The rocks there are relatively impervious granites, schists and diorites; the River Falloch had just 2.2 mg/l of calcium in 1955.

The broader southern part of the Loch, fed by the River Endrick and drained by the River Leven is shallower, more productive and has numerous wooded islands, one of which has (or had) a wallaby colony on it! It is based largely on Old Red Sandstone which is fairly calcium-rich and so lends productivity to the land and waters. The River Endrick, for instance, had 15.8 milligrams of calcium per litre in 1955. The famous Boundary Fault, separating the Scottish Highlands and Lowlands, runs from north of Balmaha on the east shore across to the River Fruin on the west shore and is made of serpentine and similar rocks.

Loch Lomond has a diverse fish fauna including brown trout, sea trout, salmon, powan (a rare whitefish), pike, perch, eels, brook, river and sea lampreys, minnows, sticklebacks, flounders and introduced roach and ruffe. The mud on the loch bed is crawling with tiny worms and midge larvae and the open water has a diverse plankton of water fleas, copepods, phantom midge larvae and chironomid pupae. Around the shorelines live many mayfly and stonefly nymphs, caddis larvae, snails, flatworms, leeches, corixids and water beetles. The stony and sandy northern shorelines harbour mosses, shoreweed, some pondweeds, reeds and rushes, flatworms, leeches, snails, shrimps, several mayfly species, stoneflies, many caddis flies, beetles, corixids and true flies. The richer southern shorelines grow milfoil, stoneworts, pond weeds, water lilies, reeds and rushes plus all of the previous invertebrates and many chironomid midges, snails, pea mussels, water lice, damsel flies and dragonflies.

The Loch is famous for its run of sea trout and salmon which ascend the River Leven, lie for a while in the Loch and then migrate up the diverse in-flowing streams and rivers to spawn. The largest of these rivers is the Endrick which is a relatively weedy mesotrophic water (as described by Maitland in 1966). Typical plants of the Endrick include water lilies, amphibious bistort, yellow flag, rushes, bur reed, Canadian pondweed, milfoil, curly and broad-leaved pondweeds, starwort and reed canary grass. The invertebrate fauna was very diverse with numerous species of worms, flatworms, leeches, shrimps, hog louse, mayflies, stoneflies, caddis flies, dipteran flies (chironomid midges, black flies, daddy long-legs, etc), water beetles, snails, bivalves, corixids and other bugs - plenty of fish food!

Peter Maitland found the trout stock to be distributed throughout the River Endrick, much of the spawning occurring in tiny tributaries, with parr living in the side streams for two years or so before migrating in April or May into the main channel or smolting and migrating down to the loch, then the Firth of Clyde and north Atlantic. Sea trout were more abundant than salmon and River Endrick sea trout caught by anglers averaged around 500g (a pound) in May and June and getting on for a kilo (around two pounds) through July to October. Brownies averaged 250g (half a pound) from March to June, 500g from June to September and 750g in October. In Loch Lomond, rod caught sea trout averaged around 3kg in March, 1.5kg in April and one kilo through May to October. Brown trout on the loch averaged about a kilo in March, 500g in April and May and between 500g and 250g for the rest of the season. This is the stamp of trout to be expected from a medium-productivity British lake system.

Peter Maitland repeated his survey of the Endrick 30 years-on (Maitland, 1996), finding that whilst the rocky upland section had remained largely unchanged, many middle river sections had suffered substantial bank erosion and channel-widening from intensive sheep grazing or ploughing and many of the lower sections having extensive deposits of gravel shoals, sand and silt. Such changes in land use and such consequent river bank and channel damage are probably very widespread in British rivers. Few have been documented by photographic surveys like Peter Maitland's. Anglers and fishery managers should routinely take pictures of their fisheries from known points so that they can monitor habitat quality over the years.

The River Don, Aberdeen (Shields, 1996)

Brian Shields provides a review of the recent status of the famous River Don brown trout fishery – arguably, the best in Scotland. Whilst the headwaters of the Don arise in the cold, hard rock Cairngorm Mountains and surrounding heather moorland, much of the middle and lower river runs through very productive, alkaline soiled, arable farmland. Many side streams are quite rich in dissolved nutrients, making the river much more productive than other Scottish waters which explains the Don's productivity for brown trout. However, habitat quality surveys revealed widespread impacts from intensive grazing and channelisation, many tributaries suffering substantial damage and indications of nutrient-enrichment being quite commonplace. During electric-fishing surveys, juvenile trout and salmon numbers were markedly lower in such areas than in areas of better habitat. The quality of the side streams is critical as this is where virtually all of the trout fry and parr live up to an age of around two years. At this age the trout gradually drop down to larger tributaries and into the main river channel where they take up residence as adults. When mature, these fish migrate back up the side streams to spawn, completing their typical large river brown trout life cycle pattern. Whilst the Don does run sea trout, it is noted more for the quality of its brown trout angling. A good parallel in Wales is the River Usk and in England the River Exe. Smaller side streams are very vulnerable to habitat damage as many of them are too small to fish and may be over-looked by both farmers and fishermen, being considered of little importance to the main river system. Nothing could be further from the truth – if you add up the area of nursery habitat available to trout in headwater and side streams, it is a very large and important resource, potentially capable of producing vast numbers of juveniles which gradually recruit into the main river brown trout fishery downstream or which smolt and run to sea.

Brian Shields set up traps on a side stream to demonstrate that emigration of young trout peaked at an age of 2 years, with fish moving downstream in the spring. Older and faster-growing parr migrated first; an exact parallel of typical smolt movements. Not all tributaries hatched trout eggs very successfully. Incubator boxes buried in the gravel showed high (over 80%) trout egg hatching success in clean upper catchment tributaries, but a lower (less than 50%) hatch in mid- to lower-river side streams where sediment levels appeared to be higher. Even at a 40 or 50% hatch, these silty side streams are miles ahead of many southern lowland rivers where gravels are horrendously silted and salmonid egg survival is probably often less than 10%.

Analyses of River Don Estate trout catch records going back over 100 years showed a decline in numbers caught in the latter part of the 20th century, compared with the early decades of the 1900s when large numbers of relatively small trout were caught. Since the 1980s the average size of brown trout caught by angling had increased which may indicate a reduction in juvenile production and increased growth amongst survivors through reduced competition for food (Shields, 1996). On the lower river, where angling effort is greatest, most brown trout are caught at around three or four years old. On the upper river, which is less fished, more older and larger brown trout are caught each season, probably reflecting the better chances of survival up amid the hills where the crowds are fewer. The best fishing months on the Don are April and May, with June also being quite good. In common with all trout fisheries, a relatively few keen anglers spent lots of time fishing and accounted for a high proportion of the catch. It is often said that 10% of anglers catch 90% of the fish – I wish I had time to be one of them!

Lake Windermere (Allen, 1935)

Lake Windermere lies in a glacial valley in the English Lake District. It is almost 17km long and divided into two fairly even-sized basins, the North basin being the deeper of the two. The trophic status of the lake has varied from original oligotrophy, through mesotrophy after enrichment started in the early 1800s and then a period of eutrophy in the South basin due to increased phosphate inputs. Most recently, an easing of this situation has occurred owing to improvements in sewage treatment works in the lake's catchment. The lake has a stock of resident brown trout and a migratory population of sea trout, including, as we have seen, those of Black Brows beck. A great deal of pioneering research has been carried out on Windermere and other Cumbrian lakes because of the location of the excellent Freshwater Biological Association, based at the Ferry House, near Far Sawrey on the eastern shore. The Association publishes an invaluable series of identification keys for aquatic invertebrates and actively promotes collaborative research on freshwater ecology (www.fba.org.uk). The Windermere brown trout stock was studied in the early days of the laboratory, during the 1930s, by K.R.Allen who estimated that the stony shallows supported about 12,000 trout, around half being three year-olds and a quarter four year-olds. The younger brown trout lived up the various watercourses feeding the lake, dropping down into the lake at ages from one to three years, but mostly as two year-olds. As usual, the fastest-growing parr migrated first. After a period of invertebrate feeding on the lake shallows, many of the larger brown trout switched to a diet of fish, growing large in the process. This pattern of migration between streams for spawning and the main lake for adult growth is commonplace amongst brown trout, paralleling the marine migration of sea trout.

The Vosso system in Norway (Bror Jonsson, 1989)

Bror Jonsson and colleagues have studied in detail the wild trout populations of Norway. The Vosso river and lake system, a well known angling destination, provides an interesting example of trout biology in this magnificent landscape. The lakes are deep and steep-sided with narrow rocky littoral (sunlit) zones, bedded with boulders, gravels and sands. These cool waters support, in various habitats, wild brown trout, sea trout, salmon, Arctic char, grayling, minnows, burbot, pike and perch. An interesting place to go fishing, to say the least! In the Vosso river system, brown trout spawn principally in the streams which feed the lake systems, the parr dropping downstream as they grow and recruiting into the lakes where they spread out to forage over both the lake bed and open waters. Few trout occur deeper than about 50 metres. Where sea trout occur (in Lake Vangsvatnet, for instance) smolts in these cold waters may be of two to seven years of age. A seven year-old smolt is very old, indicating the ultra-slow growth in these northern waters. Sea trout migrate out into coastal waters during summer, perhaps travelling 100km away from the natal system, returning in autumn to over-winter in the deep shoreline areas of the lakes. Typical brown trout growth in Vangsvatnet is around 8cm at one year, 14cm at two years, 20cm at three years, 22cm at four years, and 25cm by years five or six or seven. These brown trout have short Scandinavian summers during which to make their modest growth; they grow slowly, but tend to be long-lived. In lakes with no sea trout run, most adult trout living out in the open water zone are females, with males tending to feed more over the lake bed. On Vangsvatnet, however, many female trout migrate to sea whilst males remain to forage in open freshwater. In both cases females seem to dominate the richer feeding areas. Open water fish eat surface flies, midge pupae and water fleas (*Daphnia*). Lake bed-feeding fish take a range of invertebrate groups including crustaceans, molluscs and insect larvae. In the nursery streams, terrestrial insects, chironomid midges, black flies, stoneflies and caddis flies are all important food sources for Norwegian trout.

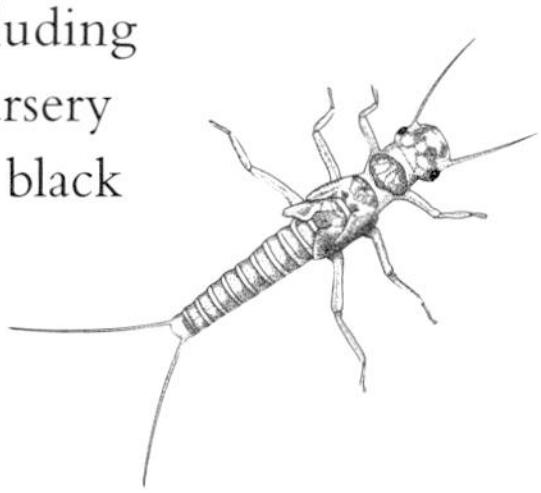

Naturally eutrophic still waters, limestone rivers and chalk streams

These fertile waters are often spring-fed and based on readily-dissolved, base-rich rocks such as chalk and limestone. Despite their richness, unless they have been polluted with fertilisers, sewage effluent or other nutrient-rich effluents, they tend not to have prolonged algal blooms, but have prolific beds of aquatic plants, reedy margins and thriving invertebrate populations. Such waters are, however, very sensitive to artificial enrichment and can soon start to produce cloudy water and algal blooms if the water entering them is carrying elevated levels of phosphorus and nitrogen. If the environmental conditions remain healthy, eutrophic lakes will grow lunker brown trout, but when over-enriched they can soon deteriorate into a turbid algal soup. Once this has happened, restoration to clear-watered conditions may not be easy and so prevention is far better than cure. Wherever possible, nutrient levels on fisheries should be maintained in as natural a condition as possible.

Typical aquatic plants found in hard-watered fisheries include reeds, rushes, sedges, reed canary grass, reed sweet grass, bulrush, reed mace, bur-reed, diverse filamentous algae, ribbon weed, several pond weeds and water buttercups, stoneworts, starworts and water lilies. Typical invertebrates include very abundant populations of midges, worms, snails, pea mussels, swan mussels, duck mussels, caddis flies, mayflies, shrimps, water louse, dragonflies, damsel flies, flatworms, leeches and, sometimes, native crayfish.

Lake Geneva (Lake Leman; see Champigneulle & colleagues paper in Bagliniere & Maisse, 1999)

Lake Geneva or Leman is western Europe's largest lake, with a surface area of over 58,000 hectares, about 40% lying in sub-alpine France and the rest in Switzerland. Despite its relatively high altitude, the lake is very productive and is classed meso/eutrophic. The fish fauna of interest to anglers and netsmen includes brown trout, Arctic char, burbot, pike, perch and roach; seventeen other fish species are present in the huge and varied catchment.

Many trout are harvested each year by professional fishermen using nets and by pleasure anglers trolling lures. The total annual catch of trout since 1950 declared by professional fishermen has varied between 9 and 32 tonnes – that's a lot of trout! In the 1990s there were 145 annual permits allowing professional netsmen to use nets of minimum mesh size of 48mm and with no catch quotas. 2,465 amateur permits allowed trolling lines with a maximum of 20 lures per boat to be used and a quota (bag limit) of 8 trout per day and 250 trout per year per permit. Since 1986, amateur anglers have been asked to declare catches and these (12 tonnes) amount to around three-quarters of the weight of trout caught by the professionals (16 tonnes). The natural trout stock is supplemented with a stocking programme. Since 1994 wild or captive Lake Geneva brood stock have been used, with around a million 5-10cm parr released each year. Additional stocking is carried out on some inflowing rivers. Trout run the many inflowing rivers and streams around the vast shoreline of the lake in order to spawn naturally in the autumn and early winter and the fishery exploits an unknown mix of naturally spawned and stocked brown trout. The Lake flows out into the upper River Rhone, but impassable barriers to migration mean that the trout population is land-locked, with no sea trout present. Unknown numbers of trout of 15-50cm leave the lake each year, presumably recruiting to the Rhone fishery downstream.

The complexity of natural spawning and the varied stocking regimes mean that accurate interpretation of trout population biology in the rivers and streams is next to impossible and that management of the Lake Geneva fishery is, inevitably, imprecise and not well understood. Young trout of one and two years of age are known to drop downstream from small stream nursery areas in large numbers in autumn, winter and early spring. Whether some of these fish are displaced from the high-gradient streams during intense spates or whether the migration is controlled and deliberate is unknown. Growth is known to be rapid in some rivers at least, for instance in the River Redon, where trout grow to 33cm and mature sexually by the time they are three years old. This is exactly comparable to wild brown trout in English chalk streams. In a protected (no-fishing) zone of the River Redon the density of adult trout present in autumn was around eight per hundred square metres of stream bed – a high figure. On fished reaches, the typical adult trout densities were around half this figure. River Redon trout of between 2 and 7 years of age are caught in traps during the spawning migration, most of the larger, older female fish having their eggs are stripped for the hatchery programme.

Lake Geneva trout seem to exhibit one or two years of moderate growth, followed by a rapid acceleration, probably linked to a dietary switch to fish-eating (of roach). Sexual maturation is often delayed to four or five years of age. This is the classical ferox life history strategy. Lake Geneva trout captured in spawning tributaries showed sizes of around 50cm at four years of age, 63cm at five years, 66cm inches at six years and 70cm plus at seven years – large brown trout. Tagging studies showed, in common with brown and sea trout the world-over, that spawners overwhelmingly return to the streams where they were naturally spawned or into which they were stocked at an early age.

Sea trout of the Atlantic French coast (G. Euzenat & colleagues, 1999)

Along the coastlines of Normandy and Picardy, a number of rivers arising in limestone or sandstone areas run to sea and have stocks of sea trout. Their biology has been studied in detail by French fisheries biologists (see Euzenat & colleagues paper in Bagliniere & Meusse, 1999).

These French sea trout migrate up and down-river throughout the year. In May to August, on limestone rivers such as the Bresle or the Calonne which have a steady (spring-fed) flow in summer, most mature fish migrate upstream well prior to spawning. On spatier schist/sandstone catchments with more unpredictable flows, such as on the River Orne, many sea trout migrate in October and November, running in fresh off the tide and straight up towards the spawning grounds on the back of autumnal flood waters. Smolts on both river types run the system downstream from March to May, peaking in April. Kelts make it back after spawning to exit the freshwater systems from December through to March. So, in any month of the year, French sea trout are on the move, a complex use of these river systems. Once at sea, trout move northwards to the English Channel and North Sea, some tagged fish being recaptured as far afield as the Danish west coast.

Smolts vary in size from 11 to 33cm, averaging 20cm and 90 grammes (about three ounces). Most smolts are one or two year-olds, exceptionally threes. Older smolts probably come from tributaries where growth is slower. Early-running smolts are generally older and the final run tends to be dominated by one year-old fish which have just reached the size threshold for migration. Adult sea trout sizes vary widely between rivers, from 25cm to 90cm; 0.2kg to 9kg (half a pound to twenty pounds) and fresh-run fish tend to be in excellent condition. Upper Normandy and Picardy sea trout mostly return to freshwater after one sea winter at some time during the following summer or autumn. The next most common group return to spawn as maiden fish after two sea winters. The oldest sea trout aged from scales have been at sea for a total of over six years, returning to spawn several times over that period – these are the lunkers. The average length of sea trout in this region is around 55cm, weighing around 2.3kg (5 pounds), a good stamp of fish.

On the Orne river system in lower Normandy sea trout run big, averaging 60cm and 2.9kg (well over six pounds) and often achieving this size after only two winters at sea. In contrast, on the River Touques, more trout return early, usually after a single sea winter at around 46cm and 1.4kg (three pounds). It has also been found that brown trout which drop down to marine areas, but without undergoing the silvering characteristic of smolts, can have a high survival rate. These trout may live largely in the estuary, so-called 'slob' trout. Toques sea trout are consistently smaller than those of the same age from other rivers which may reflect genetic or environmental differences in these populations. The Touques also commonly runs finnock in the summer - trout which have only been at sea for two or three months. Some of these finnock then remain in freshwater and spawn the following winter whilst others filter back to sea before the winter, perhaps just feeding in the estuary and lower river system. The common behaviour of finnock visiting freshwater in summer seems to be widespread, with fish often spending time in differing estuaries on their way back south to their natal rivers. This could also be the case with English Channel finnock along English south coast estuaries.

Kelt survival on these northern French rivers is high and returning previous spawners account for around 12% of sea trout on the Touques, 10-25% on the Bresle and Arques and 25-40% on the Orne. Most of the older returning trout are female. The scales of one long-lived fish revealed that it had spawned in seven successive seasons.....a very successful and fortunate individual. Guyomard (1999) explains that the River Orne was known as a brown trout river up until the 1960s, at which point it was stocked with trout from both hatchery and sea trout (River Vistula) origins. Soon afterwards, smolts and returning sea trout turned up and these fish were known to have been stocked. It may well be that the current (valuable) sea trout stock has arisen as a consequence of stocking the system with new trout strains. This is interesting and may parallel the well-known South American examples where brown trout stocking has led to the establishment of thriving sea trout stocks in Chile, Argentina and the Falkland Islands. Caution in interpretation is required, however, as it is thought that the sea trout seen on the Orne may actually be sea-run stocked fish and that these trout may not be spawning successfully at all or, alternatively, that restocking is leading to overcrowding in freshwater and the adoption of migratory behaviour by some wild brown trout (Guyomard, 1999).

At Segrie-Fontaine, south of Caen there is a small visitor centre explaining the ecology of the L'Orne and, further upstream on the Rouvre, a large tributary, there is a countryside centre and nature reserve where you can walk the banks and, perhaps, see the salmon, sea trout, otters, native crayfish and pearl mussels which make this small river so special. When we called in there on a recent trip to France it was raining so hard that I wouldn't have been all that surprised to see sea trout migrating up the path to the visitor centre!

On the Bresle system in the 1980s it has been estimated that, each winter 3-5 million trout eggs were laid and 5500 to 8300 smolts produced each spring. The chances of an egg surviving as far as a smolt were, therefore, around 0.1%; slim odds. 15-20% of tagged Bresle smolts returned from the sea to the river to spawn as marine survival was high at that time. The estimated size of the returning sea trout stock was 2,200 each year of which around 900 were netted, 140 were caught by anglers and 1100 to 1200 survived to run upstream to spawn. The life of the sea trout is a perilous one and leads to an understanding of why these fish have evolved to become so wary and cautious.

Chalk stream trout (Mann et al, 1989)

The chalk streams of England (spring creeks in the USA) are fed from springs which flow with clean, cool, clear alkaline water. Many English chalk streams also have greensand aquifer influences, these rivers being less alkaline than pure chalk-fed systems. Where chalk streams still have abundant flows and where stream habitat quality is high, they can promote startlingly productive wild brown trout fisheries. The trout tend to migrate into headwaters in November and may not spawn until December, January or even later, depending on prevailing conditions. Winter rainfall re-charges aquifers, allows winterbournes to flow and creates access for spawning trout. Where abstraction regimes are excessive, after autumn droughts and dry early winters, trout linger for longer, waiting to migrate upstream to spawn, perhaps not migrating until late January or early February. Ephemeral winterbournes naturally provide large areas of spawning and nursery habitat for wild brown trout, if they can access them. Competition from other fish is likely to be low or absent, given the fact that winterbournes dry out in summer. Where the headwaters are perennial, it is possible also to find salmon, minnows, eels, bullheads, stone loach, sticklebacks and brook lampreys. In terms of overall fish production, the trout can represent quite a small element of the fish community, despite their importance as a quarry species.

Many of these clear, productive small headwater streams in England are in Wiltshire, Hampshire and Dorset – the Bere stream, River Tarrant, Devil's Brook, Candover Brook, Bourne Rivulet, upper Meon, Gussage stream, Sydling brook, Tadnoll brook, River Till and others. Trout eggs spawned in mid-winter hatch in early spring and the resulting fry and parr disperse widely and successfully throughout these miniature systems, possibly avoiding some of the crowding problems seen on other river types. With modern intensive agriculture, chalk stream headwaters tend to be silty places and gravels are also often concreted together with lime deposits, making spawning difficult: trout egg survival is, therefore, often relatively poor. Chalk river catchments as a whole have an estimated 49% arable land use, compared with an average figure for England of 36% (Environment Agency & English Nature, 2004). Autumn cultivation leaves ploughed soils which are readily eroded by winter rain, washing soil straight into these vulnerable rivers. Further problems arise where livestock break down river banks, crumbling chunks of soil straight into the river. Much of the fine sediment which clogs up spawning gravels, inflicting consequent poor egg survival, comes from intensive agricultural sources.

Once past the early population bottleneck of siltation, trout parr show rapid growth on the abundant chalk stream invertebrate communities; typically 12cm after one year, 22.5cm after two years and around 30cm at three years, by which time they have reached sexual maturity. The relatively even temperatures and abundant plant and invertebrate production on these streams leads to sustained trout growth potential and a stable population structure. Not very many wild chalk stream brown trout survive to reach four or five years of age; it is a short life, but a merry one!

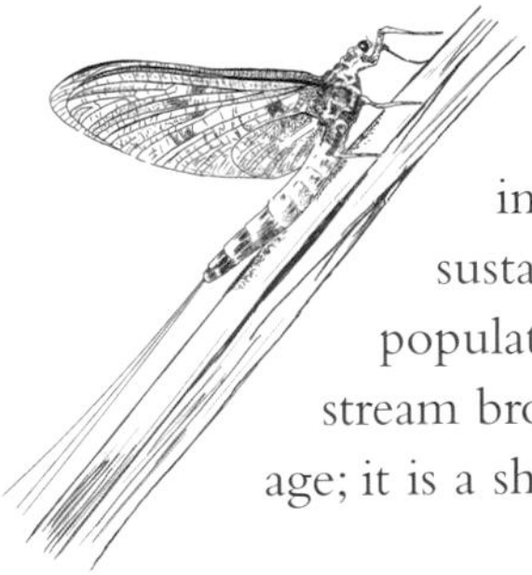

Scientific fisheries surveys show that although growth is rapid, overall densities of adult wild trout in typical, fairly uniform, chalk streams can be quite low compared with higher-gradient streams. Where habitat is varied, however, wild chalk stream trout stocks can be surprisingly abundant, especially if catch-and-release angling is practised. Habitat degradation is, however, commonplace on these rivers and there is great scope for restoration projects which aim to ameliorate or solve problems such as over-abstraction, intensive riparian land use, nutrient enrichment, localised point-source pollution, control of non-native plants and animals and low physical habitat diversity (Environment Agency & English Nature, 2004). The rapid growth of chalk stream trout needs to be set in context by comparison with other river types.

Overview of wild brown trout growth potential

In their classic book 'The Trout' (1967), Winnifred Frost and Margaret Brown provided (in Appendix 3) information on trout growth rates, calculated from scale readings, from a range of British waters. The information still makes for interesting reading. The table below considers average trout growth (length in centimetres) for various types of fishery in order of biological productivity.

	Year 1	Year 2	Year 3	Year 4	Year 5	Year 6	Year 7	Year 8
Chalk streams	12	25	32	39	48			
Limestone river and lake systems	9	20	30	37	40	47	57	
Sandstone and medium productivity waters	6	13.5	20	24.5	28	35	48	
Granite and peat bog systems	4.5	10	15	19.5	22	23	23.5	26

On average, then, chalk streams grow trout which are more than twice the length at three years of age (and far heavier) than fish from granite peat bogs. On the upper River Tees in Yorkshire, for instance, an eight year-old brown trout is hardly bigger than a two year-old from the upper Hampshire Avon. Of course, on any water, there is a considerable variation in trout growth rates, this fact being masked by using averaged information. In the table above, variations between rivers and lakes are further masked by combining a range of fisheries in each category, but I hope that the comparisons are still useful and provide a rough guide to what may be expected under natural conditions.

Bagliniere & Maisse (1999, Table 4) group French brown trout stocks from rapid to slow growers. If arranged as a series with the fastest first, we get: Poitou-Charentes, Normandy, Alsace, Alps - Leman catchment, East Paris catchment, Pre Alpes, Basque country, Massif Central, Jura and the Pyrenees. Sizes at 2+/3 years run from, at best, 35cm, down to a diminuitive 13cm. This is very similar to the size range seen in wild brown trout of three years of age in British waters although even our chalk stream trout don't quite keep up with Poitou-Charentes Region trout. Sounds like another good place for a fishing holiday!

In wild trout populations, the growth rates of immature fish and the typical size at sexual maturity are very important characteristics, probably having evolved in response to the prevalent feeding conditions and likelihood of survival as fish grow older. If mortality rates in a given river or lake increase sharply after four years of age, then there will be strong selection to mature at three. If environmental conditions dictate that long-life is typical in a given lake, then trout may evolve a life cycle which includes moderate early growth, late maturation and spawning a number of times in successive years. Big wild trout tend to have grown rapidly as parr, but mature later than usual and are often long-lived.

Take ferox, for instance, which occur in large, deep, cool lakes such as Llyns Padarn and Peris in Wales, the English Lakes Ullswater, Bassenthwaite and Windermere, a sprinkling of Irish loughs and, most famously, Lochs Awe, Quoich, Rannoch and Arkaig in the Highlands of Scotland.

Mighty Scottish ferox

Ferox 85 is a research group of keen fishery scientists / anglers who jointly aim to discover more of the biology of the stupendous piscivorous (fish-eating) trout which we call ferox. Alastair Thorne of Scotland's Fisheries Research Services (a Government Agency, www.frs-scotland.gov.uk) has kindly supplied some up-to-date information, based upon recent research carried out by himself and colleagues from the FRS Freshwater and Marine laboratories. The work has concentrated on the deep Highland Lochs Rannoch and Garry. Loch Rannoch ferox approaching 20 pounds have been caught by anglers trolling either natural baits or large spoons or plugs. This large lake has been famous since Edwardian times for producing enormous trout for those intrepid fishers willing to put in many hours of effort in small boats, battered by breaking waves in the cold, wind-swept expanses of the loch. Whilst ferox in Ireland are thought to be a separate brown trout species, the Scottish view seems to be that Highland loch ferox may be part of a genetically variable Salmo trutta stock. Scottish ferox are certainly very variable in body shape and spotting patterns. Whether such fish are a real (reproductively isolated) species or a life cycle variant of the highly adaptable brown trout probably matters little to you if you have a whopper bending your rod double!

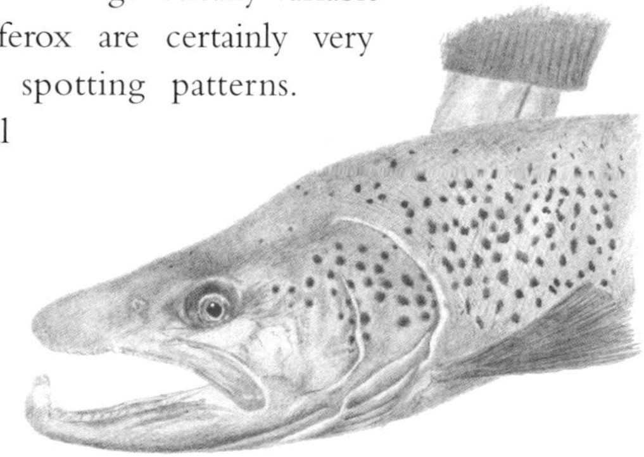

Scale reading studies show that ferox start off their growth just like average invertebrate-feeding brown trout, but show a characteristic growth spurt, corresponding to a change-over to a fish diet at a typical size of 30-35cm and an age of perhaps 6 to 8 years. These trout then exhibit rocket growth, fuelled by their usual diet of Arctic char and smaller brown trout. On Lough Corrib in the far West of Ireland the large fish-eating brown trout seem these days to thrive on a diet of roach. In Loch Garry minnows occur in the diet of ferox and these small fish may help them to bridge the dietary gap from invertebrates to fish. Once fish-eating has been adopted, the distance between the growth rings on the scales widens markedly, showing rapid length increases. Multiple recaptures of tagged fish have revealed, for example, that a 1.5kg trout caught and tagged in September 1994 weighed 6.4kg when it was recaptured in May 1998. That's rapid growth! Interestingly, this fish weighed only 4.6kg when caught again in May 2001; now over fifteen years old it had gone into physical decline. These old fish have a relatively large head and a thin body in poor condition. For many years this was viewed as the characteristic shape of ferox but, in reality, it corresponds with old age. Such fish may be losing their grip, less successful at catching their elusive prey and so more willing to take the chance of snatching at a sparkling spoon trolled slowly along in the depths of the loch. If these fish were most easily caught, they would have been viewed as being typical of the species by anglers. Before the recent scientific research interest in ferox, only anglers would have seen them with any regularity.

Ferox in their prime, when early teenagers, tend to be deep-bellied, supremely fit fish. However, even these fish vary markedly in condition, being thinner after spawning and possibly owing to high parasite burdens carried by some individuals. Ferox can be very long-lived for trout and lucky ones may survive to be old teenagers or even twenty years of age. At the time of writing the UK rod-caught record ferox, weighing just over 14kg, caught from Loch Awe by Brian Rutland in 2002, was aged from its scales at a veritable 23 years. Cold northern waters can produce really long-lived salmonids; Norwegian ferox have been aged at up to 34 years for male fish and 38 years for females.

Most of the big Scottish lochs are thought to harbour large fish-eating brown trout. Ferox distribution seems often to coincide with that of Arctic char, but some stocks occur in waters which only support brown trout. The scant information available from tagging studies indicates that, in relatively unproductive Scottish highland lochs, ferox may not be very numerous, so catch-and-release may be a necessary management strategy if we are to conserve stocks and maintain fishery performance. Whether the more productive limestone loughs of the West of Ireland support higher densities of ferox is unknown. Fortunately, many of the trout fishers of Loughs Corrib and Mask return most of their fish, so the conservation of these valuable stocks should be assured.

One of the most fascinating aspects of the research carried out by Alastair Thorne, Alisdair MacDonald and colleagues on Loch Garry involved the use of hi-tech tags which allow the repeated location of fish and data retrieval showing the depths at which fish have been swimming at differing times of day. Analyses of preliminary results appear to show no sign of territoriality as these big trout range widely, typically swimming in relatively shallow water at night and making deep dives of quite short duration during the day. The dives are probably in search of char shoals which they chase in the depths of the loch when light levels are high. Trout are, after all, primarily visual hunters and the 390 acres of Loch Garry, with an average depth of 50 feet, must make prey location a tricky business unless visibility is good. In one excellent set of data (August 2002) a 3.7kg ferox spent most of its time in the top 5 metres of water but, each day, dived down to between 5 and 10 metres, presumably whilst hunting. It could be that the char are caught in the deeper water, but that digestion is aided in the warmer surface waters, hence the daily deep-diving behaviour of these fascinating fish. There were some indications in Loch Garry that ferox may lie up using boulder outcrops for cover which could be an additional or alternative reason for so much time being spent in relatively shallow water around the margins of the loch. I look forward to future findings from this interesting line of research on these large predatory brown trout.

Scottish and Irish sea trout declines

Dr Andy Walker of Fisheries Research Services, Pitlochry, Scotland has, for many years, researched the sea trout of West Highland rivers and lochs. These fisheries, famed for their numbers and size of sea trout have, since the 1950s, fluctuated greatly in their productivity. He updated his findings in Salmo Trutta volume 6 (Wild Trout Trust 2003), noting that many factors could have been to blame for possible stock declines: increased poaching, increased exploitation by legitimate angling, increased predation and changing, less favourable, marine feeding conditions. By the late 1980s very well known sea trout fisheries such as those on Loch Stack, Loch Maree, Loch Sheil and Loch Eilt were all clearly suffering from stock declines, despite the fact that the superb Scottish countryside and mountain ecology appeared still to be in good heart. Fishery owners tightened regulations to reduce exploitation on those few adult fish which made it back to spawn. From 1990 the key sea trout research focus, both in Scotland and in the similarly affected West of Ireland turned to sea lice infestations. Trout post-smolts which had been at sea for only a short while were turning up plastered with larval sea lice which chewed away the skin from the head, back and fins, leaving the young migratory trout open to osmotic stress (drying-out whilst underwater!), secondary infections and consequent death. Numbers of parasitic sea lice were unusually high in estuaries where the cage-rearing of salmon was taking place. Fishery owners and managers therefore engaged salmon farmers in active dialogue to discuss what could be done about the apparent linkage between sea lice infestations and salmon cages.

Paddy Gargan and colleagues (2002) reported similar research results in Ireland and severe sea lice infestations were also affecting sea trout in Norway. The Irish research indicates that sea trout smolts living well away from salmon farms may have a background infestation level of around 5-10 sea lice per fish, but that very close (within a kilometre) of a salmon farm this can climb to ten times that level, threatening smolt survival.

Sea trout may, of course, be affected by many factors. Damage to freshwater habitats, sea lice, the disease Furunculosis, other parasites and diseases, nutrient enrichment of coastal waters, sand eel fisheries and climate change are all factors which may have been adversely affecting wild sea trout and salmon stocks. Escaped salmon from sea cages are also running rivers and inter-breeding with wild salmon (and, perhaps, trout), an additional concern for wild game fish stocks. In Scotland and Ireland, the importance of both salmon farming and game angling to local economies means that sustainable solutions must be found. Better management of salmon cage production may, in some areas at least, have lessened the threat from sea lice.

Now, ten years-on, Andy Walker reports that his intensive study on the Loch Sheildaig system, where both up- and downstream migrating trout are trapped and can be tagged and counted, has shown that stocked trout (of local genetic provenance) have survived well in freshwater, smolted and migrated to sea but few adults have returned. Marine survival has been very poor and studies of young smolts, only a few days at sea revealed that many were severely infected with sea lice. The levels of infection seen may well have proven fatal. Sampling revealed a relatively dense, five metre-wide band of sea lice larvae living around river mouths and the shore line. Freshly migrating smolts have to run the gauntlet of infection and it appears that this could be the key to the poor marine survival indicated from upstream trap results. A very similar view had been expressed in Ireland by west coast fisheries researchers concerned by sea trout declines in Connemara. Further Scottish research showed that the second year of the salmon farming cycle appeared to be the one which promoted the bulk of sea lice production. Salmon smolts newly introduced to cages harboured few lice and lice numbers dropped-off when cages were run fallow to break parasite and disease life cycles. With new knowledge, progress was being made.

The link between poor sea trout survival and nearby salmon cage culture appears from research findings to be one of cause-and-effect and it is now important to discover ways in which wild migratory salmonid stocks can be conserved, supporting the angling tourism economy whilst, at the same time, the salmon farming industry is not impaired to an unacceptable level. The careful use of fallowing and cage rotation in key bays, together with the use of medicated food and good coordination and collaboration between different salmon producers seems to hold out hope.

It is intended that cage salmon farming impacts can be reduced to a minimum whilst, simultaneously, a re-stocking programme with juvenile trout of the correct genetic provenance will pump-prime recoveries of those formerly famous fisheries which still have few returning adult sea trout. This is bound to take several seasons before the typical large, long-lived, multiple-spawning sea trout of these north west Highland Scottish rivers become relatively abundant once more, but the prospect of success is there. Some Highland sea trout and salmon fisheries have experienced better fishing in recent seasons and it is best to check on current form when deciding where to fish. This is a heartening example of commerce and conservation organisations working together on the basis of sound scientific research findings. Necessity is the mother of invention. With trout conservation issues firmly in mind, perhaps now is the time to consider them in greater detail: read on.

The author with his biggest River Piddle wild brown trout, caught by electric-fishing. It's much easier than with a fly rod.

CHAPTER 3

CONSERVATION AND MANAGEMENT

IT'S AMAZING how time flies. Back in the late 1980s I carried out a questionnaire survey on the status of wild game fish stocks in the British Isles (Giles (1989). The results, together with much follow-up work revealed widespread concerns over much of lowland south-east England for the health of brown trout populations. In the western Celtic fringes of Cornwall and Devon, Wales, Cumbria, much of Ireland, up the west coast of Scotland and through the Scottish Islands many wild trout stocks remained. The best wild trout waters tend to be well off the beaten track. Amongst all waters surveyed a large proportion had, at some time, been stocked. In the crowded, over-developed south of England most formerly productive wild trout fisheries had dwindled to the point where stocking was sustaining the fishing pressure and where wild fish were a rarity. Some would argue that a trout is a trout and that stocked fish are just as good as wild ones for angling purposes. Others maintain that you can't beat a wild trout as a challenging quarry for the fly rod. Also, rather importantly, the good habitat quality required to sustain a wild trout stock supports a wealth of other wildlife. The presence of self-sustaining game fish stocks tells us, therefore, that the quality of our environment must be reasonably good. Wild trout are a barometer which we should keep an eye on.

In Europe, the ubiquitous trout species is *Salmo trutta*, the brown trout. Some authorities argue, very reasonably, that we should also recognise officially (to aid their conservation) sub-species or even new species additional to *Salmo trutta*. These include ferox, gillaroo, sonaghen and the marmorated trout of Yugoslavia which has char-like markings.

Arguments for the conservation of distinctive trout races are based upon studies which show genetic differences, maintained at population level between *Salmo trutta* and these various other races of trout. Distinctive local trout stocks are vulnerable to habitat damage, over-exploitation and to stocking which results in adverse changes to the genetics of the population. It takes a long time for populations to adapt to their environment, but it may not take long to wipe out local adaptations through bad fisheries management. Sadly, there are many examples of crass fisheries and environmental management leading to the loss of important natural game fish diversity. In the survival stakes, diversity is strength.

Trout diversity has developed in both freshwater and migratory populations. The sea trout of the Caspian Sea are said to be distinctive forms and have been reported to grow to a staggering 45kg (Ade, 1989). The wild sea trout of the Caspian, Aral and Black Seas are little documented, but are known to suffer from a range of environmental problems and many stocks may have an uncertain future. In recent years major water diversions for agriculture have reduced Aral Sea water levels by around 15 metres, increasing salinity, exposing huge areas of former lake bed and wreaking major ecological damage. The sea trout are now probably gone, together with almost all of the other fish species. Another fine natural fisheries resource is lost through agricultural intensification (Williams & Aladin, 1991).

Mountainous European areas, with their cool lakes and rivers support many natural brown trout stocks; the French Pyrenees, Massif central, the Ardennes, Bavarian Alps, Harz Mountains, Swiss Alps and upland ranges in Poland, Czechoslovakia, Spain, Italy, Greece and the Yugoslavian Julian Alps all have renowned brown trout fisheries. In many cases, the local trout populations are distinctive in a number of ways, for instance growth potential. Brown trout of 15kg have been caught in Lapland's Lake Inari. Norway, Sweden and Iceland all have fabulous, diverse brown trout stocks and have migratory populations producing sea trout up to around

10kg. Sweden's River Morrum which receives lusty Baltic sea trout has a record 15kg rod-caught fish. Baltic sea trout remain common and readily catchable from many shore-based locations. Many northern European countries have large numbers of Arctic char and grayling waters, as well as diverse wild trout fisheries.

North America

North America has diverse inland game fisheries and a mix of western seaboard Pacific salmon and east coast Atlantic salmon stocks. Inland, there are rainbow trout, cutthroat trout, brook trout, lake trout and arctic char and grayling. Brook and lake 'trout' are actually species of char, in the genus *Salvelinus*. Rainbow trout have most recently been classified with the Pacific salmon in the genus *Oncorhynchus*. The fact that fish taxonomists still change their minds over exactly where to place species underlines the close genetic affinities of northern hemisphere salmon, trout and char. Closely-allied races and species can often interbreed and produce surviving offspring but, as we shall see later, such mixing of gene pools can lead to serious potential problems for wild stocks.

Brook trout are typically upland small stream fish although larger river populations and migratory coastal stocks also occur. Lake trout, as their name suggests, roam large, cold deep water lakes, sometimes growing huge and living long in the process. Lake trout and brook trout have been artificially hybridised to produce Splake. Wild cutthroat trout are native to the eastern-flowing rivers of the North American central divide, often penetrating small, unproductive side streams. Cutthroats also naturally occur along the western- flowing streams and Pacific coastline and, unlike rainbows, have not been widely stocked outside their native home range.

The cutthroat trout has been split up into many regional types, some of which have been given the status of sub-species from time to time. These distinctive local variants include Yellowstone cutthroats, Montana black spots, Pacific coast fish, Lahontan, Paiute, Bonneville, Colorado, Rio Grande, greenback and yellow-finned cutthroats. Rainbows, native only to streams flowing west from the central divide, have often been introduced to native cutthroat waters and will hybridise freely with them, threatening the survival of local races. The natural range for wild rainbow trout covers northern Alaska down through the western states to the Californian peninsula and coastal Mexican rivers. Amongst these varied rainbow trout stocks there are many migratory steelhead populations, Californian golden trout, Arizona Apache trout, desert Gila trout and Mexican golden trout, amongst others. Several of these, it has been argued, deserve full specific status, so different are they from the archetypal rainbow trout.

The folly of introductions

Of course, rather like the European brown trout, rainbow trout have now been stocked extensively over much of the world. The introduction of species to new habitats and existing wildlife communities is a risky, unpredictable business. With introductions can come diseases and parasites to which native fish have no natural immunity. Introduced species can also out-compete native fish for food and space and predatory species like trout may prove far too good at eating smaller species which have no natural defences against the incomers. Take the Falkland Islands, for instance.

Brown trout in the Falklands

Bob McDowall (2001) provides a brief review of the ecology of freshwater fishes found in the Falklands Islands based on extensive surveys which he carried out in 1999. McDowall explains how the islands native freshwater fish fauna may now be comprised of only two species, the zebra 'trout' *Aplochiton zebra* and Falklands minnow, *Galaxius maculatus*, both of which can live their entire life cycles in freshwater or migrate to sea to take advantage of the rich marine food resources found in this polar region. Whilst the Falklands minnow is still widely-distributed and common, the zebra trout seems to have become far rarer in recent decades and is now thought to occur essentially only where brown trout are absent. Concern over the conservation status of zebra trout led the Falklands Islands Government to give it complete legal protection in 1999. Brown trout were introduced into the Falklands during the 1940s, with stock coming from Chile, the USA, England and Scotland. It is thought that most or all introductions were from non migratory stocks.

Whatever their various provenances, trout liberated into relatively unproductive Falkland streams soon started to migrate to sea to feed on the prolific krill populations found around the islands. Not surprisingly, these fish grew like greased lightning and returned to spawn in the streams where they had been released, rapidly adapting to local conditions. Gradually, with natural straying behaviour, further streams were successfully colonised by brown / sea trout and now the species is firmly established, supporting well-known world class sea trout fisheries. Immaculate Falklands sea trout of 10kg-plus have been caught by visiting anglers and multiple catches of trout of a large average size are commonplace. Whilst the brown trout was finding its feet in the Falklands environment, native zebra trout populations appear to have been impacted severely, probably via both food competition and by direct predation. Unproductive Falklands rivers offer little aquatic invertebrate life for trout parr and sub-adults and so young zebra trout may have suddenly been subject to an intense threat against which they have no natural defences. Although there is little or no documentation of this interaction, there seems little doubt that the pugnacious brown trout has won the fight for natural resources in these streams. The introduction of this northern hemisphere species has had an appreciable ecological impact. A similar history has developed in New Zealand where introduced brown trout have done very well over the last 150 years, producing world-class fly fisheries in upland streams but simultaneously impacting small native fish species (McDowall, 1968).

Rainbow trout in Lake Titicaca Peru

Lake Titicaca is the highest lake in the Americas (around 3,800 metres above sea level), having risen gradually with the building of the magnificent Andean mountain chain. The lake, which straddles the Peruvian / Bolivian border was a cradle of the Incan civilisation and naturally supported a restricted fish fauna of one catfish species and a diverse group of toothed carp (cyprinodont) *Orestias* killifish species. The killifishes, which had this enormous (8,000 square km) lake pretty much to themselves, diversified widely to exploit the various habitat types, evolving in the process into a wide range of separate specialised species. Some developed into algal browsers, others into plankton-feeders, some became specialised predators on molluscs or crustaceans and a few became large enough to eat smaller fish species. This process of rapid evolution is called adaptive radiation and has also occurred amongst the cichlid fishes of the great lakes of Africa. Twenty three of the Lake Titicaca *Orestias* species are endemic to the lake and the larger ones support important native fisheries, with nets being set traditionally from the famous reed boats. A wonderful sustainable way of life, one would have thought.

However, in 1940 rainbow trout (and other species) were introduced into this natural mountain paradise, bringing with them a microscopic protozoan parasite rejoicing in the name of *Ichthyophthirius multifilliis* – try saying that after a few pints of beer! This little parasite, which causes 'swimmer's itch' in humans, thrived on the skin of both trout and killifishes alike and built up to plague proportions, killing an estimated 18 million killifish in one massive outbreak. Not surprisingly, this had a chronic impact on both the unique endemic fish fauna and on the natural fisheries: a sad example of the folly of exotic fish introductions. The silver lining to this cloud was, however, the development of a spectacular rainbow trout fishery which, although not well managed over the years, did give rise to huge catches of massive trout for the local people and a boost to the rural economy.

Rainbow trout introduction had brought with it a mixture of costs and benefits and this is an outcome which has typified salmonid fish introductions the world over. Exotic fish, once liberated can produce exciting new fisheries with little environmental damage, but they often proliferate, changing natural fish communities through competition, predation, hybridisation or the spread of parasites and diseases. When will we learn? Once the toothpaste is out of the tube, you can't get it back in.

The loss of special trout strains

Anyone who has taken the trouble to have a close look at wild trout from a variety of waters will have noticed substantial differences in shape, size and colouration. Not all trout are the same. Whether you believe in splitting trout up into many subtly different types or lumping them together as larger, very variable species, I guess what really matters is that we try to ensure the long-term conservation of the wild salmonid resource. This is vital both for its intrinsic values and for potential value to humanity as a future genetic resource. It may well be that some of the genetic variants are especially good at resisting extreme environmental conditions such as high temperatures, low pH values, low dissolved oxygen concentrations or whatever. Qualities of this type are worth conserving because they may be of critical survival value at some point in the future. Mankind must not be so greedy as to try to get more and bigger trout from all available habitats. We need to learn to appreciate what nature provides and to accept, indeed rejoice in, wild trout in all their shapes, colours and sizes. Small is better, sometimes. The history of human exploitation and manipulation of freshwater fisheries is a depressingly familiar one of greed and lack of appreciation of the limits of natural productivity.

In the following sections I consider just a few examples to illustrate some key threats to wild trout survival. These include competition for water supplies, habitat destruction, over-exploitation by angling, introductions of exotic salmonids, hybridisation and disease.

Maine 'square tail' brook trout

In the mid 19th century, massive brook trout of 2-5kg and more were discovered in the Richardson and Rangley Lake watersheds of Maine. These trophy-sized trout fed on Arctic char, now just a memory on these lakes, possibly having been predated out of existence by stocked land-locked salmon. In the early days a notional catch limit of 50 pounds of brook trout per person per day led to the killing of virtually every trout caught. Unsurprisingly, the populations were unable to sustain the gold-rush type bonanza of fishing pressure which ensued after the early fantastic catches were publicised. Sadly, many of the big bags of brookies weren't even eaten; they were displayed, photographed and buried. Anglers posed with strings of lunker square-tailed trout, rather reminiscent of big game hunters with a boot resting on the head of a shot African bull elephant.

Another probable nail in the coffin of early, thriving brook trout stocks was the manipulation of river flows and lake water levels introduced with hydro-electric power schemes in the mid 1880s. Lake draw-downs to keep the turbines spinning may have restricted brook trout access to important spawning and over-wintering streams. Concern over water management and electrical generation in this extensive area of rivers and lakes is still widely felt, with low summer flows often developing in dry years. There have, however, been fisheries management initiatives to conserve remaining brook trout stocks. Catch restrictions to one and two fish limits and, in some areas no-kill policies, have led directly to marked increases in stocks of big trout. Brookies of around 3kg now survive long enough to be caught by fishermen, a situation not seen for around half a century. Lessons from the past have been taken on board and the future for these Maine fisheries looks more encouraging (see Ted Williams article in Trout Unlimited TROUT magazine, summer, 1997).

Trophy strain trout

In the 19th and early 20th century cutthroat trout of Pyramid Lake, Nevada grew to prodigious sizes; John Skimmerhorn caught an 18.6 kg specimen there in July 1925. Did he put it back? No. Rather than conserve these amazing fish, man snuffed them out by over-fishing the stock and messing around with their habitats. In 1938, the last natural spawning run of lunker cutthroats from Pyramid Lake was reported to include numerous 10 kg plus fish, but this stock was lost when an upstream dam diverted the flow of the Truckee River to irrigate crops. Competition for water supplies was the culprit, once again. Now re-stocked, cutthroats are still present in Pyramid Lake, but the leviathans are gone. Might they have had special genetic constitutions facilitating awesome growth potential or was the feeding just so rich that a 'standard' cutthroat could have done similarly well? We will never know for sure, but Robert Behnke (TU TROUT Summer, 1997), an expert trout biologist, certainly reckons that those huge cutthroats were a specialised genetic strain. Despite continuing good feeding conditions in Pyramid Lake, recent cutthroats grow to only about half the maximum size of the past giants.

Behnke describes how wild brown trout stocks in Lake Vanern, Sweden were similarly disrupted by hydro-electric dam-building which barred access to particular spawning areas. This led to the loss of the longest-lived (16-17 years) and largest (15 kg plus) brown trout strain which had depended upon those particular spawning and nursery habitats. These separate, distinctive sub-stocks of wild trout occur commonly in large lake and river systems which haven't been messed around with too much. Careless management or a lack of management to maintain key areas of habitat can soon lead to the loss of these specialised trout.

On Kootenay Lake, British Columbia, the huge Gerrard strain of Kamloops rainbow trout naturally spawns in one river at the northern end of the lake. These trout are late maturing, long-lived, specialist predators on the little, landlocked, kokanee salmon. Trout of this strain have grown to 20kg -plus when stocked into Jewel Lake, B.C. However, Gerrard strain Kamloops rainbows seldom establish new stocks which retain their huge growth potential, probably because of interbreeding with 'normal' rainbows, with a resulting dilution of the genetic specialisation. There are good evolutionary parallels operating here: giant cutthroats feeding on very abundant lake chub, giant rainbows feeding on abundant dwarf kokanee salmon, ferox trout in northern Europe feeding on Arctic char and smaller brown trout. All survive because of access to suitable spawning rivers and probably constitute separate, unique breeding stocks. The genetic growth potential of these fish was naturally selected and developed because everything was there to support it; a dependable, rich food supply plus suitable habitats, right through the life cycle.

The implication is clear – special wild trout and their habitats need special protection, otherwise you lose them. Who knows what the future will bring and what sorts of fish people will need to call upon to provide food and recreational opportunities in tomorrow's world? As long as we remain ignorant of future needs, we must do everything we can to conserve genetic biodiversity. Extinction is, after all, forever.

Yellowstone cutthroats

In a fascinating article, Paul Schullery (TU TROUT Spring, 1996) outlines some of the history of Yellowstone Lake. He explains how Man has interfered with the natural ecosystems of the park, with the best of intentions, but with variable results. Yellowstone National Park was set up in 1872 – a far-sighted move. Contrary to the conservation ethos, however, native Yellowstone cutthroat trout were regarded as an exploitable natural resource and were fished heavily. Over the first half of the twentieth century an estimated 48 million adult cutthroats were removed and hundreds of millions of eggs stripped for hatchery use, reducing natural reproduction in the lake's fifty nine spawning streams. The 1960s saw the over-harvested stock on its knees and new fishery regulations were instigated in the 1970s to try and protect the remaining population. This appeared successful and fishing improved through the 1980s, but reports of the capture of lake trout started to circulate and were confirmed in the early 1990s. Someone had deliberately introduced lake trout into the system, presumably in the belief that he/she was doing the fishery a favour. A research programme revealed the presence of a previously unsuspected substantial lake trout stock, probably spawning successfully every year since the latter part of the 1980s. Lake trout were now a firmly established species in the Yellowstone Lake ecosystem and juveniles were, by then, recruiting into the breeding stock. A potential population explosion was on the cards. The history of lake trout introductions into large western American lakes reveals that, very often, these large-growing predatory char, once established, decimate native fish stocks. Young cutthroat trout living in the open waters of Yellowstone Lake are perfect fodder to fuel just such an ecological disaster. Expert fishery biologists reckoned that, over the twenty first century the cutthroat stock could be reduced by 70% and the annual value of the sport fishery might drop from $36 million in 1994 to less than $9 million, all because of an ill-considered species introduction.

In winter, the famous Yellowstone River cutthroat stock living downstream migrates upstream to shelter in the lake – right where the big predatory lake trout lurk. With declining cutthroat stocks, grizzly bears, mink, martens, otters, osprey, bald eagles, divers (loons), mergansers, gulls, grebes, terns, kingfishers and other species all suffer direct or indirect knock-on effects from changes in their cutthroat trout food supply. Lake trout aren't as available as cutthroats to predators (or fishermen), since they live mostly down in the depths and spawn on lake bed gravels. They do not have to run the dangerous gauntlet of spawning stream migrations. In the mid 1990s it was suggested that an intensive, selective, lake trout gill net fishery could keep the invaders in check, possibly allowing a resurgence of the cutthroat stock. In the latter half of the 1990s, research gill netting was underway – trying to catch lots of big lakers, but few of the precious cutthroats. The jury is out on the long-term outcome, but Mahony & Ruzycki (2000) report that the netting programme of spawning lake trout appears to be having a positive effect. The sizes of mature lake trout are declining, a sign that the fishery is starting to bite a useful hole in the spawner stock.

The moral of this story is clear – just because you may feel that a species introduction could be a good move, don't do it until the relevant authorities have weighed up the pros and cons. If enough sound scientific evidence isn't available, apply the precautionary principle and just don't do it.

Hybridisation problems for Bull trout

Native bull trout, *Salvelinus confluentis* have suffered a calamitous decline throughout their range in the western United States and Canada, probably from factors including over-exploitation, hybridisation with brook trout, habitat damage and man made barriers to migration. These magnificent char, classified as 'Threatened' throughout their USA distribution have attracted considerable conservation efforts in recent years. M.W. Buktenica & colleagues (2000) describe the Crater Lake National Park Oregon project where introduced brook trout (Salvelinus fontinalis) have, over nine years, been deliberately over-exploited and removed in Sun Creek by a combination of electric-fishing, trap netting, snorkel diving surveys and use of the antibiotic Antimycin ('FINTROL') which is toxic to fish. Antimycin is neutralised by the application of potassium permanganate at the bottom end of the treated stretches.

Sun Creek originates as abundant sub-Alpine cold spring feeds, high in a glacial valley overlain by volcanic ash and pumice soils originating from the Mount Mazama caldera. It's a small stream – a series of waterfalls and pools of a metre or so width in the headwaters and meandering through volcanic soils of the lower valley where it swells to around 6 metres wide. Here, it is largely over-shaded by mountain hemlock and is, therefore, cool and dark. The objective of the project is to eradicate brookies from the Creek and to prevent re-immigration, allowing a recovery of the native bull trout stock. Following early extensive electric-fishing operations, many of the bull trout were removed from the stream and carefully held in nearby waters while Sun Creek was deliberately polluted with Antimycin to kill brook trout. After this combined onslaught, stocks of brookies plummeted, whilst most bull trout survived the various fisheries operations and continued spawning each winter. Recent results are that the bull trout stock in the Creek has increased from around 200 in 1992 to nearly 800 in the year 2000 and that distribution has expanded from a nucleus of around 2 kilometres to 14 kilometres. With protection, the population is increasing, but at considerable cost. Just imagine how much work would be involved in extending this operation to further former bull trout strongholds. Remember – all of this has proved necessary because of the introduction of 'generic' hatchery brook trout into native trout waters.

Arizona Apache trout

Imagine it's the 1800s and you are looking out over pristine montane habitat of the White Mountain region of east-central Arizona (see Ruiz & Novy, 2000). The headwaters of the upper Salt and Little Colorado rivers gather here and flow away down the rocky slopes, towards the arid heat below. Above about 1800 metres it stays cool enough to sustain salmonids and here you would have found spectacular indigenous yellow-bellied, heavily-spotted rainbow trout finning in the crystal waters. Originally, it is thought that about 1000 kilometres of stream supported these Apache trout, but by the 1950s, their distribution was probably pegged-back to less than 50 kilometres. That's not much habitat for the world population of a species. Currently, around 200 kilometres of isolated headwaters above natural barriers allow these delicate trout continuing existence and it is hoped that the recovery programme currently underway will expand this range to up to 500 kilometres, securing the future of this threatened species. In 1955, fishing for Apache trout was closed on their only remaining known wilderness streams at Fort Apache Indian Reservation. By the early 1960s a reintroduction programme had been initiated and by 1974 the species had gained legal protection, but was subsequently downgraded to 'Threatened' status. In 1992, all stocking with 'generic' rainbow trout was stopped within the natural distribution of Apache trout. A recovery plan was written and implementation started. This involved addressing the genetic purity of remaining stocks, establishing a pure broodstock hatchery programme, elimination of stocked exotic trout which had hybridised with Apaches and targeted habitat improvement projects. The goal of the programme is the de-listing of the species, indicating a relaxation of its conservation status. This will be considered when at least 30 self-sustaining natural stocks are alive and well, all known stocks are replicated and when current risks to the species have been eliminated. Of the 39 stream systems ear-marked in the recovery programme, 31 will be actively managed for genetic purity by protection from stocking with exotic species. Nineteen streams on federal and tribal lands have been fenced to remove cattle grazing pressure and to allow a re-establishment of the delicate desert flora. Logging issues are also being addressed in these and other areas. Ten further streams and 14 small cold water reservoirs will be stocked with Apaches, specifically to encourage sport fishing for and a widened appreciation of this spectacular-looking trout.

By 2000, 26 artificial barriers had been constructed on 21 streams to protect Apache stocks from colonisation by non-indigenous salmonids.

Nineteen streams had been chemically treated with FINTROL to remove non-native brook trout, brown trout and rainbow/Apache hybrids. Every ten years, monitoring will be undertaken on all Apache trout streams which will include fish and habitat quality surveys, invertebrate sampling and assessments of the condition of surrounding meadowland. Physical fish barriers, in-stream structures and runs of fencing are to be examined annually to ensure the continuing success of conservation initiatives. Good luck to them.

Whilst some fish introductions can bring great benefits, as we have just seen, others can be an unmitigated (or difficult and expensive to mitigate) disaster. Take the spread of Whirling disease in north American rivers, for instance.

Whirling disease

Whirling disease is a parasitic condition caused by the protozoan *Myxobolus cerebralis* which infects the cartilage of young trout, both in hatcheries and in the wild. Discovered in Europe in 1903 and the US in the late 1950s, the disease seemed only to ravage juvenile hatchery trout and was kept largely under control by destroying infected stocks. First found in Pennsylvania in 1958, it was then discovered in Nevada, Connecticut, Virginia, California and, by 1966, Massachusetts. Since then the parasite has turned up in at least 22 American States which shows how fish parasites and diseases can soon get around, once liberated (see Thomas Brandt's article, TU TROUT Spring, 1998 and Nickum & Bartholomew, 2000).

Rainbow trout are chronically susceptible to whirling disease. In laboratory experiments, brook trout and cutthroats were also found to be susceptible to infection, but brown trout appear to have a high degree of natural immunity. These matters remained largely academic until, suddenly in the early 1990s, the disease broke out in the wild rainbow trout stocks of the Colorado and Madison Rivers and both populations suffered sharp declines. It would appear that the spread of the disease from hatcheries to north American rivers had been influenced by the widespread stocking of hatchery-produced trout which carry and transmit parasite spores to wild fish populations. Once introduced to a wild rainbow stock, the disease, which has a spore stage in tiny freshwater *Tubifex* worms can cause high levels of mortality in trout fry and parr which lose their balance and whirl in the water when startled. Infected fish often have characteristic curved spines and darkened tails.

Rainbow trout may have suffered more than brookies or cutthroats because many of their streams and rivers are relatively warm and silty, providing a perfect home for the parasite's intermediate *Tubifex* worm host. Cool, rocky, mountain streams may have few *Tubifex* and so not harbour the disease to the same degree. Habitat type and quality may, therefore, partly determine the vulnerability of a fishery to infection. A further complication seems to be the presence of whirling disease spores in many rivers, but a lack of trout kills. It may be that the disease doesn't hit wild trout stocks unless a suite of suitable factors develops. The spores need to infect young trout not long after they have emerged from the gravel and so water temperatures during incubation and around the time of emergence may be critical. Whatever the actual cocktail of environmental factors may be, when they coincide, they can trigger a devastating whirling disease outbreak. Much remains to be discovered and understood about this condition.

Nickum & Bartholomew (2000) explain how the impacts of parasites and diseases on fish populations are often unpredictable; it is better to be safe than sorry. If in doubt, don't stock. Unfortunately, the history of trout stocking hasn't always followed this maxim of precaution in the face of unknown risks.

The importance of genes

Trout are, by nature, a variable species, whose variability extends from external appearance, through body chemistry to behaviour. Some trout are characteristic of upland peaty, acidic catchments, others of alkaline limestone and chalk stream habitats, others of estuarine and marine conditions. Some migratory stocks have to negotiate steep-gradient spate rivers, spawning amongst large cobbles in fast flows, whilst others simply trundle a few miles up a low-gradient spring creek (chalk stream) and dig a redd in small gravel. These differing environmental constraints produce different sorts of trout. This is true of European brown trout, North American rainbow trout; trout the world-over. The differences we see in trout appearance and behaviour are important aspects of the ability of the fish to survive and reproduce. Some of this variation is inborn (genetic) and some is determined by habitat (environmental). Like us, fish are the complex product of nature plus nurture. Wild animals must have the correct range of characteristics to survive and those which thrive best leave many descendents as the successful products of natural selection. Natural selection acts through a vast number of processes. Examples include abilities to survive in particular chemical and physical conditions, to learn from experience, to find and capture food, to avoid predators, to compete with other trout for territorial space, to migrate to specific habitats at the right time of year, to attract mates and to breed successfully. All individuals vary in these and in many other abilities and only those with the best overall mix of attributes will have genotypes which tend to prevail in a wild population through succeeding generations. Over many generations, natural selection acts (blindly) to hone given populations into a successful inter-breeding unit of particular types. Over each life cycle, those individuals which breed most successfully, the 'fittest' in the evolutionary sense, will be best represented genetically in the next generation. Organisms can be viewed simply as vehicles which transport their DNA from one generation to the next (Dawkins, 1989). With time, populations become specialised – adapted to suit their environment and such adaptation is important for the overall long-term survival of species and its DNA. This is the process of evolution.

Local variation in the appearance and behaviour of trout can also be due to random genetic change (so-called 'genetic drift'). We must be careful not to assume that all observed variation is truly adaptive or that the introduction of any new genetic stock is necessarily damaging. Guyomard (1999), whilst acknowledging the importance of adaptation to environment, emphasises the view that geographical variation in trout is not necessarily adaptive and that re-stocking seems generally to be ineffective so that threats from stocking can, perhaps, be over-emphasised. As with most areas of biology, there are probably examples to back up most arguments. In the opinion of many fish population geneticists, however, the evidence which we have for important genetic differences and local adaptation in trout and salmon stocks is compelling (see, for instance,Youngson et al, 2003). Conserving the genetic diversity represented by local wild trout populations is, therefore, a worthwhile and urgent component of trout fishery management, even if, at present, it is driven primarily by the precautionary principle – read on.

The research of Professor L. Laikre (1999) revealed that, of the vertebrates studied to date, the brown trout shows the greatest degree of local genetic structuring; something like ten times that of Atlantic Salmon. Wild trout are genetically highly variable and, whilst by no means all of this variability will have adaptive significance, much of it probably does. To establish how important these genetic differences are to the survival of trout stocks in the long-term, a huge long-lasting research effort would be required. In the meantime, it is important that we don't risk damaging the priceless natural genetic resources which the world still has to offer.

The excellent genetic research of Professor Andy Ferguson (Queen's University, Belfast) has taught us much of the basis for trout variability and of the importance of conserving genetic diversity (see Ferguson, 2004). Take wild trout in the British Isles, for instance. After the last Ice Age (about 14,000 years ago), sea trout re-colonised British and Irish freshwaters from at least four glacial refuges in North-West Europe, namely the Atlantic, Mediterranean, Danubean & Adriatic areas. All present day British brown trout populations have arisen from these four (or more) genetically distinct stocks. The colonists which founded new populations in pristine post-glacial river and lake systems gave rise to offspring which have subsequently proliferated and adapted to local conditions so that extensive genetic diversity has evolved rapidly, both within and between catchments.

Lough Melvin

In what has become a classic study of population genetics (Ferguson, 2004), Prof Ferguson and his fellow researchers have unravelled the evolution of the wild brown trout of Lough Melvin which lies in North-West Ireland. Not all Melvin wild trout are alike, but they do fall naturally into three categories; ferox, gillaroo and sonaghen. These are all brown trout, but ferox spawn early in the depths of inflowing rivers, sonaghen later in shallower sections of inflowing rivers, whilst gillaroo spawn in out-flowing rivers of the lough. This separation of spawning habitat and in the timing of breeding effectively maintains these three types of trout as separate genetic populations within the one water system. It is reasonable to argue, therefore, that Melvin has three distinct brown trout species; ferox – *Salmo ferox*, gillaroo – *Salmo stomachius* and sonaghen, *Salmo nigripinnis*.

Ferox tend to be long-lived, growing to large sizes on a diet of Arctic char or similar prey and to live in large lake systems in Ireland, Scotland, Wales, the English Lake District and other northern European areas. All known ferox stocks appear to have arisen from the same post-glacial genetic lineage and have similar, distinct genetic characteristics.

Gillaroo ('red fellows'), with their muscular stomachs and bright red and black spotting are well camouflaged amongst gravely shallows and rocky

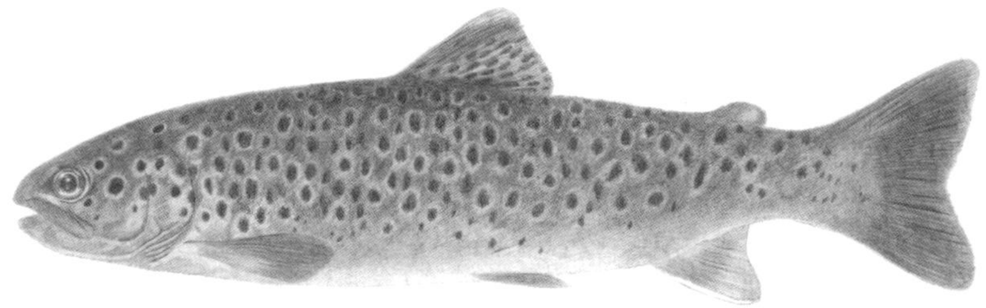

shoals where they feed extensively on invertebrates, often including lots of snails in their diet. Gillaroo are recognisable in many waters other than Lough Melvin and they too probably have a distinct genetic constitution.

Sonaghen are typically silvery, with small black spots and with long dark fins, blending easily into open water where they exploit plankton and emerging flies. Each type of trout is beautifully adapted to cope with the specific rigours imposed by its particular micro-environment within the lough and associated river systems.

This localised evolution of brown trout is not unique to Lough Melvin. It has occurred in a myriad of complex ways throughout the wide distribution of the archetypal brown / sea trout - *Salmo trutta*. Physical differences are most obvious in brown trout, but even though most sea trout look fairly alike, there are substantial variations in genetic make-up both within and between their populations. Much of this genetic variation is likely to be of adaptive importance. The practical value of this diversity is that wild trout have become separated into distinct groups which together exploit all available habitat types. Each population expands to fill available niches. Isolated Arctic char populations in large lakes do similar things, evolving specialised bottom-living (benthic) and open water (pelagic) forms. If these specialised trout (or char) are lost, their genetic diversity goes with them and the sum total of the natural resource which we term 'wild trout' is so much the poorer. The moral of this story is that the conservation of genetic diversity is a very worthwhile goal and we ignore it at our peril. Luckily, Nature is surprisingly resilient.

The persistence of wild trout gene pools

Stan Guffey (2000) describes an interesting study of Great Smoky Mountain National Park where, between 1940 and 1974, all but twelve park streams were stocked with hatchery brook trout of various sizes, from fertile eggs to adult fish. This was a response to a 70% decrease in stream mileage occupied by native brook trout over the Twentieth Century. In 1974, within a new National Park Service policy of managing only for native fauna and flora, the stocking programme was stopped and genetic studies were undertaken to try and understand the status of the brook trout stocks. Guffey concluded, after quite extensive, but not exhaustive electrophoretic protein studies, that diagnostic hatchery alleles (genes) were detected in only 11 out of 40 samples from streams known to have been stocked. Where they were detected, hybrid samples had low frequencies of hatchery genes. Whilst many people claim that years of stocking must effectively obliterate distinct wild trout stocks, the evidence here is to the contrary. Native trout genotypes appear to be surprisingly persistent; a greatly encouraging view for trout conservationists everywhere.

Andy Ferguson (2004) has found that wild trout stocks are still present over much of the natural range of the species and that, whilst some populations appear to have been swamped by stocked farmed fish, very many haven't. Genetic diversity is still present (especially in the north and west of the British Isles) and that diversity confers strength to our wild trout stocks.

Hybridisation of farmed and wild salmon

We must not, however, be complacent, as the work of Phil McGinnity and colleagues (2003) has revealed. This large group of co-workers has, over ten years of study, cleverly analysed the breeding success of both wild and escapee farmed Atlantic salmon on the Irish west coast at Burrishoole, County Mayo. They note that, each year, an estimated two million cage-farmed salmon escape into the wild of the North Atlantic – this figure amounting to around 50% of wild Atlantic salmon thought to be present at sea in any one year! Obviously, many of these cage-reared salmon will be eaten by their many potential marine predators, but many manage to survive and these fish can reach sexual maturity and find their way into salmon rivers. Because of their history of artificial selection for fast growth rates, farmed salmon tend to be bigger than wild ones and could represent a competitive threat. McGinnity and colleagues wanted to know what happens to these fish – do they spawn successfully? Do they interbreed with wild salmon? How well do their progeny do in the wild? Using state-of-the-art DNA profiling techniques it proved possible to establish the parentage of salmon and to answer all of these questions. The answers are, to say the least, interesting.

Interbreeding of escapee farmed and wild salmon does take place, producing hybrids of the two strains. In this study, egg batches from multiple families of first and second generation hybrids were planted-out in the Burrishoole River system or reared and released as smolts at sea and their fates monitored. Parr, smolts and returning adult salmon were sampled from the wild using traps, angling and nets and their parentage established. Because all groups were reared and released into equivalent environmental conditions, any observed differences in survival are due to genetic differences between groups. Farmed salmon were found to have both genetic and competitive impacts on wild salmon. Selective breeding of the farmed fish has reduced their ability to survive in the wild, especially at sea. Over their lifetimes, farmed salmon were estimated to have only 2% of the success of wild salmon. Hybrids had intermediate success. Second generation hybrids mostly (70%) died as embryos, due to genetic incompatibility of parents.

The conclusion reached, after also assessing other researchers findings was that hybridisation between farmed and wild salmonids (trout and salmon) leads to reduced survival of hybrids under natural conditions. As many of the young fish produced in the wild can be hybrids from farmed x wild spawnings, populations can dwindle. On top of this, any salmon parented by farmed fish were faster-growing than wild fish and tended to displace them competitively so that wild salmon parr densities were also reduced. Over the course of several generations, the overall impact of hybridisation between farmed and wild salmon could potentially be the extinction of vulnerable wild salmon stocks (McGinnity et al, 2003). This is true whether the farmed salmon are escapees or whether they are deliberately stocked in enhancement programmes. By stocking juvenile farmed salmon in an attempt to bolster wild stocks, it is actually quite likely that you could be doing much more harm than good. Phil McGinnity and colleagues believe that their findings and conclusions are just as relevant to the stocking of farmed brown trout (of all sizes) into wild brown trout populations. Whilst farmed brown trout may not have been so stringently selected for fast growth as salmon have, they have often been selectively bred in captivity over many generations. Any impact of stocked trout on wild trout populations will vary with local circumstances, but it is likely to be negative, rather than positive, for the welfare of the wild trout population (see McGinnity et al, 2003).

Where stocking farmed trout may be inappropriate

Eighty years ago Harry Plunket Greene (1924) wrote 'Where bright waters meet' a lovely description of the Hampshire Bourne Rivulet, a short stream which joins the River Test between Whitchurch and Longparish. Amongst his many concerns for the stream, he noted with deep regret the impact which over-stocking had on the wild trout. With too many fish in the water the formerly finely-conditioned big trout literally wasted away within a very few months, leaving an impoverished stock. Plunket Green's view was, that as long as the spawning habitat is good and pike numbers are controlled, the surviving trout stock is available for exploitation by anglers. Good habitat and limited predation leads to an exploitable surplus in the wild trout population. Who can disagree?

The stocking of farmed trout can affect fisheries in many ways including: interbreeding with wild trout and affecting the population genetics, competition with wild trout for food and space, predation on wild trout and other species, introduction of parasites or diseases, increasing fishing pressure or attracting predators, all of which can drive down wild trout numbers. The stocking of substantial numbers of relatively large farmed trout into salmon and wild trout spawning and nursery areas may be best avoided, because of the risk of increased predation on wild juvenile salmonids. This may be especially important where natural salmonid stocks are already at a low ebb. The decision on whether to stock farmed trout into a fishery, especially one with a wild trout or salmon stock, should be carefully considered. Even if the answer is yes, it requires expert knowledge and judgement to assess where and when to stock, appropriate numbers, sizes and the best provenance of stocked trout.

Stocking effects on wild trout populations

Richard Vincent (1984) describes the situation from 1955 to 1969 on the four mile Varney section of the Madison River, Montana where 1,200 – 1,600 catchable-sized (20-30cm) rainbow trout were stocked annually to increase angler catch rates and to increase trout stocks perceived to be below carrying capacity. The river here, below Hebgen Dam, is braided with a complex of channels formed from long riffles, fast runs and a few pools. There is a substantial gradient. The stocking, which had gone on for fifteen years was officially stopped in 1970 as an experiment to see whether wild brown and rainbow trout stocks increased and, if so, which classes of fish responded to the disappearance of stocked rainbows. Unofficially some stocking occurred in 1972, but none after that. The results of the field experiment were startling. When stocking was stopped, brown trout of two years and older were around 150% higher in numbers and 120% more in biomass (weight). For rainbows, by 1976, two year old and older fish had increased in number by 800% and biomass by 1,000% - ten times the weight of wild rainbow trout present with stocking.

Vincent interprets these results as a probable relief for the wild trout from the upsetting of their normal social behaviour by stocked trout. Stocked fish probably fought for lies and disrupted the settled dominance hierarchy which regulates natural trout populations. These views are supported by other studies. Bob Bachman (1984), for instance, did some pioneering research with wild brown trout in Spruce Creek Pennsylvania. As mentioned previously, Bachman observed that, when hatchery brown trout were stocked into the wild population, they simply didn't know the social etiquette. Instead of fitting into the stable pecking order for prime stream locations, they set about fighting all the time, thoroughly upsetting the stability of the wild trout population. As a direct response the wild brown trout stock declined to levels previously unrecorded. Once again, stocking suppressed the native trout stock. S. L. McMullin (1974) recorded that, along a section of the Big Hole River, after stocking was stopped, wild brown trout increased 83% and wild rainbows 325% - paralleling Vincent's results. T. Thuember (1975) saw wild brook trout stocks almost double in Pike River, Wisconsin, after stocking with hatchery trout stopped. All of these people can't be wrong: stocking isn't necessarily going to improve your fishery or your fishing.

If you have a fishery with virtually no wild salmonid productivity, then a careful stocking programme should cost-effectively sustain well-judged angling pressure. Where you have moderate wild productivity, however, you may well be better off improving conditions for wild trout, rather than introducing more fish to poor quality habitat. Very careful consideration should be given to the pros and cons of stocking on a case-by-case basis. Let's not go-overboard, however; where stocking densities are well-judged and where the right sort and sizes of trout are introduced, stocked fish can be harvested efficiently and there need be no serious environmental problems. How do we reach this desirable state of affairs?

Stocking trout in England and Wales

In England and Wales fish stocking (other than into fish farms) requires prior Environment Agency consent under Section 30 of the Salmon & Freshwater Fisheries Act (1975). Decisions on consent applications take into consideration costs and benefits to the fishery, including possible detrimental ecological impacts. Aprahamian and colleagues (2003) have reviewed the pros and cons of salmonid stocking and propose the following categories:

- Mitigation stocking: to mitigate lost production from an irreversible scheme or factor such as damming a headwater to impound a reservoir (eg Kielder Water, Northumbria, UK) or development of hydro-electric schemes.
- Restoration stocking: carried out after the removal or reduction of a factor previously limiting natural production. For example, the successful stocking of sea trout smolts into the River Mawddach, Wales, after a pollution incident. Local provenance stock should be used.
- Enhancement stocking: to supplement an existing stock where production is less than the water body could potentially sustain. This can involve ameliorating low-flow effects, ranching migratory salmonids, stocking migratory fish above impassable barriers (to increase smolt and returning adult runs), compensating for degraded habitats (eg acidified areas, silted gravels or historic land drainage schemes), or supporting a put-

and-take fishery. Local provenance stocks are important where wild trout exist.

- Creation of new fisheries: stocking to transfer fish into new water bodies or new species into existing fisheries. Obvious examples include the successful reservoir trout fisheries for rainbow and/or brown trout such as Blagdon, Rutland Water, Wimbleball, Draycote, Bewl, Grafham and many others. Grayling introductions into new river systems provide another example of this form of fish stocking.
- Research and Development (R&D) stocking: used to answer key conservation and management questions; for example, sensible stock densities.
- Conservation: to support a wild stock of fish below its target conservation level.

Current areas of research include assessing risks from stocking, survival and return rates for stocked fish and cost-effectiveness of stocking programmes. Aprahamian et al (2003) provide numerous examples of observed return rates and costs per fish from a wide range of salmonid studies – a paper well worth reading.

Artificial fry production and stocking

It is sometimes suggested that catching wild hen trout close to spawning, stripping their eggs and fertilising them with milt from wild cock fish from your fishery and then rearing the young in outdoor incubator boxes or in a hatchery is a viable approach to increasing trout stocks. This can work well in the right circumstances. Experience shows, however, that whilst incubator boxes can have very high hatching rates, catching up and stripping a representative sample of wild trout close to the point of breeding is easier said than done. The task is not impossible, but it is by no means easy and really requires inputs from fishery scientists to make sure that a genetically robust breeding programme is set up. Looking after your broodstock so that they mature sexually in captivity is not straightforward either – the combined stresses of capture, relocation, changes in water quality, diet and un-natural holding facilities all take their toll. It is very common for such fish to succumb to fungal and /or bacterial infections or to fail to produce good quality eggs or milt.

To circumvent this, some people advocate the use of eggs from fish farms. If large numbers of young trout fry produced from relatively inbred farmed trout parents are involved, this is simply a case of intensive stocking with its potential attendant risks to any remaining wild trout stock. Even if they are well spread out over suitable gravel shallows, farmed trout fry may be bigger than their wild counterparts and could, therefore, out-compete them for suitable juvenile habitat. As we have seen from Malcolm Elliott's work, suitable lies for trout fry on a stream bed can be far less abundant than appearances suggest. Where possible, it is best for a fishery that all available good quality habitat is occupied by wild fish, rather than by trout which have been subject to artificial selection. This is the best way to promote long-term sustainability.

Introduced fry derived from farmed parents grow into well-finned trout which are difficult or impossible to distinguish by eye from wild fish.

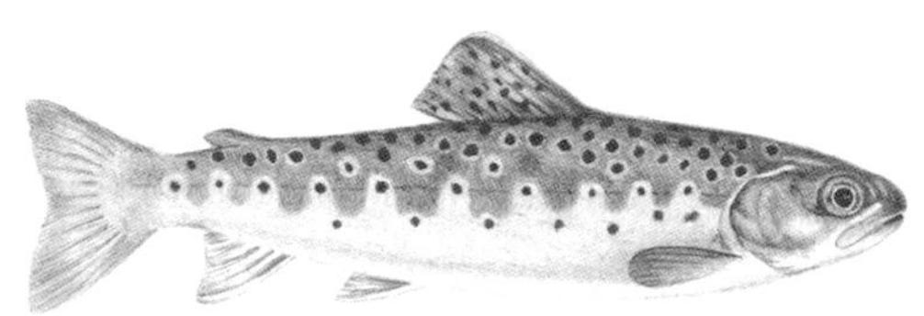

Whilst such trout give an impression that all is well on a fishery and are fun to fish for, they don't help with population assessment because you then have an unknown mix of trout from wild and stocked origins. It then becomes virtually impossible to tell what is going on with the natural fish stocks. Also, when introduced trout fry grow to maturity, they may change the genetics of the local stock via interbreeding. As we have seen, this could potentially be disastrous (see McGinnity et al, 2003).

Despite this view, some strains of stock fish may prove to be better than others in differing fisheries and it is understandable that, where natural trout production is sparse the temptation to supplement wild stocks is appreciable. This is especially the case where fishing pressure is high. If most stocked trout are caught and killed soon after introduction, then their ecological impact on the fishery will be minimal in any case. Because they are relatively easy to catch, these fish may also have protected any wild trout from potential over-exploitation. If the wild trout present migrate a long way up side streams to spawn, then interbreeding with any stocked trout remaining at the end of the season may be unlikely because the stockies don't know where to find the good spawning habitat. If little successful spawning is taking place on your fishery, however, it may well be better to improve spawning and nursery habitats for wild fish and / or simply to stock with takeable-sized stock fish, rather than to introduce large numbers of juvenile farmed fish. If the takeable stockies are sterile, posing no genetic risk to the wild stock, then so much the better. Because of the wide range of trout fishery types and circumstances found all over the world, it is essential to tailor management strategies to local conditions.

The Environment Agency National Trout and Grayling Strategy

In England and Wales, trout fishery management has recently been revamped under the auspices of the Environment Agency National Trout and Grayling Strategy (2004). The Strategy is available at www.environment-agency.gov.uk/fish or from Agency Offices. Key elements of the Strategy include social and economic aspects, conservation of wild stocks through habitat improvement, regulation of exploitation, classification of fisheries including the recognition of native trout waters, the designation of protection zones and changes in stocking policy. It is planned that 'Wild Fisheries Protection Zones' will be set up, with local consultation, and that these areas will have no trout stocking, allowing owners to protect wild trout populations and / or salmon and trout nursery habitats. Anglers fishing these zones will know that any trout which they catch will be wild ones. This is important for many anglers as the pursuit of wild trout is increasingly popular amongst UK fly fishers.

Outside these protected zones, all other trout fisheries will be classified into 'native trout waters' – those which produce significant numbers of wild brown or sea trout or are connected to such waters and 'other waters' – those where wild trout production or access is considered insignificant. In order to protect wild trout stocks, stocking into 'native trout' waters will be consented provided that it is consistent with practice over the last five years, or that stocked fish are (sterile) triploid females, or the stock fish are derived from local, naturally produced brood stock under a suitable rearing regime.

The potential of triploid trout

During the production process, fertilised trout eggs can be subjected to heat and / or pressure shocks which cause them to retain a triple chromosome content. This does not involve the introduction of new genetic material (genetic modification or GM) – it merely causes the eggs to keep a third set of their own chromosomes which would be discarded during normal reproduction. Triploided female trout look essentially similar to diploids (with the normal double chromosome compliment), but they are infertile and do not develop eggs or exhibit reproductive behaviour. Triploid trout are reported by producers to grow well, maintain condition throughout the year and perform well in lowland fisheries. Some producers report, however, that these fish can be delicate when faced with sharp fluctuations in water temperature and dissolved oxygen concentrations. Triploids potentially represent an excellent solution to the interbreeding problems of wild and stocked trout, but their performance in all fishery types (including spate rivers) does need thorough checking. Also, of course, trout farmers need reassurance that triploid production is feasible, efficient and economic.

Whether triploid female brown trout fare well in all English and Welsh fisheries and whether they perform adequately compared with diploid farmed trout is the subject of continuing research. Provided that the results of this work are positive for triploid fish, further constraints on the stocking of fertile (diploid) farmed trout into 'Native trout' waters may be considered by the Environment Agency.

Criticism has been levelled at the Environment Agency that this is a covert plan to ban all stocking on native trout waters, but this simply isn't the case. The key to happy resolutions of disagreements over stocking is to establish fair regulations based on sound science and then to assess the relevant facts on a localised, case-by-case consultative basis. Because of the history of trout fishery management in much of the British Isles and the fishing pressures presently operating, especially on lowland waters, stocking will inevitably play an important role for the foreseeable future. What is intended is that this stocking should be carried out in sustainable ways. If the various strategic measures are implemented successfully across England and Wales, trout and grayling fishing should have a better future.

The proposed new trout and grayling fishery policy initiatives from the Environment Agency seek to promote sustainable fisheries, ensuring adequate conservation of wild stocks whilst, at the same time, encouraging the success of all types of trout fishery whether wild, supplemented by stocking or wholly stocked. Their measures of success include:

- The increasing presence of thriving wild trout and grayling populations with genetic diversity protected long-term,
- Improved habitats,
- More opportunities for and participation in trout, sea trout and grayling fishing for a wide range of anglers and
- The increased economic benefits which all of this will bring.

It's hard to argue with objectives like those.

Triploid rainbow trout in Idaho

Dillon et al (2000) review the success of stocking triploid rainbow trout into Idaho fisheries which provide takeable trout for anglers, whilst reducing potential genetic impacts on wild trout stocks. In the year 2000 around 40% of Idaho trout stream stocking was in streams also containing wild trout stocks. Lake and reservoir stockings also often overlap with wild trout populations and so it was decided to investigate the utility of sterile, triploided stock fish there, too. The survival and performance of triploid and control group diploid rainbow trout was studied in 18 stream and 3 lake fisheries and, overall, triploids appeared to perform as well as normal rainbow trout. Encouraged by these positive findings, from the year 2001, Idaho authorities intended to produce or purchase about 17 million triploid rainbow trout eggs annually to meet stocking requests for all fisheries state-wide. Sterile cutthroat trout are under development for mountain lake stocking and sterile rainbow x cutthroat hybrids for the Yellowstone Henry's Lake cutthroat trout fishery. Gamblin et al (2000) explain how the stocking of sterile hybrids into the Henry's Lake fishery should reduce rainbow trout genetic introgression (hybridisation) into the wild cutthroat trout stock to less than 1% within ten generations (around 40 years).

Triploid rainbow and brown trout are already used on many UK still water and lowland stream trout fisheries and it will be very interesting to see whether their use becomes widespread over the seasons to come. Hopefully, the need for stocking trout into natural waters will decline in any case as wild populations respond to better habitat quality and to better fisheries management. Where recovering wild game fish stocks are unable to withstand any degree of harvesting, the imperative for releasing most or all fish caught becomes more urgent. The advent of routine catch-and-release (C&R) of adult samon and trout as 'the right thing to do' was pioneered by the visionary American fisherman Lee Wulff. He pointed out that salmonid fish are far too valuable to be caught only once and this allowed a springboard leap to healthier wild trout and salmon stocks world-wide. Take the USA, for instance.

Catch & Release in Montana

Jerry Wells (1987) provides an overview of Montana C&R trout fisheries performance. C&R was instigated on a long stretch of the Madison River as early as 1978 in an attempt to conserve brown and rainbow trout of over 32.5cm. The results were spectacular, these large trout increasing in numbers from two to six-fold over the years. It appears that, with C&R, trout populations can tend to get 'top heavy' with lunker fish for a while. When these individuals die, there is a subsequent rebuilding of the numbers of young, fast-growing trout vying to occupy the prime vacated lies. Whilst they are there, the big, old fish tend to get very wary and hook-scarred. Some anglers don't like this although others like the challenge of catching so-called 'educated' trout. Angler satisfaction tends to oscillate in parallel with the trout stocks – 'yer pays yer money and takes yer choice'. What is very evident, despite gripes from some fishermen, is that the C&R water on the Madison attracted, and continues to attract, large numbers of visiting anglers. C&R is, undoubtedly, an economic success.

On the Big Hole River in the early 1980s a similar attempt to increase stocks of big brown and rainbow trout was made on a 15 mile run of river. A slot limit was introduced so that anglers could take fish of under 32.5cm and one trout over 55cm. Once again, the results were very good: browns over 45cm increased from 25 per mile in 1981 to nearly 130 per mile in 1986. Over the same period, wild rainbow trout 32.5cm and larger also increased very markedly on the C&R section, to more or less double compared to a section of river where anglers were allowed to kill five fish a day. Most anglers were happy with the imposition of C&R, acknowledging the boost to wild trout stocks and the improved catches which it produced.

On the Yellowstone River from 1982 to 1987, numbers of large, wild cutthroat trout built-up very encouragingly on the Mill Creek C&R section. Cutthroat trout respond particularly well to the protection provided by C&R. On the Gallatin River, however, the same restrictions as those brought in on the Big Hole failed to work. The reason was probably the canyon habitat which imposed slow growth in cold water and high winter mortality. The trout stock wasn't resilient enough to respond positively to the changed management regime. Habitat quality needs to be adequate to sustain the high trout densities expected in C&R fisheries; a valuable lesson.

Catch & Release in Arkansas

John Stark & colleagues (2000) describe how, in 1988 at Dry Run Creek, Arkansas, youth and disabled anglers were encouraged by giving them access to a half mile C&R section of trout fishing. The Beaver tailwater fishery had a 40cm lower size limit for brown trout imposed and a bag limit of 2 fish per day. This protected wild brown trout from harvest until they reached three years of age and had a chance to spawn at least once. Size limits are usually designed to allow wild fish a spawning opportunity. The initiative was extended state-wide in 1990. Brown trout migrating upstream to find spawning grounds from November 1 to January 31, previously often killed for trophies, were now protected by mandatory catch-and-release. Many very large trout were caught and returned but not all were handled well and hand-shaped fungal infections afflicted some fish. Significant mortalities occurred, for instance, at Bull Shoals Dam and fishery closures of vulnerable stretches have subsequently been imposed to protect these valuable trophy-sized fish during spawning runs.

C&R good practice

When releasing trout or salmon, key points to remember are:

- Use tackle of adequate strength – don't over-play fish.
- Avoid landing fish unless absolutely necessary. Unhook them in the water using your finger nails, forceps or an unhooking tool and don't squeeze them too hard.

- If a fish is deeply hooked, cut the line close to the mouth. Hooks, especially barbless ones, can work their way back out to be regurgitated or may cause little lasting harm to the fish, even if they stay put.
- If you want a photo, take it with the fish in the water, if you want a record of size, measure the length – this can be converted to a reasonable weight estimate later: read on.
- Support the fish head-upstream until it has recovered enough strength to swim away on an even keel.
- Ideally, fish C&R when water temperatures are cool. Exhausted trout or salmon in warm water have a real battle to regain their 'breath' where dissolved oxygen concentrations are relatively low.

The C&R conservation initiatives in Arkansas helped more mature brown trout to survive and reach the impressive sizes (9kg plus) for which the White River system had become justly famous. In 1995, five White River catch-and-release sections were designated to help conserve rainbow trout. Numbers of 40cm or bigger rainbow trout increased from between 10 to 58-fold in these areas and anglers were six to eight times more likely to catch 40-45cm rainbows here than in undesignated areas. C&R stretches were fished 2.6 times more than other stretches and generated about three times the income per mile than undesignated areas. Rainbows grew to weights of 4.5 – 7kg and wild productivity rose as a result of successful management. Despite this, and the support of 70% of surveyed anglers, the designation of further catch and release areas has not been easy because of influential lobby groups who are opposed to no kill policies. Anglers always were a disparate (and desperate) bunch!

Most anglers, however, wish to record the size of a specimen fish when they catch it.

How much did my C&R trout weigh?

If you catch and release brown trout or sea trout and measure the length from the tip of the snout to the fork of the tail against marks on your rod butt or against an accurate tape measure, you can get an estimate of the likely weight of the fish from the table below. These estimates are calculated from an equation for Welsh River Dee sea trout kindly provided by Ian Davidson of the Environment Agency. They should also provide a reasonable guide for brown trout in good condition.

Length (inches)	Weight	Length (inches)	Weight
8	4 oz	21	4lb
9	5.4oz	22	4lb 9oz
10	7.3oz	23	5lb 4oz
11	9.7oz	24	5lb 15oz
12	12.5oz	25	6lb 11oz
13	1lb	26	7lb 8oz
14	1lb 4oz	27	8lb 6oz
15	1lb 8oz	28	9lb 5oz
16	1lb 13oz	29	10lb 5oz
17	2lb 2oz	30	11lb 6oz
18	2lb 9oz	31	12lb 9oz
19	3lb	32	13lb 12oz
20	3lb 7oz		

A recent whopper Yorkshire River Wharfe brown trout of 25 inches weighed-in at 6 pounds eight ounces. The table gets this quite close to the mark at 6lb 11oz. You may like to compare some lengths and weights for fish from your waters so see how this table works. I hope it provides a useful 'rule of thumb'; all feed-back welcome!

Catch & Release in Wisconsin

Bob Hunt (1987) compared trout catch statistics from three Wisconsin C&R trout fisheries with similar information from six normally-regulated waters where most of the trout caught were browns. The three C&R waters were regulated differently, as no harvest, one fish over 32.5cm per day(a size limit) or one trout between 35 and 42.5cm per day (a slot limit). C&R was successful on all three fisheries as the angler use was high, catches were very high for brown trout waters and the total seasonal catch exceeded the pre-season abundance of trout present. C&R waters were intensely fished with many of the anglers travelling from out-of-state, fishing with fly, rather than spinner and bringing extra income to the neighbourhood. Average catch rates per hour on the C&R waters were 1.33 to 1.96 which is very productive fishing.

- Bob Hunt reviewed other American trout fisheries where C&R was emphasised, finding the following average catch rates per hour (most recent data are quoted for a given river).
- For brown trout: 0.41 (Oatka Creek), 0.4 (Battenkill River), 0.43 (Wiscoy Creek) and 0.66 (East Walker River).
- For rainbow trout: 0.44 (Cheesman Canyon), 0.9 (Henrys Fork / Snake River) and 0.53 (brown & rainbow trout, Meramec River).
- For Cutthroat trout: 1.06 (Yellowstone River) and 1.03 (Slough Creek).

These results are worth bearing in mind – a two hour trip on these American trout waters in the latter quarter of last century would have yielded one or two trout, except in Wisconsin where the C&R waters were producing three to four trout per trip. How do these catch rates compare with current trout fishing in Britain?

Analysis of trout rod catch data – English river examples

During the course of my fisheries consultancy work, I am sometimes asked to analyse and comment on rod catch statistics. The results of these studies shed interesting light on the figures just quoted from the American literature. We can learn a lot by taking just five examples from English lowland rivers: Surrey's River Wey, Hampshire's River Itchen and the Wiltshire Rivers Avon, Nadder and Wylye.

The River Wey

The south River Wey system has both chalk and greensand influences and much of the main river suffers from extensive swathes of shifting sand, offering poor habitat quality for aquatic plants, invertebrates and trout. Densities of wild trout appear to be low and stocking is widespread. The North Wey, which is a gravel-bedded chalk stream, has much better habitat with extensive *Ranunculus* beds, good invertebrate communities and a substantial population of wild brown trout. The fisheries which I have surveyed in recent years have included ones on both the North and South Wey and have had a mixture of stocked and wild brown trout. On the better quality habitats of the North Wey, catches of around 1.5 trout per visit seem typical whilst on the South Wey, the average catch, despite the poorer habitat, has tended to be only slightly less, perhaps 1.4 trout per visit, the stocked trout helping to bridge the gap in habitat quality.

River Nadder

The River Nadder fishery, a greensand-based stream situated quite close to Salisbury, has a good wild brown trout and grayling population and is stocked each season with a small number of 30cm brown trout. The stocked trout are consistently present in catches, but do not dominate them. Over the last ten years, fishery performance remained, on average, very stable with between 1 – 1.5 trout caught per visit, plus occasional grayling.

River Wylye

The River Wylye fishery (between Salisbury and Warminster), based in good quality chalk stream habitat with gravel beds, deep pools and glides dominated by water crowfoot beds is stocked each year in early May with a moderate number of adult brown trout. There is a fair head of wild brown trout present. Once again, typical catch per day is around 1.5 trout (plus 1 or 2 grayling).

River Avon

This quite heavily-stocked stretch lies north of Salisbury on the main Avon. Adult (30-33cm) brown trout are stocked each month and anglers are allowed to take a brace per visit although many trout are returned. Catches in 2004 amounted to 4,579 trout from 2,904 fishing visits: 3,300 trout were caught and returned and 735 were reported killed. Overall, this gives an average of 1.6 trout caught per visit: once again our rule of thumb holds true.

River Itchen

The River Itchen fishery, comprised of a section of main chalk stream plus associated carriers is stocked fortnightly from April to October with adult brown trout. There are very few wild trout present. Regular stocking and the spreading out of stocked fish leads to very stable long-term fishery performance; again averaging around 1.5 trout per day.

The way it was on Hampshire chalk streams

Hampshire's famous Rivers Test and Itchen have a chequered history with respect to trout stocks, stocking and catches. Prior to the 1850s, wild trout stocks were abundant, angling pressures were relatively light, the season short and catches during the mayfly sometimes prolific, including occasional wild browns of three pounds-plus. From around 1850, wild trout catches on many stretches of these prized chalk streams declined in response to various factors – water pollution, runs of cold wet springs and summers, agricultural recession and a general lack of stream management (Hayter, 2002). Tony Hayter reports in his excellent biography of F.M. Halford, pioneer of chalk stream dry fly fishing, that in 1879, mostly fishing on the Test, Halford caught 50 trout (weighing a combined 41 pound 10 ounces) in 37 days fishing – around 1.33 trout per day. In 1892, at Houghton, Halford caught 39 trout in 34 days – 1.15 trout per day. Halford's overall average weight for Test trout was 1lb 12oz and 1lb 4oz on the Itchen (see Hayter, 2002).

By the end of the Victorian era, many clubs and syndicates had rented the best of chalk stream fishings, instigated active management and improved catch rates, but often with the liberal use of hatchery-bred trout. Over the intervening century, much has remained the same on these renowned rivers with fishing remaining expensive. Today's trout fishermen on many stretches of either the lower Test or lower Itchen are still very likely to be fishing primarily for recently-stocked, rather than wild brown trout. I am pleased to say, however, that if you know where to look you can still find affordable chalk stream wild trout fishing in Hampshire, Wiltshire and Dorset.

Wild trout on Lough Corrib

In Trout and Salmon magazine, Peter O'Reilly regularly reports Irish trout fishing results and prospects, including those on my favourite water, Lough Corrib. Here are a few examples to get a feel for what one might expect to catch. In April 2003 a group of six trollers, over the course of a week, took 17 ferox trout which weighed 171 pounds, 77.7kg (including 9 to 19 pounders). What a haul of specimen fish! In the same month, at the north end of the lough, the average catch per day for over 500 anglers was 0.72 trout. In mid-May 2004, not a good year for the mayfly, a good sample of anglers caught an average of 0.76 trout per visit from the north of the lough whilst, later in the month, the average was 0.73. This sort of figure is quite commonplace amongst the reports although the average daily catch rate can often rise to between 1.5 and 2. On really good days fishermen come off the Corrib having caught between 5 and 10 good trout, but I suspect that these were pretty competent anglers fishing in good conditions.

Reservoir fishery performance

In 1980, Rick North (1983) found that, at Draycote Reservoir (Rugby, Warwickshire), of around 33,000 trout stocked, just under 70% were declared caught. 78% of rainbows and 44% browns were recaptured. 90% of trout caught came out within 45 days of stocking, 50% within 8 days. Over the season the average daily catch rate was 1.21 with peak catches of up to 5.3 trout per day happening soon after stocking. In order to maintain an average catch rate of 1-2 trout per day, re-stocking needed to be carried out every 8-10 days. More recent practice at Draycote (2001) was to stock twice weekly with a wide size range of fish – the reservoir is an excellent Severn Trent Water PLC fishery.
On Chew Valley and Blagdon reservoirs, run expertly by Bristol Water PLC, average daily catch rates from 1976-1986 were between 1.4 and 2.3. In 1995, average daily catch rates were 2.4 for Chew and 2.2 for Blagdon. In 2003 Chew yielded nearly 23,000 trout at an average weight of two and a quarter pounds (about a kilogram) to just over 9,000 rod returns (2.5 trout per rod day). Blagdon produced over 21,000 trout of similar average weight to 7649 rod returns (2.76 trout per rod day). Both reservoirs produce fine quality still water trout fishing, year-in, year-out, providing a great recreational resource on these public water supply reservoirs.

At Rutland Water, in recent years, around 100,000 trout have been stocked at around 80 per hectare per year (25-30 trout per hectare at any one time). This generates good catch rates, for instance 2.6 per visit in July 2004. Siblyback reservoir in Cornwall recently produced a rod average of 3.5 trout, as did Grafham Water in early July, dropping back to

2 later in the month, whilst, over the same period, Stocks Reservoir in Lancashire maintained a rod average of 3.2 and the Lake of Menteith in Scotland, 3.6 . In Trout & Salmon magazine I read of average daily returns of 4.7 fish per rod in early June 2004 at Bewl Water, Kent and 5.3 fish per rod on Esthwaite Lake in Cumbria: that's very productive summer still water trout fishing!

Clearly, lowland reservoir trout fishery managers now have things well organised and average catch rates are carefully maintained by regular stocking regimes. Compared with river fishers, reservoir fly fishermen, on average, catch more trout per visit. On heavily-stocked smaller still waters, catch rates can be higher still and average trout size can be much larger. These specialist big fish waters tend to be expensive, purely because of the limited space available, the high cost of stocked fish and the high likelihood of them being caught.

Tentative conclusions on trout fishery performance

What can we conclude from all that frantic fishing and record-keeping? Both in England and on many U.S. stream and river fisheries, trout anglers tend to average one or two trout per trip. Within these overall averages, there will be very many regional and personal variations. Catch and release waters, in particular, can increase this average markedly, sometimes doubling it. On Lough Corrib, decent-sized wild trout tend to be caught at rates of 0.7 to 1.5 a day in April and May although much depends on the weather and method

used. Skilled anglers on a good day can record much larger catches. There are massive ferox there for those happy to troll away for hours on end. On stocked English lowland reservoirs, average daily bags are often around 2 or 3 and on smaller still waters, where stock densities are higher and fish are more accessible, they can be much higher. The world over, the best and keenest anglers catch many more fish than the rest and, unless you live or fish out in the wilds, you tend to get the fishery performance which you pay for.

Predation

A difficult area of trout fishery management concerns predation; is it acceptable to kill predatory animals to conserve salmonid fish stocks and fisheries? Part of understanding the ecology of river and wetland systems involves an appreciation of the natural role of predation and the pros and cons of predator management. Whilst predatory species are spectacular and popular, an uncomfortable fact is that, in our managed countryside, natural balances controlling animal populations have often been lost. Some predators can become very abundant and have severe impacts on particular prey populations. Where prey species like wild grayling, trout or salmon are particularly valued by man and especially where wild trout are sparse, conflicts often occur. Given that predators are a natural part of the trout's biological environment, should we step in to try and tip the balance in the trout's favour? I suggest that everything depends upon local circumstances.

Whilst it is irksome to see your precious trout disappear down a predator's throat, remember that many predatory species are rare and protected by law. Substantial fines or jail sentences can be imposed on those who break these laws. At the time of writing (2005), anyone found guilty of illegally killing protected birds such as cormorants, herons or goosanders in England can be fined £5,000, jailed for six months, or both. Where everything else has been tried, such as scaring away or excluding birds or creating safe cover habitat for fish, it is sometimes possible to obtain a licence to kill a small number of protected predatory species, but even this isn't guaranteed to work. In many areas the numbers killed are soon replaced by immigrants. One may be killed, but two come to its funeral. Under such circumstances, there is little point in destroying rare birds.

Cormorants

If your fishery is on a cormorant flight path, you will be visited by these birds in their quest for fish. Cormorants are shy, intelligent and learn quickly. They often hunt in small groups, very early in the morning or at dusk and are stealthy, quietly fishing either lakes or rivers. Their favourite prey is fish the size of your hand, often small carp family species (cyprinids) or eels, but they will tackle juvenile salmon and all sizes of trout and grayling when they get the chance. Cormorants eat about 500g of fish a day. Larger fish can be attacked and wounded with characteristic slash marks on their flanks and may often succumb to their injuries or to subsequent infections.

In 2004 around 17,000 cormorants were reported to over-winter in England (23,000 in Britain overall). Whilst shooting does scare them, you need to be out at all hours to keep cormorants at bay for any length of time. A useful alternative approach can be to provide your fish with lots of places to hide. Pack lake margins and shallows with submerged dead wood cover, felling suitable trees into lake margins. On rivers build in (with appropriate consents) lots of marginal dead wood habitat: trout love this, cormorants (and herons) don't. Think broadly about the many ways in which you can tip the balance in favour of your fish, keeping enough stock to sustain your fishery.

On Anglian Water reservoirs in the mid-1990s, around 8% of trout caught by anglers showed signs of cormorant damage. By 2001, this had been reduced to around 1%. How did they manage this? By delaying stocking until closer to the start of the season, increasing the size of stocked trout, distributing stockies over wider areas and by mooring boats containing scary pop-up dummies here and there on the reservoir. The sight of a self-inflating pop-up dummy may help to confirm to the non-angling public just how bizarre fishing can get, but it does scare off quite a few cormorants. By moving the boats around, the birds didn't quickly get used to the presence of the inflatable dummies and the deterrent lasted longer. Well done David Moore and Anglian Water colleagues for achieving reduced predator problems by using a raft of non-destructive techniques.

There is no doubt that cormorants cause severe problems for many coarse and game fisheries, especially those close to large inland roosts or to the coast. Goosanders, a species of saw-billed duck are also specialist fish predators and can take large numbers of salmonid parr, especially in upland river systems. Like cormorants, they are currently on the increase in Britain and are protected by law. There are situations, such as the loss of salmon smolts on rivers which are way below their conservation limit, where predation by fish-eating birds really is a knotty conservation problem which needs a long-term solution. Recent work is summarised at www.cormorants.info and the Salmon & Trout Association (S&TA www.salmon-trout.org) are active in the political debate surrounding the relative conservation merits of birds and fish.

In November 2004 the S&TA reported that a relaxation in the rules governing the issuing of licences to shoot cormorants had been announced by the Government's Fisheries and Conservation Minister, Ben Bradshaw. The number of birds licensed by DEFRA to be shot annually was to be raised from around 600 to 2,000 or more, if deemed necessary. Licences were to be allowed to run over two years, extending to May 1st in any year to try and conserve migrating wild salmon smolts where they are scarce. The presence of cormorants is now to be regarded as proof of their potential to impact on a fishery. Previously, actual evidence of adverse impacts on fish stocks or fishery performance had been required before a licence was issued. This is a controversial ministerial decision. The Royal Society for the Protection of Birds (RSPB) is reported to be considering challenging these new rules as they may contravene EU bird protection legislation. Ironically, the cormorant, protected under the EU 'Birds Directive', is known to eat wild Atlantic salmon smolts on certain European Special Area of Conservation (SAC) rivers where these fish are protected under the EU 'Habitats Directive'. Which species should be regarded as the most important for protection? In the end, it always seems to be the lawyers who benefit most from these arguments! Luckily, with good fisheries management, predation impacts can be reduced and not always with resort to the shot gun.

Pike – Tolpuddle martyrs

Experienced trout river keepers have long been aware that a dense pike population, especially in relatively small, clear rivers equates with low wild trout stocks. Harry Plunket Greene (1924) noted the importance of controlling pike in small and medium-sized trout streams and the trout which were then spared a toothy death would be available in large part to the anglers. I'm sure that he was right.

Whilst pike characterise slow river habitats and like to lie in wait in reedy margins and bays, their stocks can build up to surprising levels even in rapid waters. For instance, on the River Test at Houghton in 1893, after a period of less assiduous management by a previous keeper, William Lunn and helpers removed between 600 and 700 pike of up to 27lbs (12kg+). In the same year, F.M. Halford organised the removal of over 2,000 pike from the upper Kennet at Ramsbury, many of these fish being small 'jacks', considered to represent a serious threat to juvenile trout stocks (Hayter, 2002).

At Tolpuddle on the River Piddle where I began the Game Conservancy Trust's trout research in 1993, we found fairly high numbers of pike and low numbers of wild trout. Surviving trout usually had characteristic U-shaped bite marks on their bellies, indicating close encounters of a pikeish nature. When the gape of the bite scars was compared with the width of the jaws of the resident pike, there was a close agreement. It is possible to make these sorts of detailed observations on relatively small rivers when you are regularly electric-fishing the water. Pike, it appears, are very good indeed at sneaking up on wild trout from behind and seizing them across the under-belly. Only the most fortunate or determined trout had survived. Because our key objective was wild trout conservation, and because pike aren't exactly rare, each time we electric-fished to survey the trout stocks at Tolpuddle, we routinely removed all pike caught. Comparing trout numbers in 1993, when pike were present, with numbers in subsequent years, we found a steady increase. In 1993, Tolpuddle adult trout densities were less than 1 per 100 square metres of stream bed. By 1995, they had more than doubled and by 1997, in some areas, they were six times the starting density. By 1999, on some stretches, they had increased even further. Pike removal wasn't the only factor involved as we also improved habitats in a variety of ways, but I believe that pike removal made a substantial contribution to these startlingly good results.

I have absolutely nothing against the pike, by the way; I like them a lot and regularly fish for them each winter, but on trout streams, they can be an undoubted menace. It is worth noting in passing that pike control on larger, deeper rivers can be difficult and inefficient, often with only the large pike succumbing to the electric-fishing approach. As pike are often cannibalistic, the removal of large pike alone can lead to an explosion of jacks which then set about eating lots of trout parr and yearlings. If you tread the predator control path, you need to be aware of the potential pitfalls.

Predator control is a contentious topic and I have always held the view that it is best to try and improve habitat quality to the point where the prey have a good chance of escaping, rather than to kill predators. However, as I gained experience of practical field ecology and learnt what goes on out there in the wild, I realised that better habitat quality is not always enough.

Some predators, in some habitats are just too good at catching their prey for the prey population to do anything but hang in there at very low densities. These low densities can mean that it isn't worth going fishing, people don't look after that piece of water and it falls into an unmanaged state.

Humane control of predator populations can reverse this situation until you still have the predatory species, but not so many individuals. As a consequence, you will have more of the species which you are trying to conserve, for instance, wild brown trout. It's a question of balance.

We have now considered trout biology, habitats, conservation and aspects of freshwater ecology. The next step is to make the important link between biology and trout fishing.

The four key elements of fly fishing are:

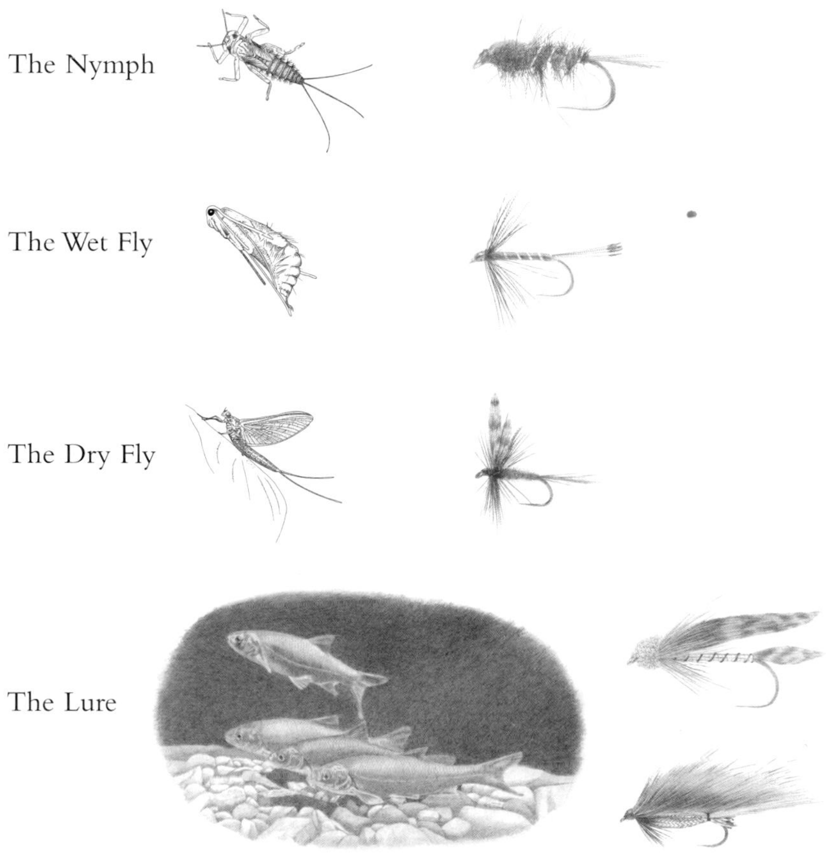

It's time to go fishing.

CHAPTER 4

GONE FISHING

THIS chapter weaves together some trout fishing experiences, plus a little background knowledge and some useful fishing tactics and wrinkles which will, I hope help you along the road to enjoyable trout fishing. For readers who wish to mug-up on detailed 'how to do it' trout fishing topics, I recommend the following books detailed in the bibliography: Clarke, 1975, Falkus, 1977, Goddard & Clarke, 1980, Harris & Morgan, 1989, Weaver, 1991, O'Reilly, 1997, Greenhalgh & Ovenden, 1998 and Lapsley, 2003. If you want to understand the principles of casting, I recommend Lefty Kreh's 'Ultimate Guide to Fly Fishing' (2003). For good reads on trout fishing from a philosophical perspective, it's difficult to beat the books of John Gierach and Tom McGuane. Peter Gathercole's Fly Tying Bible (2003) will set you off on the right road to tying that completely irresitable fly.

Seeing them before they see (or hear) you

One of the most important factors in successful trout fishing is making sure that you don't scare the fish. This is especially important where wild trout are the quarry – they are generally much scarier than stocked fish. Because of its cone of vision, a trout lying just under the surface has a more restricted view of people on the bank than one lying deeper in clear water. Where fish are hugging the stream bed, they may see you coming from a long way off. It is best, therefore, to stalk slowly upstream, ideally with the light coming over the shoulder away from the stream, taking your time and keeping your eyes well-peeled. A broad-brimmed hat and polarised glasses reduce glare and help to optimise your view. Move around so that you avoid shine on the surface and can see right down to the bed. When stalking, try to blend into the background, treading softly, as the vibrations transmitted through the bank and water are easily picked-up by trout and grayling. Don't forget that, because liquids are pretty much incompressible, sound waves travel through water much more efficiently than they do through air. Fish have sensitive lateral lines which are specifically adapted to help them hear and feel trouble coming.

When stalking you may not see fish immediately, but if you persevere, they will materialise slowly, especially if you pick up the movement of a fin, a flash of flank or the white gape of the mouth as they take a nymph. Trout and grayling have a very effective combination of colour-camouflaged skin plus reflective scales which change with prevailing conditions. The scales act as tiny mirrors, reflecting the surroundings and allowing the fish to blend superbly into their background. Grayling are not known as 'grey ghosts' for nothing; often you will be unaware of their presence until they are scared and mill around in a small shoal at the bottom of a pool or glide. The speckled skin of brown trout is made to disappear over a gravel bed, natural selection helping them avoid the ever-vigilant herons. Silvery smolts and sea trout blend into open oceanic waters where they must avoid a wide range of predators but sea trout progressively revert to a typical brown trout colouration when they return to freshwater to spawn. Colouration is an important attribute in the fight for survival.

It takes time to see and mark-down feeding fish, but this time is far from wasted. If you ignore the reconnaissance approach and fish blindly, you will almost certainly scare many more fish than you catch. Given that it usually takes quite a while to find a decent-sized trout on the feed, you shouldn't begrudge many minutes spent working out the most likely way to catch it. Softly, softly is always the best approach. Scared trout and grayling do not necessarily leave their preferred lie, but tend to sit tight, relying on their camouflage. In this state of mind they will not take a fly. After a clumsy, heavy foot-fall or botched cast it is very easy to keep casting at these fish, assuming that they don't know you are there. Believe me, they do!

If you can't see rising or nymphing trout, then you may have to fish the water, carefully trying likely spots. Remember that most fish will tend to be found where the habitat brings food to them, rather than them having to go looking for it. Wind or stream-driven currents generate these conditions, so try to imagine where the food conveyor-belt is running and the best places for trout to sit, intercepting tasty morsals. A final factor to be appreciated is that trout in streams are territorial and defend the best feeding lies. The biggest trout will be found in the best lies. Bolt holes are happily shared by scared trout, but a good feeding lie is the trout's usual sole preserve and requires defence. By learning to recognise good holding spots, you are giving yourself a big advantage in finding the trout of your dreams.

By walking or wading very slowly upstream, heron-like, keeping as quiet as possible and out of sight, you will stand the best chance of spotting trout on the fin. Watch your step when wading and wear studded waders on slippery rocky beds. A wading staff is a very useful piece of kit, especially in thigh-depth or deeper water. Fishing by wading along very gently, minimising ripples, is a pleasant experience and keeps you off the skyline, bringing you down to fish level. It allows you to see hatching flies float past, helping you match the hatch and it can allow access to little streams tunnelled by trees which are unfishable from the bank. Despite these facts, however, it is sometimes best to stay out of the water because trout are so good at picking up vibrations that even the most stealthy wader is bound to cause some bad vibes. Once you scare one trout, it will usually bolt off upstream, taking others with it. If you decide to wade, do so with care.

If you are fishing from a boat, remember to minimise noise, don't motor straight across your next drift (or across someone else's drift). It is better to move gently around using oars than to rev up your engine even for short distances. Stay sitting down, keeping a low-profile: trout are less likely to be scared by seated anglers and seated anglers are less likely to fall out of boats. Remember, that whilst a life jacket may not look trendy and could hamper casting movements it does come in pretty handy if you take a tumble out of the boat. This is especially relevant early season when the water is very cold and in windy weather when it may not be easy for your buddy to loop back upwind and pull you out of the water. Sadly, every year anglers are drowned in avoidable accidents.

From boat, bank or river bed, cover water close to you before you extend your casts. It is much better to show the trout your fly first, rather than your fly line. Lined trout seldom take flies. Whilst all trout are capable of spotting you in daylight (so wear drab clothes), sea trout seem to be able to spot anglers even at night, so tread softly and keep off the sky-line. When possible, fish into moonlight, rather than being silhouetted by it.

Night, day and the evening rise

Anyone who has fished for sea trout at night knows that these trout can see well enough underwater to distinguish between different flies when we have difficulty seeing our hand in front of our face. On natural lakes too, very big brown trout are abroad after dark, especially when sedges are hatching. Big, fat, juicy sedge pupae, when hatching in good numbers, get trout moving up in the water. Whilst much of their food is gleaned from lake or river beds, specimen trout will rise for flies when the rewards are high enough and conditions are safe enough. Swarms of big flies hatching or coming back to the water to lay their eggs around dusk or after dark are a case in point. Large predatory brown trout also seem quite happy to go marauding in the half-light. At this time, prey fish may find it more difficult to see a fast-moving predatory trout, reacting too late to save themselves. A good deal of predation occurs around dawn and dusk, but it isn't just lunkers that wake up when light levels are low.

There are two big benefits for trout of all sizes of feeding when dawn or dusk approaches: relative safety from visual predators like herons or cormorants and an increased insect food supply. As we have seen, most trout feed on invertebrates drifting in or on the water and many flies hatch as light levels fall. Also, and very importantly, many nymphs and larvae hide under stones during the day, migrating around to the tops of their rocks to graze on algae as evening falls. As these billions of nymphs undergo their daily mini-migrations, many lose their footing and drift off in the current. Scientific studies pick up these peaks of invertebrate drift which occur at low light levels. Trout, being very observant, know all about these things, too. The evening rise has a firm basis in stream ecology.

Low light levels and turbid rivers

Darkness brings with it relative safety for migrating trout of all sizes. Both low daylight levels and increased water turbidity can trigger trout movements. Tiny trout fry disperse from the area of the redd in spring, mostly at night. Downstream-migrating trout parr in autumn and smolts in spring also move mostly at night, often en masse. In clear water, upstream-migrating adult sea trout wriggle up and over gravel shallows to seek the shelter of the next pool after dusk has fallen. Spawning occurs in winter, often in turbid spates during the day when underwater light levels are low, or around dawn and dusk in clearer water. There is circumstantial evidence that both brown trout and sea trout may be able to detect low barometric pressure, starting their moves upstream in anticipation of substantial rainfall and rising waters.

In a spate, sea trout and salmon migrate in numbers and can be vulnerable to a fly or lure when freshly settled into a new lie. As spates recede and there is still a tinge of colour in the water, migratory salmonids become especially vulnerable to the rod. These fish have just run up into pools and colour in the water gives the angler cover, reduces river bed light levels and masks terminal tackle: now is the prime time to fish. Waters just beginning to colour-up after rain can also be good times for deceiving wild brown trout on the nymph or wet fly. Many nymphs are swept away in the drift during periods of high water and turbidity can do much to hide you and your leader from the fish. Heavy nymphs with a bright spot (such as a gold bead) to aid visibility can work well under these conditions. Whenever you decide to fish, an appreciation of where you might expect to find feeding trout will help you to succeed.

Reading trout streams

Running waters are much easier for the trout fisherman to read than still waters. Key points to remember are that trout, wild trout in particular, always seek the proximity of cover from predators and shelter from the current in choosing their feeding lies. Unlike us, trout have the advantage that their medium supports their weight, especially as they have a gas-filled swim bladder which effectively makes them more or less neutrally-buoyant. A trout can, therefore, hover in midwater expending very little energy, especially if it keeps out of any strong currents. Trout in good condition can starve for weeks and still survive and so their hunger is readily tempered by caution. Being cold-blooded gives these fish a further advantage in the food requirement stakes. Whilst a small warm-blooded mammal or bird must feed every few hours to survive, trout are a very different kettle of fish.

However, despite their modest food requirements, fish do not waste energy. Constant swimming against a current requires effort even for a beautifully streamlined creature like a trout and so tends to be avoided wherever possible. Energy carelessly spent needs replacing by feeding out in the open where the trout themselves may get eaten. Feeding is, therefore, a risky business. Precious energy is conserved by all animals and behaviour which achieves this has vital survival value and will be naturally selected for. Big, old trout didn't get that way by being careless. An ideal feeding lie has a position where the fish can sit in a relatively slow current, but is able to nose out into faster water to intercept drifting food items. As a rule of thumb, a brown trout likes to lie with a current speed of around 10cm per second on its nose, but close by a flow of around 30 cm per second or more, bringing the food along at an acceptable rate. If the stream is a rich one, say a spring creek (chalk stream) with abundant insect populations and fringing grasses, laden with grasshoppers, caterpillars, spiders, bugs and beetles, then a trout may be able to afford to live in a faster-current – both exspending and absorbing energy at high rates. This will be a fit, active fish. On the other hand, in a cold mountain lake, a brown trout may be inclined to just fin around in its glacial bowl at the gentlest of paces, searching for bottom-living invertebrates, drifting plankton or wind-blown surface flies. Whilst trout in these contrasting types of habitat may ultimately reach similar sizes, the mountain lake fish will take many more years to get there.

Rising to the top

A rise to a fly in a stream simply involves the trout angling the pectoral (breast) fins into the current, rising to the surface, catching the fly, angling the fins flatter and gliding back to the bottom a little way downstream. The fish then fins back along the bottom to its lie, with minimal effort. By keeping close to the bed it uses an area of slow-flowing water and keeps its distance from dangers such as herons. The behaviour is honed to be as efficient as possible, saving precious calories. A good lie is occupied very accurately and consistently – in just the right spot to maximise advantage. The trout has to minimise energy expended and maximise energy taken in whilst taking as few risks of being eaten as possible. Trout are able to disregard feeding opportunities when they feel nervous. Only a relaxed, confident trout will rise repeatedly to flies during a hatch or hold station in open water, waiting for drifting nymphs and emergers. If the trout does not detect your presence, you have a good chance of catching it, especially if it is hard on the feed. If you un-nerve your quarry, it will probably sink lower in the water and refuse to rise to a dry fly or to nip at a nymph. If you really scare it, it will disappear under its favourite log or undercut bank in a puff of silt. A partially-scared trout tends to flick its fins in an agitated way – such fish are best left to settle back down for at least ten minutes before you try your next cast.

Fishing the dry fly

Dry flies vary greatly in design; conventional patterns with vertical hackles behind the eye, double fore-and-aft hackles, Griffith Gnats with palmered hackles, parachutes with horizontal hackles, hackle-free paraduns, elk hair or CdeC-winged patterns, flat-winged spinners and others. We all have our favourites and the key to success lies in getting the size, shape and colour somewhere about right and the presentation exactly right. If you have confidence in the fly, you will take the trouble to fish it well. Good presentation involves letting the trout see your fly acting in a natural manner whilst the fish is completely oblivious to your presence. If you get this right, you will catch lots of fish.

Often, when dry fly fishing, you will either have the light coming from behind you, at which time a dry fly with white wings will shine like a beacon, or the light will be in your eyes when sunglasses plus a dark-winged fly will solve your problems. These basic rules, (which also apply to float fishing) really make a difference if you are on the water for any time at all and wish to avoid eyestrain and attendant headaches. If you want to stick to a particular pattern of fly which has poor visibility under prevailing conditions, try moving your position relative to the sun. In a boat; turn around, on the bank, if the situation permits move up-or downstream. Rather than struggling to see your fly, squinting into a rippling glare, think carefully about your options. Fishing should, after all, be fun – not purgatory!

If light and ripple conditions conspire to hide your fly and moving position isn't a possibility then watch the water, not the fly. Tighten into any disturbances that you see; splashes, swirls, head and tail rolls or delicate shimmers emanating from fish just sub-surface. Very often, you will be as surprised as the trout to find yourselves attached to each other. Another ruse is to fish a large, highly visible, bushy dry fly on the dropper as an indicator and your actual, smaller, less conspicuous imitation, close by on the point. This is a very useful way of fishing tiny ant, midge or aphid patterns which are too small for you to see but which trout will very often take with confidence. A good deal of natural trout food is really rather small.

Trout on top

When dry fly fishing, don't forget that the closer a trout is to the surface, the closer your fly needs to be to his nose before it enters his cone of vision. Trout on the river bed see a fly (and you) coming from miles away. Mid-water trout retain a fair degree of water surface and bank perspective, but surface-finners really are effectively myopic. It follows that accurate and delicate casting is vital if you are to have a serious chance of catching these fish. It also follows that your leader need only be short and that, as long as you are quiet, close approach from downstream or from opposite the trout is possible. For trout on the stream bed, fish fine and far-off. For trout on the surface, fish fine and close-to.

Life can be a drag

Finally, when dry fly fishing, always remember that real flies don't get dragged across the surface on the end of a line and so your imitation should not either. If you have trouble with drag, waggle the rod just before the line touches the surface during a cast. This will add wiggles to your leader which delay drag on the fly as the current straightens them out. A second drag-delaying tactic is to throw an upstream mend (curve) into your cast. Added seconds of drag-free drift make all the difference between regular dry fly success and failure. Drag-free flies catch trout.

Let's summarise some key pointers to increase your dry fly fishing success:

- Wear drab clothes, soft-soled footwear, polaroids and a peaked cap or hat.
- Take your time, sit back or stroll very slowly upstream, watching the water so that you can spot feeding fish before you even try to make a cast. Good fly fishers spend as much time looking as fishing. You can't catch a scared trout.
- Watch your feeding fish – is it nymphing, taking emergers or surface flies?
- Have you got the right sort of fly on the end to imitate the current food item? If not, change it.
- Having selected your fly, does it cast OK and the leader turn over nicely? If not, lengthen or shorten the leader accordingly, then de-grease it.
- Get as close as possible to your target fish, keeping low down and very quiet.
- Aerialise only enough line to cover your trout with the tippet plus fly, not your fly line.
- Try to land your fly about a metre directly upstream of your trout so that the fly floats right over his nose, not appreciably to one side or the other. Otherwise, if the trout is close to the surface, it simply won't see your fly.
- Make as few false casts as possible and cover your target trout once or twice only before resting it for a few minutes. Two or more refusals indicate the need for a change of fly.
- Believe me, you will catch a lot more trout using this stealthy approach and by taking your time than you will by racing around over-enthusiastically, 'chasing rainbows'.

Much of the skill in fly fishing lies in fish location from afar.

Under cover agents

As we have seen, the position of good stream trout lies depends primarly on physical cover and current speeds. Physical cover can be a log, rock, weedbed or undercut or it can be provided by relatively deep water. Classic holding spots are found below waterfalls where depth and surface ripples provide cover and in corner pools with undercut banks. Fast glides with either ample deadwood or tree roots along the margins or with rough boulder and rock-strewn beds are also good. Big rocks provide separate, high quality trout lies both immediately up and downstream. Trout may not lie immediately behind a rock, but further back where they are still in sheltered water and can easily pop out into the torrent to pick off prey.

Creases occur where a log or rock causes the current to be pushed across channel, leaving a slow water lie next to the main flow and such places are well-liked by a range of fish species, including trout. The narrow zone between the slow and fast currents is often shown up by a line of bubbles trapped in the surface tension; this is known as the drift line and is well worth fishing wherever you find it on a stream. Drift lines on streams are analogous to scum lanes on lakes – there are generally plenty of insects caught up in the foam and the trout know it.

Seams form around river bends where water flows more rapidly around the outside of the bend than around the inner line. If the bend is sharp, the seam can end up flowing in a circle back around the inner bend to form a backflow, eddy or, on a really fast river, a whirlpool. Trout in back eddies effectively face downstream and are difficult to approach from the usual direction – you may need to detour out in a loop and then stalk in low to the ground from upstream in order to make an effective cast.

Fishing pools

Trout like the cool, well-oxygenated water of shady pools where they are safe near the bed or tucked-in under banks. The searching out of well-oxygenated, shady water seems especially important to sea trout and this is worth bearing in mind when choosing where to fish. A deep, well-covered pool below a fast riffle will generally be better in summer than a series of long, relatively slow glides. Under warm conditions the turbulent, bubbly water of riffles is sought by trout even during the day, especially if dissolved oxygen concentrations fall appreciably.

Trout usually move up to the pool lip (the bottom of the riffle upstream) or down onto the pool tail (the head of the riffle downstream) to feed towards dusk. Riffles are packed with insect nymphs, larvae and pupae: they are fly production factories. Sea trout and big brown trout will usually lie deep in a pool, under tree roots or rock cover during the day and venture out onto shallows in the evening. When sea-trouting, it is best to wait until after dusk before casting a tentative fly across the shallow pool tail. Remember that it is the thwack of the fly line hitting the water which seems usually to scare fish. Minimise this risk by casting gently, aiming your cast just above the surface so that the line straightens out, stopping just above the water and then falling softly onto the surface. Use the lowest weight line you can get away with and the longest, lightest leader which you can handle under prevailing conditions. Tapered leaders turn over far better than level monofilament and make a big difference for dry fly fishing on clear streams.

The strawberry on the railway line

There is an interesting debate on whether trout can see your leader, however fine, but are not scared by it or whether they will only take a fly when they fail to see the leader. If the former explanation is correct, then what really matters is probably the drag-free drift of a dry fly. This is the 'strawberry on the railway line' theory – trout see the line, but can't resist the strawberry. The alternative explanation is that finer, clearer leaders work mostly because the trout find them hard to see and so the fly looks to be out there on its own, behaving naturally just like a real one. My guess is that there is probably merit in both views: use the least conspicuous leader you can get away with, cast gently and ensure, as far as possible, that your artificial fly follows the normal line and speed of the current as it approaches a feeding trout. This is sound for a dead-drifting fly. If you are fishing an active nymph, then a slow, variable, twitched retrieve works well. If you are fishing a sedge hatch, then a dry imitation twitched across the surface at dusk can be deadly. Sometimes, when you are letting a dry fly sit out there on a calm still water, just tapping the rod butt will send ripples out from the fly and these can be enough to provoke a take from a trout closely inspecting your offering – it's great fun when it works!

Do you need to match the hatch?

A trout which has been feeding on a range of food species may well be tempted by a generalised, likely-looking fly such as an Adams or Hares ear nymph. But a trout which is keyed-in to a particularly abundant and juicy food item may well require something quite similar for it to recognise the fly as potential food. You know yourself that if you are looking for something in particular, say a screwdriver in a box of tools, you visualise the screwdriver and then go looking for one. All vertebrate animals may search for prey in this way – by forming a so-called 'search image'. If this is the way trout recognise food and decide whether to accept flies, then your imitation needs to conform to the image in the fishes mind. This image may have just a few key components, perhaps the right size, shape, colour and behaviour. Very often, trout take emerging flies rather than those which have fully emerged and are sitting on the water surface. This may be why emerger patterns are often more successful than traditional hackled dry flies. Where trout are being choosy, generalised patterns will be very hit or miss, whilst patterns which try to match the hatch or, at least, match the current search image, should stand a better chance. Fly patterns which exaggerate search image features might be even more attractive than natural insects and so become super-effective flies. See Bob Wyatt's 'Trout Hunting' (2004) for a thoughtful discussion of this and related topics.

Use your eyes to observe both flies on the wing and floating on the surface. Ideally, watch trout feeding to see just what they are taking. A compact pair of lightweight binoculars come in useful for this close observation work. Start your stalk by short-casting and gradually extend your range. This avoids lining and scaring fish which may literally be under your feet. Away from pools, on relatively uniform stretches, stream-wise trout hug the cover afforded by banks. Here, they find overhead shelter and take advantage of the fact that the current speed is slowed by friction, creating a series of suitable feeding lies. A short cast upstream along your own bank can be executed very gently and accurately, keeping just the tip of your leader and fly near the trout. This is a deadly tactic in the right hands. When there are no trout rising, they are probably nymphing down below and you need completely different tactics to reach them.

Get on down

Cobbled river stretches and depressions in a smooth gravel or rocky bed have a slower current zone near the bottom than that found above. Here, working deeply fished nymphs can really pay off, especially early or late in the season when the water is cold or in bright conditions on a sunny day. Teams of leaded nymphs fished deep for grayling or trout work because of the natural bed-hugging behaviour of the fish. A shot nipped a foot above the fly plays hell with your casting technique but it does get your fly down to the fish. It really is very easy to fish over the top of torpid fish in deep water. I speak as someone who has wasted many precious hours on the river bank doing just that. Whilst a shot on your cast may not appeal to the purist, it does allow you to bump the weight across the debris on the bottom whilst your slightly buoyant nymph drifts with the current just above the bed, right on the trout's nose.

Reading lakes

The term 'still water' is a misnomer as all pools and lakes have wind or temperature-generated currents to varying extents. When a stiff breeze blows across a wide lake, a considerable water circulation is set-up, bringing deep, cool water to the surface at the up-wind (windward) end of the lake. If the lake has stratified in summer, with the formation of a stable upper warm layer (the 'epilimnion'), a cool lower layer (the 'hypolimnion') and with a narrow zone of rapid temperature change between the two (the 'thermocline'), then a stiff summer wind can cause the upper layer to pile-up at one end of the lake and then to rebound in a series of oscillations or 'seiches'. All sorts of complex currents and temperature differences are then happening down there and the trout will react accordingly, moving to their preferred temperature, dissolved oxygen and food-supply stations. This makes the business of trout location on large lakes pretty tricky stuff. If you have limited time and are searching a big lake by boat for trout, this is where a little echo-sounder can really produce the goods. Otherwise, you may need to pick the brains of generous-spirited local anglers or engage the services of a good ghillie.

If you visit a particular water frequently you can invest time in finding out the answers for yourself and it helps to keep a fishing diary as the memory can play tricks. It really is very satisfying to get to know a local water in all its moods so that you can begin to predict when and where you are most likely to succeed. Don't expect local anglers to give away such hard-won knowledge too freely, if at all! Going fishing with a like-minded buddy halves the work as you can try different spots and differing tactics, comparing notes. A mix of solitary contemplation and friendly banter makes for a happy fishing season. In the end you can get to know a water like the back of your hand, but be careful, if the fishing gets too predictable, it loses its challenge. Fortunately, fishing has so many variables affecting success that the chances of really getting to the bottom of the problem of catching fish with any degree of consistency will remain just a dream for most of us mere mortals.

On any lake, there are natural features which will generally attract trout. These include drop-offs where fish can cruise in the safety of deep water, but still be close to shallower, more productive hunting ground, rocky or gravely shores which are rich in snails, caddis larvae, shrimps, water lice, etc and islands, especially those with richly varied shorelines. Bays which grow abundant weed beds will be rich in insect nymphs, snails, etc. Expect good olive hatches there. Deeper water over a silty bed is where abundant bloodworm (midge larvae) populations live and where thick hatches of buzzers (duck fly) will happen. These areas are worth fishing close to the bed with suitable nymphs (buzzers or Diawl bachs) or surface fishing with teams of buzzers, wet flies, spider or dry midge patterns. Silty bays on limestone systems will also be good for mayfly (Greendrake) hatches. Bays with deep reed beds often get good falls of black gnats and these are well worth fishing, especially on breezy days.

Most man-made lakes have features on the bed which trout use for cover – old stream channels, ditch systems, tracks, hollows, etc. Reservoir trout fishermen who know the lie of the underwater land catch a lot of big trout from old ditches, etc where there are often fence lines and sunken bushes which provide cover for wary brownies (read Arthur Cove, 'My way with trout', 1991). Deep, clear, open water, accessible from a suitable promontory or from a boat is often the haunt of *Daphnia*-feeding trout. Remember that little crustaceans like *Daphnia* swim down deeper in bright light and rise towards the surface at dawn and dusk. The trout follow, often necessitating the use of a fast-sink line on a bright day and an intermediate or floater in the evening. *Daphnia*-feeders, especially rainbows, are often susceptible to flies incorporating orange in the dressings. Because red wavelengths of light do not penetrate the depths, orange and red flies actually look dark grey or black when fished deeply. The orange fly in your hand may, really, be acting as a black lure when you plumb the depths; strange, but true.

Both inflowing and outflowing streams are natural focal points for trout in lakes – especially around dawn and dusk when wary fish will work their way into shallower water to pick-off food from these conveyer belts. I well remember fishing Scotland's Loch Avish where bigger than average wild brown trout cruised stream mouths in the gloaming. In Connemara, the Cong Canal, which was an attempted man-made link between Loughs Corrib and Mask produces specimen brown trout each year to anglers fishing its clear flowing waters. The stream concentrates trout because it concentrates their food supply. Sea trout passing through river and lake systems also tend to linger around river mouths and these are well worth a drift, especially during breezy, overcast evenings.

On lakes, winds form bands of static bubbles and foam which trap insects in the surface tension. These 'wind lanes' are prime feeding areas for both brown and rainbow trout. On lake fisheries, trout feeding on or close to the surface tend to work upwind, slowly cruising singly or in shoals, picking off flies as they go. Under still conditions, the presence of rising fish will be obvious, even though the rises will be gentle. When there is a ripple, watch out for splashy rises or glimpses of fins or tails as fish roll over. Shimmer or the flattening of a patch of ripple is caused by fish swimming just below the surface, often indicating an approaching pod of rainbows, picking off swimming nymphs or taking still emergers. By watching the progress of trout patrolling upwind, you can anticipate their route and lay out a delicate cast well in front of them. Aim to fish your flies across the nose of the fish, rather than straight at them. This is a productive tactic and it often pays to let your dries, emergers or nymphs dead-drift on the breeze, watching the leader, fly line tip or indicator for takes. Often, all you will see is a gentle draw of the leader away from you – tighten up before the trout feels the resistence of the rod and the fish should be yours.

Fishing from the shore, you can let a big dry fly drift out downwind on the breeze. This windward zone collects insects blown off the land and so is a hot spot for surface feeding trout on the look-out for black gnats, daddy long-legs, grasshoppers, beetles, etc. Don't put your rod down unattended, however. A friend of mine saw this happen on Pitsford Reservoir in the English Midlands; a big trout grabbed a daddy long-legs on the long drift and raced off, hooking itself in the process. All would have been well, except for the tangling of the line around the reel handle and the consequent loss of a set of gear down into the depths. I hope the trout got away, the angler was left both speechless and rodless.

An alternative to drifting flies downwind is to deliberately search the shore which the prevailing wind is blowing on to the lee shore. Here, you are where the floating flies, both terrestrial and aquatic, pile up providing a feast for wary margin-patrolling trout. Needless to say, you must stand well back and fish a short line for quite a while before wading in. Very often you can pick up a really nice fish from water just deep enough to cover its back, but you will only accomplish this by stealth.

Once the margins have been carefully fished, you can extend your casts further. Remember, when casting into a wind, you should aim the fly at the water and stop it suddenly before it hits, keeping your line moving fast and shortening your leader, if necessary to obtain decent turn-over. Contrary to instinct, it can be more successful to fish a lighter, rather than heavier line when punching into a stiff breeze, but it is critical to keep the casts low, tight and energetic to attain sufficient line speed to overcome the resistence of the wind.

Calm

Under still conditions, you may well be driven crazy by the completely unpredictable routes which rising still water trout can take, zig-zagging around after flies. If you are boat fishing and decide to motor slowly over to a pod of rising fish, as sure as eggs are eggs, they will melt away and start rising somewhere else. If you aren't careful, you can end up on a wild trout chase, getting little useful fishing done. Before this happens, try staying-put and casting out a well-oiled, bushy dry fly on a completely de-greased leader, letting it drift around well away from the boat or bank. It really is quite surprising how often trout will have a go at such apparent free offerings. Arthur Cove used to do very well in calm waters by covering both his leader and the first few yards of his fly line with a fine smear of clay so that the whole thing fished just sub surface. By retrieving very slowly indeed, he could avoid line wake. Otherwise, he would put a dab of grease on the leader about a foot above each fly and let them sit still. Nowadays, of course, you can buy lines specifically designed to fish just beneath the surface (intermediates and their like) but, back then, Arthur was way-ahead of his time (Cove, 1991). He would often fish a team of small (size 12) black spiders to imitate the dark chironomids which are so common on all trout fisheries. When necessary, he would slowly twitch back his sparsely-tied, deliberately ragged nymphs, to great effect. The key in calm conditions was to avoid line wake at all costs and to fish with flies imitating the likely prey of the trout. Wherever trout are feeding, some knowledge of their likely current diet will stand you in good stead.

Trout diet: you are what you eat

Trout diet varies with the size and life style of fish, with habitat type and with changing weather conditions. If you like trying to 'match the hatch', see Pat O'Reilly's (1997) and Malcolm Greenhalgh's (1998) excellent books. Pat O'Reilly's book is illustrated with fine insect photographs by Melvin Grey and Malcolm Greenhalgh's with excellent paintings by Donald Ovenden, both allowing the identification of many flies and suggesting suitable imitations. John Goddard's 'Waterside Guide' (1988), with numerous insect photographs by John and drawings by Charles Jardine is also excellent, follows a similar approach and is small enough to keep in your jacket pocket or creel. The sections below cover food items likely to be on the trout's menu, a few examples of what trout were actually found to eat in scientific studies and finally, a stroll through the year on streams and still waters to see what's likely to be about.

Use your eyes, plus your knowledge

How can you determine what a trout or grayling is likely to be feeding on today? Observations whilst on the water go a long way to telling you what might be happening. Clouds of mayflies, buzzing midges, skating sedges or daddy long-legs whirling along on the breeze are good starting points. Trout crashing into marginal weed beds towards the back end of the season encourage the still water angler to reach for a slow-sinking line and some fry patterns. Swirling fish, working slowly up the breeze amid a hatch of midges, calls for the floating line and a team of buzzers, grenadiers, soldier palmers, hoppers or similar patterns. Sedges popping out over reservoir shallows call for suitable emerger or invicta type patterns. The rise form of the trout often provides some good clues as to the stage of fly being taken.

Trout flash underwater when chasing nymphs, bulge under the surface when grabbing pupae, head-and-tail rise after emergers, sip down spinners and often make a mad dash after a retreating mayfly dun or skittering caddis taking to the wing. Often, when observing trout, it is easily possible to guess the right food species but to fish the wrong stage of the life cycle. You could be fishing a dry mayfly very unsuccessfully because trout are actually on the ascending nymphs or emergent duns. Close observation will help distinguish just what is going on. You don't need several degrees in freshwater ecology to be a good fly-fisher but, if you learn the basics of fly identification, it will open-up a whole new area of appreciation and enjoyment of the sport. If you haven't got the time or inclination to acquire this knowledge, that's OK, you can still catch lots of trout by fishing something sensible under the prevailing conditions. Knowing the Latin name of the species is, for practical fishing purposes, irrelevant. If you are observant and have good eyesight, you can inspect flies hatching on the water, on the wing or perched on bank side vegetation, sorting through your fly box until you find something similar. Some ultra-keen fishermen carry a small aquarium net to catch natural flies with – I haven't got to that stage, yet.

Many very successful anglers limit themselves to half a dozen, or less, deadly patterns and learn to cast and present them to perfection. Almost always, careful presentation is more important than a close match to the natural. A perfect imitation of what the trout are eating, belted-out on a chunk of overly-heavy leader by an angler standing on the edge of the bank in a bright orange shirt and white hat probably won't lead to much success. A delicate cast, presenting something sensible, often will. One of the best known trout fishermen in the UK limits himself to two small dry fly patterns, one black the other brown in sizes 14 and 16; on these, he catches plenty of chalk stream trout. Of course, good presentation, plus a well-tied and chosen fly is the best of both worlds, and the most satisfying, especially if you tied the fly yourself. Budding fly-tiers are recommended, once again to read Peter Gathercole's excellent 'Fly-tying Bible' (2003).

A trout's reaction to your fly varies considerably with the type of fishery which you are exploring. Trout in rich habitats and trout which have been caught and released are a fair bit harder to persuade than upland fish which are lean and hungry. The ability of trout to learn after being caught and released can make a big difference to fishery performance and, in extreme cases, only champion fly tiers and casters can catch such 'educated' fish regularly. This is, however, an extreme circumstance. See Bob Wyatt (2004) for an interesting discussion on the extent to which trout may be able to learn about the dangers of being caught on artificial flies; the trout's brain is probably unable to generate much in the way of what we call thought. Whilst trout are super-tuned to the appearance and natural behaviour of their food organisms and to a whole range of potential risks from predators (including us), as far as we know, they can't count or reason-out problems. Fish certainly can, however, learn from experience and where anglers are commonplace, trout can get very wary indeed. Matching the hatch can be important on such fisheries.

Wet fly on freestone streams

Spatey, boulder and shingle-strewn rivers and streams can be very difficult to fish with the dry fly because of a lack of good drifts in the pocket water and virtually instant skating, owing to the fast, swirling currents. This is where 'North country' wet fly fishing comes into its own. Small, soft (often partridge) hackled flies, including the many 'spider' patterns can be fished upstream, straight across or across and downstream to tempt trout on the fin. Upstream fishing usually involves wading, casting a short-line with a team of spider patterns and raising the rod to keep in touch with the flies as they tumble back towards you on a dead drift with the current. There are parallels here with the deadly 'Czech-nymphing' technique used for grayling. Upstream wet fly fishing lends itself to a steady rhythm of gentle roll-casting, searching-out trout from undercuts, under bank side bushes and from little runs and pools, it is a delicate and skilful art. As you lift the rod, your flies rise in the water and you can induce takes from trout and grayling which may have been viewing the flies with a degree of suspicion until that point. A steady upward movement of a nymph or wet fly may be a passable imitation of an emerging nymph or pupa – who knows what a fish thinks?

Wet fly fishing down and across the current offers several chances of fish. As you cast straight across the current and throw an upstream 'mend' into the line, you may instantly rise a trout. You can often get a sharp take from fish as your flies flash across their noses whilst swinging across the current and then, finally, you may also receive some interest from fish along your bank as you retrieve slowly before casting again. With care, you can effectively fish continuously, taking a step or two downstream between casts. On a cast of three flies, the top dropper can be a bushy bob fly, the middle a spider and the point fly a generalised heavy nymph or flashy attractor like a Williams favourite. In faster water, the heavy nymph may be needed to get the flies down. By changing flies and keeping an eye on hatches, you can get firmly into the groove and really catch some fish, most of which will probably be small and turned off the hook whilst still in the water. Some, though, may require the landing net, this isn't just a technique for snatching parr. Whilst many 'upstream dry fly purists'may deride this approach, it is very deadly in the right hands and downright skilful. Some knowledgable pundits say that the good wet fly fisher needs to be a better angler than the good dry fly man. Who cares, as long as they both enjoy their sport and treat their quarry with respect?

Where to start

My best advice at the start of a trout trip is to sit down and watch the water before you tackle-up. Look for feeding fish, look for hatching flies or lots of flies on bankside vegetation (or in spider webs). Sit back and drink-in the atmosphere; you aren't in a race. If the clues present themselves, then follow them up. If all is quiet, this must mean that fish aren't actively rising and you may decide to go prospecting. Try a small dry Adams or a small, unleaded hare's ear nymph. Cover the water very slowly and carefully, it's surprising how well you can do with a simplified approach. If you manage to catch a trout without using a specific fly and you decide to kill it, sample the stomach contents with a marrow spoon soon afterwards.

Long, thin marrow spoons recover recently-eaten items from the back of the throat and stomach, allowing you to identify the flies and then choose a suitable imitation from your fly box. Once you have learnt to identify the key invertebrate groups, even if only approximately, then you are streets ahead. If you have made a survey of your fishery with a pond net, then you will already have a mental list of what's likely to be on the trout's menu. If you know something of the biology of the insects, this can also help you with your fishing tactics. A marrow spoon full of shrimps or caddis larvae indicates the use of a deeply-fished nymph. A thick mass of midge pupae should see you making up a cast of buzzers, size and colour-matched to the naturals. A tightly-packed ball of hawthorns, adult mayflies or craneflies should see the dry fly box emerge from the tackle bag. A belly full of small fish indicates that a streamer, muddler or floating fry may do the trick. A marrow spoon is a good investment if you are taking fish for the pot and can, therefore, investigate their inner workings. Marrow spoons must not, of course, be used on live fish!

Trout diet on upland waters

Trout are carnivores which seize food items with the sharp small teeth on their jaws and tongue; they eat a wide variety of prey species. In their fine book 'The Trout' (1967), W.E.Frost and M.E.Brown provide lots of information on brown trout diet. On the upper River Tees, for instance, brown trout ate various terrestrial insects, midge and caddis larvae and adults, stonefly and mayfly nymphs and adults, beetles and bullheads. In Three Dubs Tarn most invertebrates eaten were midge pupae and caddis fly larvae plus pea mussels, midge larvae, mayfly nymphs, and the rest alder fly and dragon fly nymphs. On Wise Een Tarn, caddis larvae, water fleas, midge pupae and larvae, dragonfly nymphs, mayfly nymphs, alderfly larvae, water lice, shrimps and terrestrials were commonly found in trout stomachs. On the Aberdeenshire River Don three quarters of food items found in trout stomachs were blackfly larvae and adults (smuts), and most of the rest mayfly nymphs, midges, caddis flies and shrimps. On Lake Windermere, trout often ate midge pupae, stonefly nymphs, caddis larvae and terrestrial flies and beetles blown onto the lake surface in spring and summer. In autumn and winter they ate water lice, shrimps, snails and, in November, char eggs. This switch from the lake bed in winter to more open water feeding in summer is often observed.

Trout parr in the Altquhur burn, River Endrick, Scotland (Maitland, 1966) ate about 25% crustaceans (shrimps), 25% dipterans (midges), 15% mayflies, 15% caddis flies, 10% stone flies and a few beetles and other animals. Salmon parr ate around 45% mayflies, 20% stoneflies, 20% diptera, 5% caddis flies and sundry worms, shrimps, beetles, snails and other items. Note how the young trout took large numbers of shrimps from the river bed whilst the salmon almost always took drifting or surface insect prey. This dietary difference between young salmon and trout is commonly recorded in fisheries studies.

On Llyn Tegid, North Wales, Ball (1961) recorded a wide variety of brown trout food items, including shrimps, caddis larvae, mayflies, midges and water lice. As usual, the trout concentrated on lake bed invertebrates in winter and spring and surface food in summer. Summer food intake was far higher than that in winter. Grayling on the same lake probed in between stones for caddis larvae and molluscs whilst trout took species more often encountered on the surface of the lake bed. The grayling's mouth, which can be extended into a sucking tube, allows it to reach places which trout simply can't. In this way the two species probably avoid strong competition for food. The sharp teeth of the trout allow it to grasp small fish; in this lake bullheads are eaten quite frequently. Whilst grayling do occasionally eat fish, trout do it regularly. On Llyn Alaw, Anglesey, P.C. Hunt & J.W. Jones (1972) found brown trout to concentrate on shrimps, water lice, leeches, snails, corixids, caddis flies and sticklebacks. Larger trout ate more fish than smaller ones, a widespread observation.

Trout diet on lowland waters

On Ireland's River Liffey at Ballysmuttan, surface flies and other insects were again important in summer, together with black flies, midge larvae and mayfly nymphs. In the cooler months of the year brown trout worked the river bed, foraging mainly on stonefly nymphs and caddis larvae. In the River Fergus (Co. Clare), fly-caught trout had been feeding on terrestrial insects, adult mayflies and nymphs, caddis flies, larvae and pupae, midge pupae, blackfly larvae, shrimps, water lice and snails. In Lough Inchiquin (Co. Clare) water fleas (Daphnia and friends), midge pupae, water boatmen, adult mayflies, caddis flies and other flies were taken in open water, whilst snails, water lice, shrimps and caddis larvae were gleaned from the lake bed. On Dorset's little River Tarrant, brown trout parr concentrated on Baetis olive mayfly nymphs, chironomid midges and a range of caddis fly species (Richard Mann & colleagues,

1989). In a small still water fishery in Surrey, M.C. Lucas (1993) found, early in spring, that both browns and rainbows fed deep down on caddis and alder fly larvae. In summer, rainbows often ate water fleas, adult and pupal midges in open water, whilst, perhaps because of competition from the rainbows, the browns continued to skulk in the depths foraging for various larvae, beetles, water lice and sticklebacks. Despite their sharp protective spines which can be locked into place, sticklebacks often fall prey to trout.

Paddy Fitzmaurice (1979) found that, on Lough Sheelin (where there are no rainbow trout to compete for food), brown trout come up into the open water to take large numbers of water fleas, surface flies and water boatmen. These trout are very cute, selecting the bigger species of water fleas, rather than the little ones. Even here, though, trout feeding over stony shallows were hunting sticklebacks, small perch, corixids and mayflies. It is clear that, whatever the type of fishery, trout are both opportunistic and adaptable in their feeding behaviour.

During the filling of Rutland Water, in common with all lakes, millions of worms were forced to the surface and eagerly gobbled-down by newly-stocked young brown and rainbow trout during winter. These fish switched to shrimps, snails and midges in spring and summer. Now, many years later, in the mature reservoir a wealth of midges, caddis flies, water fleas, beetles, corixids, water lice, shrimps, snails and small fish make Rutland a good, varied feeding habitat for stocked trout, year-round. Some huge browns, over-wintered for several years patrol the depths for fish prey, falling sometimes to large, deeply-fished lures.

This short review provides a brief insight into natural trout diet and how it varies between waters and through the year. Let's now consider how this can inform our fly fishing trips.

Fly-fishing through the season

The following section describes fly hatches and insect falls likely to be encountered on British trout fisheries. I have included some Latin names for those readers who want to brush-up on their aquatic entomology and the common names are there, too. Hatches seen in North America and other countries will be similar in overall pattern, but will differ in detail and are described in appropriate local literature.

Rivers

As we have seen, trout living in flowing waters are opportunistic, taking whatever they can catch without expending too much effort or exposing themselves to too much risk. Good hatches or falls of flies, especially big, easily-caught ones, like March browns, Olive uprights, *Ephemera* mayflies or large dark olives, tempt out the specimen fish. Blue-winged olives and Iron blue duns can provoke intense rises, if you are lucky enough to be there at the right time. Remember that, at any one time, many trout are likely to be nymphing, rather than surface-feeding and so looking for surface rises alone will reduce your chances of success. As you wander the fishery, always look both above and below the surface for indications of feeding fish.

March – April

In spring, many trout will be intercepting midge pupae or sipping down hatching chironomid midges (duck flies). Pheasant tail and hare's ear nymphs, small buzzers and Cul de Canard ('C de C') emergers should work well. CdeC feathers come from around a duck's oil preening gland and are naturally very buoyant; they make brilliant thorax and soft wing materials. Many stoneflies, for instance *Perla*, *Nemoura*, *Perlodes*, *Dinocras* and *Isoperla* emerge early and mayflies such as large dark olives (*Baetis rhodani*), large brook duns, March browns and Olive uprights (*Rhithrogena* and *Ecdyonurus* species) and Iron blues (*Baetis pumilus* or *niger*) may be on the wing. Grannom sedges (*Brachycentrus subnubilis*) and Sand flies (*Rhyacophila dorsalis*) are abundant now on some sandy and gravel-bedded rivers. Hawthorn flies (*Bibio marci*) and black gnats (*Bibio johannis*) often get blown onto the water from hedgerows or reedbeds and can provoke a good response from hungry trout.

May-June

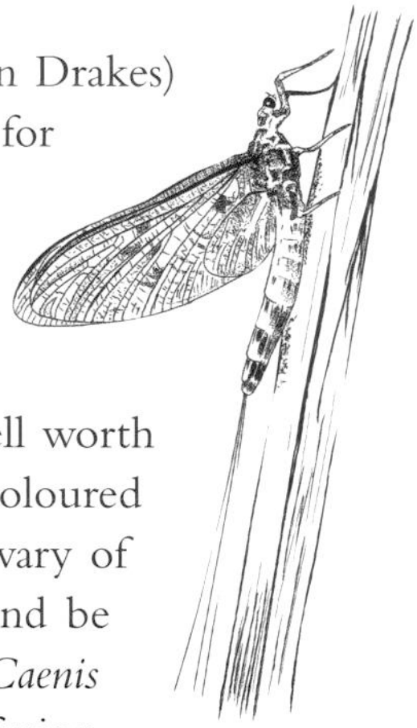

In early summer, large *Ephemera* Mayflies (Green Drakes) will get even the biggest trout out and looking for surface food. 'Duffers fortnight', in late May – early June, when Mayflies are normally on the wing, accounts for many specimen wild and stocked trout every season. Remember that, especially early on in the Mayfly season, it is well worth trying an olive nymph, rather than a larger, pale coloured mayfly nymph which wild browns often seem wary of in the early days. On silty rivers you will see and be frustrated by the Angler's Curse or Broadwings (*Caenis* species), little white mayflies which hatch in profusion and get the trout rising avidly, but are very difficult to imitate successfully. Other mayflies seen at this time of year may include Yellow May duns (*Heptagenia*), Medium olives (*Baetis vernus*), Olive uprights (*Rhithrogena semicolorata*) and 'pale wateries' (mixed small mayfly species, *Baetis fuscatus* and *muticus*, *Centroptilum luteolum* and others with transluscent wings). Many stonefly species continue to hatch, especially on rocky upland waters. Sedges (caddis flies) also get going now, including the Welshman's Button (*Sericostoma*), Cinnamon sedge (*Limnephilus*), Silver sedge (*Lepidostoma*), Marbled sedge (*Hydropsyche*), Grannom, Sand flies and several species of brown sedge. Many beetles and alder flies are also on the wing and can end up on the water, together with reed smuts (*Simulium* species), chironomid midges and black gnats. A good box of dry flies and emergers, some light tippet material and a 5 weight rod should serve you well at this time of the season.

July- August

As summer progresses, tail end hatches of *Ephemera* mayflies, Green duns (*Ecdyonurus*), Dark duns (*Heptagenia*) and Yellow duns (*Potamanthus*) and False March browns (*Ecdyonurus venosus*) occur, together with blue-winged olives (*Serratella ignita*), *Caenis* and various pale wateries. Summer evenings often bring a fall of upwinged spinners – egg-laying females returning to the water. These flies, when spent, lie flat on the surface and can provoke intense rises towards dusk. Trout will move right out onto open shallows under these conditions. Try a small polythene-winged imitation, a sherry spinner, or similar. Mid-summer also brings with it many more sedge hatches – Caperers (*Halesus*), Cinnamons, Sand flies, Marbled and Silverhorns. These hatches can be electric in the evening as the pupae swim actively towards the surface. Try an amber nymph, Invicta or suitable bushy dry fly skated across the surface. Tiny microcaddis (*Hydroptilidae*) also abound on many waters, but don't bother with these, unless you have laser-vision, sit back and smoke your pipe instead. Stoneflies continue to emerge in the uplands at this time. Midges, mosquitos, reed smuts, black gnats, beetles, flying ants, caterpillars, grasshoppers and daddy long-legs can all also be part of the trout's menu. No wonder wild trout are in prime condition at this time of year. Keep your eyes open and try to work out what's happening, it's a fascinating piece of detective work. If you fail, retreat to the pub and drown your sorrows. You may well find me there.

September - October

Even now, hatches of Blue-winged olives, Iron blues, Pale wateries, Large dark olives and False March brown mayflies occur, together with similar species of sedge and terrestrials to those seen in mid-summer. At night, under cover of darkness, big brown trout will be abroad and you can sometimes intercept them on their travels with a big streamer or surface wake fly like a muddler or cork-backed lure. These fish-eating trout need to sustain themselves on large food items and can take lures savagely, leaving you in no doubt that you have something substantial on the end of your line. By this time, however, wild trout will be maturing sexually and starting their spawning migrations – be careful not to kill 'unclean' fish. It is traditional in Britain not to fish for trout as they colour-up for spawning, but many north American fisheries include opportunities to fish for all kinds of trout on their upstream spawning migrations, with anglers using streamers and other lures to trigger aggressive responses from territorial fish, often males. Angling traditions and regulations vary widely between countries. What seems odd to me in Britain is that, whilst many shake their heads in disapproval at fishing for brown trout on their spawning migrations, these same anglers are the first to be out on the water chasing salmon and sea trout on their upstream spawning migration.

Still waters

Much less is known of trout foraging behaviour in still waters than on rivers. Brian Clarke's 'The pursuit of still water trout' (1975) remains a fine read on the subject. It seems unlikely that feeding lies are occupied or defended on lakes. Young trout may mostly feed close to weed beds or boulder cover on the shallows but adult fish probably roam widely, foraging for whatever is plentiful and easily-caught.

March – April

On still waters the chironomid (Duck Fly) is King, bringing up big brown trout on Irish Loughs and stocked trout on reservoir fisheries. This is an area where English reservoir trout anglers, well used to buzzer fishing, can do very well with wild fish. An interesting variety of approaches is available, ranging from traditional wet fly fishing through various chironomid pupa imitations, to the use of small wet flies such as the Mallard and Claret and various dry midge patterns. All prove deadly in the right hands and under the right circumstances. Sepia duns (*Leptophlebia*) and several large stonefly species hatch from boulder-bedded lakes in early spring. Brown and black sedges are also on the wing.

May-June

Ephemera Mayflies, Claret and Sepia duns (*Leptophlebias*) and Pond and Lake Olives (*Cloeon* species) come along in early summer, bringing out nymphers, wet fly fishers, dappers and dry fly anglers, all enjoying the best of the season's 'on-the-top' fishing. A good olive hatch gets trout in a lively feeding mood. A wealth of midges will be around and teams of buzzers on floating lines continue to score. If you are very lucky, you may see early hatches of the Great red sedge (the Murrough, *Phryganea grandis*) and the Green Peter (another *Phryganea* species). These juicy caddis flies really get the big trout interested in the late evening when they scuttle across the surface after they hatch. Try a well-greased high-floating G&H or Elk hair sedge pattern on a strong leader. Longhorn (*Oecetis*), Cinnamon, Silverhorn and Brown sedges and Grousewings (*Mystacides*) may all be common at the lakeside. Sedge fishing into the dusk on an Irish Lough is a treat which every fly-fisher should indulge in while they can. The ubiquitous chironomid midges are still high up on the preferred menu, as are black gnats. A good fall of black gnats (terrestrial flies), especially when they are clumped-up, mating will bring a rapid response from trout. This happens most often in the relative calm of a windward (upwind) lake shoreline, especially if it is fringed with dense reed and rush beds where these flies are generated. Another fly which is blown onto water from land as an adult is the alder fly (*Sialis* species). These large dark brown flies which look quite like sedges, have predatory aquatic larvae which crawl out of the water to pupate and emerge as adults on land. Occuring on both lakes and rivers, they are a tempting treat for a trout on the cruise in spring.

July- August

The tail end of Mayfly hatches can still be seen, *Caenis* are still (unfortunately) around, and Pond and Lake olives still make their very welcome appearances. All the usual sedge suspects are still at large, as are mixed midge and sedge hatches. During the heat of the day, many trout will drop down into the mysterious depths in search of swarms of water fleas and ascending midge pupae. Occasionally, certain snails migrate across lakes and reservoirs by trapping air inside their shells and setting sail. At such times trout really home-in on them and this can create very frustrating fishing unless you realise what is going on. Dick Walker, observant as ever, devised a small, dark cork-bodied fly for such occasions. Many terrestrials are very abundant at this time of year, including grasshoppers and beetles on some still waters, making 'matching the hatch' even more testing. It's time to dust off the dapping rod, a much neglected and deadly piece of kit. Dapping either a bushy artificial or a natural fly is great fun and children can have a go at catching trout without having to learn proper fly-casting. Once hooked, they can learn the finer points as the seasons tick by.

September - October

Pond and Lake Olives can still put in an appearance and sedges are still very active on warm September evenings. Midges continue to be important in still water trout diet. At this time, dapping a daddy long-legs or grasshopper can make for an interesting breezy afternoon's fishing. Fry-feeding trout will be chasing juvenile roach, perch and sticklebacks, both on natural lakes and reservoirs. Now, trout really pack on weight to reach peak condition prior to spawning.

What can we conclude from this brief consideration of trout diet and fly hatches and how does this inform our approach to fly fishing?

Take home messages

The concentration on dry fly fishing, often seen on some waters, bears little relation to what trout are actually likely to be doing for much of their time. Don't forget that trout, especially wild trout, are very wary and may require substantial amounts of surface food to be available before they will risk regular rising to flies. Emergers are often targeted by actively feeding trout, perhaps because they are vulnerable and easy to catch. On brighter days and when hatches are sparse, trout will mostly stay deeper, picking-off drifting nymphs and pupae or foraging over the river or lake bed.

Early and late in the season, when the water is cool trout are usually feeding deep down on invertebrates, on or very close to river and lake beds. Sinking lines, leaded nymphs and slow retrieve rates will all pay off.

In early spring and summer, midge larvae and pupae (duck fly or 'buzzer' hatches) are very important, both on lakes and rivers. Small patterns imitating pupae or emergers fished on floating lines should work well. On lakes, trout feeding on midge larvae and pupae often stay deep during the day and here a very slow retrieve with a sinking line, leaving nymphs static for a while over the front of the boat 'on the dangle' can really pay dividends.

Through spring and summer, trout will line-up to pick off nymphs, emergers and adult flies from seams, creases, bubble lines, scum and wind lanes. Close observation will reveal what they are after at any one time and whether you should be fishing a nymph on a dead drift, an emerger in the surface film or a dry on top. This is the cream of exciting, testing fly fishing sport. Deft presentation is the key to success.

In summer and early autumn, a whole range of terrestrials including caterpillars, beetles, grasshoppers, flying ants, daddy long-legs, grasshoppers, etc can end up on the water surface. These trigger a good deal of surface activity from hungry trout and dapping is a method which is well worth remembering under these circumstances.

In mid-summer, trout in lakes often forsake the brightness of the surface layers and cruise the depths, picking off midge pupae ascending to the surface, swarms of water fleas which can be very abundant in productive lakes or shoals of small fry. These deep cruisers will respond readily to flies, especially orange or red ones, provided that you get down deep enough to find them. On some lakes, larger perch and roach fry are on the menu by this time and a deeply-fished lure, like an appetizer, zonker or minkie can score well.

At the back end of the season on most still waters there is an annual bonanza available, with trout concentrating on larger fry. These trout behave in a very characteristic way, making lightening-fast dashes into shoals of fry hiding in weed beds, stunning small fish which then drift away just sub-surface or on the top. The trout then circle back to pick off their prey at leisure, often taking them as delicately as they do a dry fly. Floating fry patterns, white muddlers and minkies or zonkers can all score. These trout are in absolutely prime condition and usually head-off on long powerful runs when hooked. Exciting stuff.

Post cards from fishing days

It was a fine day in May in the late 1960s, I was a young teenager out with partners in crime Yeato and Jeff, walking the upper Wellow Brook in Somerset. The small fields were bounded by thick hedgrows, alive with nesting song birds, the grazing was rough and varied, supporting just a few dairy cattle. Wild flowers, butterflies and grasshoppers were abundant, grass snakes hunted frogs in wet hollows and barn owls quartered the evening meadows for voles. We had no permission to fish, but nobody minded as the little brook with its wild brown trout was just part of the rural landscape. It had always been there and was taken for granted by generations of fishing lads. Much of it was deep-shaded by scrubby briars, hazel and willow and you could just about jump across it at its narrowest point. As youngsters we spent care-free, sunny afternoons turning over flat stones in the crystal shallows, catching bullheads, stone loach and crayfish. Over the gravel shallows hung clouds of pristine minnows, the males fabulous in their spring spawning colours, the females plump with eggs. But all of those small fish were subordinate to the job in hand – catching a decent-sized trout for tea.

In my hand was a little green solid fibreglass spinning rod, a Milbro Spinwell, matched with an Allcock's Aerial centrepin reel bought in Crudgingtons of Green Street, Bath and purchased after many months of diligent pocket money saving. On the business end was a size 10 Model Perfect eyed hook, tied on with a half blood knot; that was it. No tackle bag, no landing net and no worries. We were free to roam in the countryside – a precious childhood. In my pocket was a Balkan Sobrani tobacco tin of my Dad's, filled with wet moss and lobworms collected from the front lawn the night before. Stalking worms on the lawn was a little like stalking trout along the brook; walk slowly and softly, crouch down and attack with precision. Like the trout, the worms will beat a hasty retreat if they sense your presence; survival reactions honed by generations of blackbirds, thrushes, snuffling badgers, foxes and hedgehogs.

The wild brownies in the brook were even shyer than the lobworms, having grown up amid kingfishers, herons and possibly otters, although I never saw one there. These trout lived in clear shallow water, their excellent camouflage and wariness making them hard to spot. When undisturbed, they ventured out from the safety of their log or tree roots to feeding lies where they picked-off nymphs and surface flies. As I lay on my stomach in the long grass, a water vole paddled across the surface with a mouthful of reed sweet grass and a trout melted away from its feeding station into cover, scared by the overhead movement.

Mayflies started to trickle off the edges of slower glides and were picked off in mid-air by flycatchers and along the margins by wagtails. The duns which made it to bank side hazel bushes shed their dull waxy skins to step out as shiny spinners, keen to join the dancing, mating swarms above the shrubby vegetation. As time trickled by, in the way of a young chap with his life ahead of him, I whiled away the time, just absorbing and learning from the scene before me. Gradually, as I refocused on the stream bed, my trout was back on station having recovered from the fright of the swimming vole. At around three quarters of a pound, it must have taken the best part of ten minutes for him to come back out from the dark safety of the undercut bank. He started rising for Mayflies, confidently taking a mixture of nymphs, emergers and duns riding the current before take-off. My underhand cast was good, the worm landing five yards upstream of the trout and I teased it downstream in the current, trundling it over cobbles and fronds of water crowfoot, gently retrieving line. The worm stopped abruptly next to a flat stone and I gave it a tweak only to find an irate fat bullhead clamped firmly to the tail end. A worm that size was a lottery win for a bullhead and it would not let go. I reeled him in and, as he passed the trout's lie there was just a puff of silt where the trout had been. I released the bullhead and walked on upstream, deeply unimpressed.

Bumping into Yeato and Jeff, I discovered that they had both caught several small trout, all of which were returned. A plan was hatched to walk about a mile downstream to the big stone weir and the pool below. We wandered slowly through the languid afternoon heat, pausing to catch and admire slow worms which were out on their early summer walk-abouts. These really are spectacular creatures and we sat for ages, just watching them. All of a sudden, it was late afternoon and the weir pool beckoned. We approached with the upmost caution and as Jeff was oldest, he had the first cast. Jeff had taken off his hook and tied on a small Ondex spinner which he lobbed way over to the far side of the pool – all of fifteen yards, with his recently acquired Intrepid Elite. His judgement was fine, feathering the spool with a finger tip and stopping the flight of the spinner exactly at the point where it dropped next to a bramble bush which overhung and dangled into the deepest part of the pool. The spinner dropped into the sparkling four foot depths and was arrested just before it hit the gravel with a sharp turn of the reel handle which set the blade spinning. The flashing lure had travelled no more than two yards before a blur of black spots and flashing yellow flanks grabbed it, bending the little spinning rod double as the trout fought to get back to its thorny lair. It almost made it too,as Jeff had his four pound line tangled-up around the bale arm and this took a precious few seconds to sort out but he had cleverly walked back up the bank, drawing the fish into open water. That brown trout, the biggest any of us ever took from the Wellow Brook, was over a pound and a half – an absolute whopper and eaten, I'm sure, with reverence. It was probably close to the end of its natural days anyway and had done its job. I caught a trout myself on the way back upstream but, at half a pound, it was given the benefit of the doubt and the chance to grow into a takeable fish for us to try and catch next season.

Mells

A couple of years later, still armed with my Milbro Spinwell rod, now matched with a gleaming black Intrepid Elite reel with a furry edge to the spool to stop the line getting caught behind and with a proper roller bale arm, I was bitten early by the tackle bug. I had cycled many miles from home to go poaching with an old pal Pete who lived close by the upper end of the Mells River. This sparkling little stream, spring-fed from the Somerset Mendip limestone, was packed with small wild brown trout and we would wander for miles through lightly grazed, unimproved pasture land. The EU Common Agricultural Policy, which has done so much recent damage to the British countryside via subsidised intensification, wasn't even a gleam in the politician's eye back then. Farming was gentler, less greedy and more sustainable in those days.

Pete and I were going slowly, taking in the scenery, when quite suddenly, I caught sight of a truly massive grass snake lying coiled up in the sun on a rocky ledge. It was the mother of all grass snakes and, even allowing for fading memory and a fisherman's tendency to exaggerate size, it must have been between four and five feet long and as fat as my wrist in the middle. That's a big one. I edged towards it, sure that it was comatose, basking in the warmth on its rock and I got to within about ten feet before it shot off like a rocket, gone in a whirl of dry leaves and leaving me with just a crystal-clear memorised snap shot, imprinted forever. I hope the Mells river valley still has as many snakes as it did when I was a lad, grass snakes are becoming a rarity now. I recently made an advisory visit to the valley some way downstream and was delighted to see wild brownies still finning away in the current. Thankfully, some things never seem to change.

After a couple of hours stroll, Pete and I came to a pool which had been dug off-line from the river, but remained linked via a sluiced channel. As with so many Somerset pools lying within limestone stream systems, little trout had found their way in and had grown rapidly into big fat trout - trout of interest to teenage boys. Small spinners were blood-knotted to lines and stealthy casts were made, allowing the Mepps spoons to nudge the gravel bed, throwing up tiny plumes of attention-grabbling silt. Wham! We were in business from the word go and the trout were stonking great two pounders – all four of them. Only later did we pause to think that their tatty fins and uniform size probably indicated a hatchery, rather than wild origin. I hope the owner isn't reading this. At least we put the small ones, probably the wild ones, back in again and so we weren't entirely criminal in our enterprise. An abiding memory of the Mells River, absorbed during pauses to soak our toes in the cool water, was the abundance of freshwater limpets, flattened stone-clinging mayfly nymphs and caddis larvae with intricate sand cases which plastered the rocks and pebbles. Those streams were certainly clean – I didn't know then that the mayfly nymphs would have been Ecdyonurids, but I did know that you didn't see them where the water was smelly. When people comment now on declines in aquatic fly life, I can only agree. Back in those days stream life had a chance to thrive and there were more flies than you could shake a stick at.

As a young lad, I regularly used to cycle several miles through the Somerset countryside to a small lake which was connected to the Kilmersdon Brook and which had a great wild trout stock. This little fishery, owned by a benevolent retired Estate Agent who didn't mind young lads poaching his trout, was weedy, clear-watered, full of invertebrates and splendid wild brownies up to two pounds and more. The trout were prolific. I imagine that they spawned in the stream and then dropped down onto the pond where they grew fat on the varied aquatic life until we came along with our worms and spinners, unceremoniously hauling them out. I have to confess that, in those days, all sizable trout were killed with a solid whack on the head, carefully wrapped-up in damp grass or dock leaves, laid in the bottom of a willow creel and cycled back home to a waiting buttery frying pan. I wonder whether young Somerset lads still fish that clear pool for its trout? I hope so; it's more fun for them than staring at a computer screen and that's what fishing should be about - simply having fun out there in the fresh air.

Chew

My dear old Dad had done a deal with a colleague at work who was tired of fishing (how can anyone get tired of fishing?) and had come home with a Sharpes Scottie, weight 7, two piece bamboo rod, a reel and floating line – proper trout fishing tackle! I was beside myself with glee and expectation; surely no trout would now be safe.

Early one April I cadged a lift over to Somerset's lovely Chew Valley Lake, having saved up for a day's bank fishing ticket. After several years of wandering brooks and small pools with cans of worms and small spinners, a graduation to fly fishing seemed the logical sequence of events. I had managed to tackle-up and tied a size 10 white lure on the end of my sturdy leader, thrashing the water to foam in an attempt to get the thing further away from the bank than about ten yards. My arm had started to ache, a blister appearing on the inside of my thumb and fellow anglers had retreated to a safe distance, carrying their straw bass bags full of fine trout with them. Still, I persevered, putting in enough raw energy to scythe several fields of mustard, but I still couldn't cut it with the trout. Blisters then began to appear on both the palm and thumb of my right hand and frustration was rising. It all seemed so unfair – I had a bamboo rod and some flies, I was fishing on Chew around 1970, casting like a dervish and surely I deserved at least one trout!

A kindly-looking neighbouring angler with a floppy hat all covered in nymphs and dry flies wandered over for a chat.'How are doing?' he asked 'Not well' I replied.'What are you using?' 'White lure on a floating line'. 'Ah, I see....ever consider getting yourself a sinking line?' 'A what?' It was explained to me that, being early April and the water still cold, the trout would be lying deep and any angler wishing to take home some trout should be fishing either a very long leader on a floating line or a short leader on a sinker. Nymphs or small lures would work fine, as long as they were fished deep. Ah, OK!

My only option, given my single fly line status, was the longer leader, kindly assembled for me by my new found friend. This I proceeded to lash around the nearest tree on my back cast, destroying it immediately. Leader number two was made up and I was positioned on a bit of bank without a tree right behind – progress. A Herculean bit of whip-cracking hurled out the leader, fortunately straightened by the breeze and my white lure was allowed to sink down onto the realm of the stroppy stockie cock rainbow trout which seized it with attitude and wriggled eel-like back to shore. I fell on that fish with my home made priest - it must never have known what hit it. Milt oozed from its vent and it started to go black immediately, but none of that mattered, I had caught a trout on a fly, trying to match hatches could come later.

That was the only trout I did manage to catch that day but boy, did I learn a few things about reservoir fly fishing. Virtually everyone else on the Woodford Bank that spring day went home with limit bags of rainbows and browns. I went home with a trout, several blisters and a determination to save up for a sinking line and to get better at casting. How could you time that subtle double-haul and what the hell was a shooting head?

The hedgehog

By the following season, I had read everything I could get my hands on regarding trout fishing and had been down in the fields practising my casting. My Triumph 500 motor bike had been given the once over and the engine oil topped-up to replace the vast quantities which it had sprayed over my boots, last time I went fishing. It was time to learn more about the mysteries of Chew Valley Lake, first hand and, on a mild late April day I was wandering along the path to the north of Heron's Green Bay on the west side of the reservoir. This bay has varied depths, prolific weed growth, good hatches of midges and sedges and always holds plenty of trout. Early migrating swallows and martins were skimming the surface for hatching flies and a cuckoo called from a willow next to the shoreline reeds. A brilliantly coloured green woodpecker was hopping along in search of ants in a meadow full of buttercups and the resident

Canada geese were honking loudly and chasing each other in their annual pre-nesting displays. It was good just to be out walking briskly along in the fresh air, tackle bag bouncing on my back and rod in hand. What more could you want? In April, my fervent hope was to contact some of the splendid full-finned, over-wintered rainbows for which Chew is famous. These three to four pound fish are difficult to find but are a real prize when you do manage to catch one.

The path led me along past a small wood on my left, past a creosoted timber bird watching hide with the observation flaps solid with spider webs plastered with small black midges and onwards towards the point. The sun was warm and there were swarms of chironomids hovering over bank side bushes and trees.

Laying back on the bank, smoking cigarettes were two seasoned trout fishers, each with a well-worn waxed jacket, thigh waders and battered hat festooned with flies, mostly bedraggled nymphs. Each also had a wet, bulging straw bass bag and sticking out of one bag was a square, spotted spade tail belonging to a very solid rainbow trout. With the natural inquisitiveness of a teenager, I walked over to ask a few questions. 'Those look nice fish' I said, receiving a reply that 'They certainly were, and there are plenty more where those came from'. This was the sort of conversation I liked. I sat down at a respectful distance and took in the scene.

Each angler had a rod laid flat on a large flat black plastic sack, with a shooting line heading off into the depths and a stout hazel twig hammered down vertically in front of the reel. This wasn't the sort of set-up which you come across in standard books on fly fishing and so I looked-on with interest. The two friends paid no attention to their rods, they just chatted away and smoked, enjoying soaking in a few rays of spring sunshine. Every so often one of them would chuckle in appreciation of a joke or observation; a more relaxed approach to catching trout could not be imagined. And so the minutes ticked by and I set up my own rod with a floating line, long leader and a team of buzzers to imitate the midge pupae which must, by now, have been wriggling upwards in the cool waters. Those swallows and martins must be catching something.

I was scanning the surface for rising trout, but had seen nothing more than a nice pair of great-crested grebes performing their courting dance which involves a lot of head-shaking and looking deeply into each other's eyes and a fat cormorant which was fishing along the margins, coming up regularly with small perch. I wished that I could catch half as many fish as him. The sun was quite warm by now and, snug in my Barbour jacket and rubber waders, I was starting almost to nod-off. Just as my eyelids had started to droop, a screaming ratchet shattered the tranquillity as one of my fellow angler's rods tried to take off like an Exocet missile. With remarkable calm, the fisherman got up, strolled over to the rod which was, by now, literally hopping up and down against the hazel twig, and latched into a racing trout. No strike was required as the fish had hooked itself but the bend in the stout fibreglass rod, arching right through into the handle, told me immediately that this was another very substantial fish to add to their already considerable catch. In due course a fine over-wintered rainbow slid into the net and was landed, cleanly despatched with a weighty priest and placed in the bag.

Beside myself with interest I walked over to try and discover the secret of this magic technique. I must confess that I wouldn't have been surprised to see a bunch of maggots on the end of the hook or a big fat lobworm. But this was doing the anglers a great disservice as nothing could have been farther from the truth. The rig consisted of a stout nylon leader, a split shot about six inches from the hook and a long-shanked, close-clipped deer hair nymph with a red tag at the bend of the hook. With a knowing grin, the anglers explained the reasoning behind their approach. They, too, wanted to catch big, solid rainbows in peak condition and such fish fed along the deep margins on sedge larvae, shrimps, snails, etc. Because it was still only April, the water was cold and the fish would undoubtedly be lying deep. Hence the sinking shooting heads and split shot: these served to pin the line down on the bottom. The slightly buoyant deer hair nymph would hover just above the bed and be moved around very slowly by any currents. The red tag would be an eye-catcher and certainly proved to be a fish catcher! To prove their point, out came a marrow spoon and, sure enough, the stomach of the rainbow which must have pushed four pounds, was stuffed with caddis larvae.

Whilst many a dry fly-only man might have shaken his head in disapproval, this use of the hedgehog as the fly was known, seemed rather clever to me.

Afloat on Blagdon

A couple of seasons later, I had got myself a carbon fly rod, built up from a kit. I just had to stick on the handle and whip on the rings, getting them almost straight. I had cut-price, mill end floating and sinking lines and a mega-box of flies, some of them bought, some cadged from mates and some tied, very inexpertly, by myself. Everyone has to start somewhere. The vast majority of these flies I would never use, but I didn't know that then. In deference to my new-found pile of tackle, I decided to visit Blagdon reservoir – 440 acres of Victorian splendour nestling in a Mendip valley of the little River Yeo. The reservoir, constructed for public water supply over 100 years before, had matured into a beautiful fishery, stocked with prime trout from the Ubley hatchery. Here, Dr Bell, a local GP, is said to have come up with enduring fly patterns including the grenadier, buzzer and amber nymph. He used his scientific observational powers to deduct that chironomid midges and caddis flies were top of the trout menu on this water. They are still.

I was afloat on Blagdon for a summer evening with Merv, an old friend of the family. Merv wasn't a fisherman, but fancied a go, so I had set him up with a dapping rod (actually a coarse fishing float rod) and a big, bushy daddy long-legs which he was bumbling patiently across the surface on the breeze. It seemed to both of us that, as long as trout aren't scared of the boat, dapping has a good deal to commend it – you can relax, tangle-free, working just the fly in the surface water with no leader touching to give the game away. No tricky casting, just the good fun of waiting for that exciting rise.

Some time had passed as we drifted before the wind (I needed a drogue to slow the boat down) and several fish had swirled at the dapped daddy, but none had stayed attached. This was because of an understandable tendency for excitement and striking too early on Merv's part. I remembered the maxim of saying 'God Save the Queen' before striking and passed this on to Merv who nodded appreciatively. More time passed during which I flicked my cast of three wet flies around with little effect (the boat was going too fast to keep up with the retrieve). A shimmer had appeared in the water very close to the daddy and, sure enough, a dorsal and then tail fin broke surface as a trout rolled over the fly, a pause, a strike.....God Bless the Queen! Merv's first rainbow trout headed for the horizon, most surprised by the sudden restraint of rod and line. At just under two pounds he was par for the Blagdon course, in prime condition and sat gleaming in the wetted straw bass bag on the boards of the boat. All was well with the world.

Unscrewing the marrow spoon from the handle of my priest, I examined the trout's stomach contents finding masses of buzzers (midge pupae), many still alive and kicking, mostly dark green and about a size 12. Out came the fly box, off came the Soldier Palmer, Invicta and stick fly - they had seemed sure-fire winners earlier - and on went a team of green buzzers. The point fly had a little lead under the dressing, the middle one was standard, the top one was tied as a dark green soft hackled spider which was dibbled across the surface at the tail end of each retrieve. We decided to anchor up for a while to give Merv's dapping arm a rest and to allow me to drift my flies around on the breeze with a floating line (always my favourite line).

By now, my casting had improved and I could even give the line a well-timed double-hauling pull, adding a few useful yards on the shoot. I aimed to cast about a metre above the surface to give the line and leader time to straighten out before dropping gently onto the water. I had also learnt the importance of a slow retrieve when buzzer fishing. Chironomid pupae aren't Olympic swimming gold medallists, they just drift and wriggle their way upwards towards the surface. A leaded point fly gets well down and, with practice, it is possible to judge when it is around the bottom and when to start a very slow retrieve, keeping the flies just moving without snagging-up. I had learnt the vital importance of watching the tip of the fly line to see the magic drawing forward which indicates a take, although this can be difficult to see in a ripple. Now, I would add a blob of flourescent floating putty to aid visibility in choppy water.

Nothing happened for quite a while and we had another drift to try the daddy again. No joy, so we anchored-up again, this time in a reedy bay and watched the house martins and swallows swooping for hatching flies. I noticed that there are gazillions of midges and some sedges about now and wonder what the likelihood was of a trout even noticing my flies, let alone grabbling one. As my attention drifted, I stopped pulling my fly line without realising it and my flies just dangled static in the water.....Wham! Down went the rod tip as a fine rainbow pushing three pounds made a serious mistake.

As has happened to me so many times since, I realised that during a day's nymph fishing, it is just so easy to fall into a mindless mechanical rhythm of cast and retrieve – you drift into autopilot mode, your flies moving in unlifelike ways and the trout aren't impressed. When you pause, either accidentally or on purpose, your flies move extremely slowly with the drift of your line, rather as they might if they were alive and trying to ascend to the surface to hatch. This is what the trout are used to and your fly may well be picked-off confidently as just another small snack. Experienced nymph fishers appreciate this and fish slowly with intense concentration, watching the tip of the line like a hawk, but only for relatively short periods. Then, they wade out of the reservoir margins, often with a trout in the landing net to take a break and absorb the atmosphere. Trying too hard can lead to headaches, frustration and a lighter bass bag: less time fishing can, believe it or not, equal more trout caught.

Avington

I entered a fishing phase which included wanting to catch a whopper rainbow, stalked in clear water. This, I realised, would cost me an arm and a leg, but I had earmarked cash for the purpose. An old pal Steve, had recently gone down this road with mixed results. He ventured into deepest Wales to a put-and-take water where 'the trout are all as long as your leg' (see John Gierach, 1991). The chosen tactic was to hurl out a massive leaded Montana nymph on a ten pound leader and sinking line, hauling it back at a high rate of knots. This process was repeated, metronome-like for a couple of hours until Steve's arm was almost wrenched out of its socket and a huge, fat stockie rainbow raced through the peaty waters. Perspiring-freely, Steve applied the brakes and, after some hectic moments managed to fold the immense beast into his modest landing net and stagger up the bank with it. The coup de grace having been delivered, Steve spooned his fish (presumably looking for leaded Montanas) only to find part-digested trout pellets. The thrill of the chase diminished somewhat at this point.

Never one to be downcast for long, Steve decided that the fish which really was pretty big – around ten pounds I think and with OK fins - should reside for posterity in a glass case. He'd heard about a quite well known local taxidermist who wasn't too expensive, dropped the frozen fish in on him and forgot about it for several weeks. The phone went in due course and a voice said...'your trout is ready for collection'. Excellent! A long section of mantlepiece was cleared of family photographs and long-forgotten important memo notes and the cased trout was duly collected, wrapped in protective brown paper and tape. The family was assembled and the ritual unwrapping took place. To Steve's horror, what looked back at him was not what he remembered of his prize trout, but a hideous glaring red, white and black enamelled monstrosity with its tail bent around to fit it into an under sized case. A dull plastic eye, three sizes too big, stared out over the hearth, reflecting Steve's disappointed face. He later expressed the opinion to me that 'it looked like the bugger played for Manchester United'.

Notwithstanding Steve's experience, I went to Avington in Hampshire, close by the hallowed River Itchen, to hunt for my own monster rainbow. The fishery was immaculately kept, with large trout cruising the clear waters. I watched a middle-aged chap with a bamboo rod flicking out a small nymph at passing trout which studiously ignored his nicely presented fly. To everyone's amusement, he let his back-cast drop a little low and it landed on the back of a springer spaniel which had been minding its own business, sniffing around after frogs in the long grass. The dog was rather taken aback by the arrival of a metallic fly and headed for the hills with a howl, providing a fine fight on the cane rod. Luckily, successful catch-and-release was adopted, with the dog none the worse for his experience, but remaining well away from the lake for the rest of the day.

I returned to my quest and found a quiet corner where trout of enormous proportions were nosing around, apparently chasing green damsel fly nymphs. Nervously, I tied a size 10 longshank, leaded damsel to my six pound leader and cast it about five yards ahead of a mega-cruiser. The trout whipped up to the fly as it sank and then, distainfully ignored it. Hmmm.....stocked rainbows aren't necessarily a push-over it seemed. I tied on a similar-sized light grey, leaded rabbit fur nymph which I could see down in the depths and went on slow patrol. My method was to keep low, moving softly and casting short lines ahead of cruising trout. This was very interesting as many fish had a close look at my fly before turning away and swimming on. I wondered to myself just how often this sort of thing happens on less clear-watered fisheries where I am fishing 'blind'? A good deal of the time, I suspect.

Hours passed and many large flies were tried: big trout, big fly, right? Wrong. Finally, I tied on a well-chewed, short shank size 12, hares ear nymph with a four pound clear mono leader (this was well before Fluorocarbon days). As is so often the case, fining-down did the trick and the fly was eagerly accepted by the then biggest trout of my life (8 pounds 6 ounces) and I was delighted. The trout was eaten for supper by a gathering of friends and it tasted just fine. This seemed a better epitaph than being entombed in a glass case, whichever football team the trout might have played for.

I didn't pursue lunker stocked rainbows again until, many years later, I visited a small still water fishery near Mere in Wiltshire in the company of a well-known trout fisherman and angling writer who proceeded to catch trout right, left and centre. Brian was stalking with a short line, using a pale-bodied, leaded mayfly nymph with an articulated abdomen which wriggled on the retrieve. What a difference a bit of life in the fly made! Another useful lesson learnt. I struggled that day until I was encouraged to lighten and lengthen my leader, tying on an 'Oxford & Cambridge' nymph. This little-known pattern, a bizarre late evening creation of my own, has three pairs of mobile, white rubber legs poking out through the dubbing of the thorax and does a pretty fair imitation of rowing along on a twitched retrieve. That subterfuge was enough to fool my only ever double figure trout – a rainbow which put up a battle Royal, before folding into the net. Those two big stockie rainbows were enough for me, I had got that tee shirt and now wanted to pursue some wild brown trout.

Bonnie Scotland

In the late 1970s I carried out fisheries research at Glasgow University for my Ph.D. and, in the process, gained experience of many highland river and loch fisheries and of the fine folk of the Outer Hebrides (Western Isles). My base was at the University Field Station at Rowardennan on the east bank of Loch Lomond and this provided a wonderful introduction to the diversity and splendour of Scottish freshwater fisheries. The loch has a resident population of brown trout, a healthy sea trout stock and a reasonably prolific salmon population. All of these fish populations rely primarily on in-flowing rivers and streams for spawning habitat. There are no Arctic char in Lomond, but there is an abundant population of powan, a Coregonid whitefish or 'freshwater herring' which feeds mostly on plankton and other invertebrates. Whilst whitefishes are uncommon in the British Isles, they are widespread further north in Scandinavia.

Much of the sea trout fishing on Loch Lomond is carried out from boats drifting around the islands in the broad southern half of the loch, with anglers using long, limber rods, floating lines and traditional attractor pattern flies. This approach can bring mixed catches of trout and grilse, the larger salmon more often falling to trolled spoons and plugs. During my three years in Scotland, I was befriended by a couple of local anglers who regularly fished the River Endrick for its sea trout. These men knew the river extremely well and only bothered to fish when a particular rock, close by a bridge in the village of Fintry, was covered with water. When there had been little or no summer rain and early-running fish had long settled into pools to sit-out low water conditions, these guys mowed their lawns, dug their gardens or watched sport on television. Many years of effort had taught them that Endrick sea trout run up-river with spates and that fresh fish are most vulnerable to capture during or soon after those bursts of migratory activity. Fresh, silvery fish are best for eating and stale, dark fish, well-advanced with egg or milt maturation are best left to spawn in peace.

Despite the fact that sea trout, like salmon, generally eat little whilst in freshwater, they will still take a fly, bait or spinner at certain times. Perhaps, soon after taking up residence in a new lie, these fish become a little territorial and defend their new position. A flashing spinner or attractor fly, a big dark lure close to the bed or a wake-making surface lure may all elicit an aggressive response from a fresh fish. Fishing for migratory salmonids is generally weather-dependent, unpredictable and often unproductive. However, nobody who has thrilled to the power of a fresh-run sea trout or salmon will tell you that it is boring! For my money, there is a good deal more watercraft and interest involved in fly fishing for brown trout than in fishing for salmon, but sea trout certainly have me under their spell. Maybe it's the sheer unpredictability of sea-trouting which makes it so much fun.

On the Endrick, it was common practice amongst locals to roll cast a team of wet flies right in underneath overhanging alder bushes and then to let them fish down and across the flow. Those sea trout showed the typical bank-hugging behaviour of the species and casts had to be very well-judged, landing just by the bank edge and then swinging slowly in under overhanging vegetation. Sea trout often respond to a fly swinging across their nose and favourite patterns included teal blue and silvers, silver butchers and black pennels, all in sizes 10 or 8. Many times, two or three maggots were attached to the point fly and this, I was told, could make a fearsome difference to the bag at the end of a tiring night.

I suppose this indicates that sea trout in freshwater do not entirely lose their appetites. The fact that they will happily gobble down a worm or two also backs up this observation. Of course, sea trout in estuaries and the lower stretches of rivers are routinely taken on both trotted and legered baits, often those intended for other species. Perhaps, the closer trout are to the sea and the less time spent in freshwater, the hungrier they remain, their appetite waning with prolonged residence in freshwater. It has been pointed out by many biologists that a predatory fish like a trout migrating back to its spawning beds would not do the survival of last year's progeny any favours by feeding actively in freshwater. Maybe this is a key evolutionary reason why salmon and sea trout shut down their food intake and fast for periods ranging from weeks to months whilst on their annual reproductive migrations.

Another reason could be that such big fish would hardly self-sustain in low-productivity streams in any case and would be vulnerable to predation if they spent much time out in the open looking for food. Fasting may be the safest solution. Whilst sea trout quite often recover from this imposed fast, recondition as kelts and return to spawn again, rather fewer Atlantic and no Pacific salmon achieve the same feat. Breeding is usually a one-off activity for salmon.

During my time in Scotland I was fortunate to see many of the steep, spatey west coast highland rivers, with their long-lived multiple-spawning Atlantic sea trout and the gentler east coast rivers, such as the Tweed and Tay with their shorter-lived, rapidly-growing North Sea fish. As Andy Walker has pointed out; differing sea trout stocks have differing life cycle strategies, probably relating to variations in local environments. Spawning batches of eggs sequentially over a number of years allows fish to 'spread their bets' on unpredictable spate systems. There, powerful floods can wash out redds or prolonged drought can shrink areas of nursery habitat, meaning that juvenile survival is low in some years, but high in others. Spawning several times, over a range of years, would appear prudent. However, going for broke with a single 'big bang' reproductive effort may be worthwhile in the slower-flowing, more productive East coast rivers where trout fry will find equable conditions in all years and so there is little risk of failure, as long as you produce lots of eggs. Despite superficial appearances, not all sea trout are the same; stocks in differing rivers show subtle localised adaptations and these may be critically important for the long-term survival of these wild game fish populations.

Scottish brown trout are immensely variable, from the small, dark, slow-growing peat bog fish which seize virtually any fly, through to the sleek, fat, choosy fish of the limestone lochs, surrounded by food in clear weedy waters. This latter group of brown trout, exemplified by the

Durness limestone loch populations, fished from the Cape Wrath Hotel, can be as difficult to catch as any wild chalk stream brownie and very considerably bigger. Contrast this with the more usual conditions in Loch Avich, for instance, which drains into the west coast Loch Awe system. There, any reasonable team of nymphs or small dark wet flies fished in 'soft weather'on a light leader will catch trout. On Loch Avich and most other moorland waters, you are likely to basket a leash or two of half to three-quarter pounder brownies. By contrast, in the Durness area, you might hope for a hard-won three pound or bigger specimen trout from the testing Lochs Borralie, Caladail or Lanlish.

Whilst researching Outer Hebridean fish populations, I was given permission to fish for trout by the Factor of the North Uist Estate and I made occasional use of this freedom in the evenings before escaping the biting midges in my tightly zipped-up tent. North Uist seems to have almost more water than land and the lochs vary tremendously from alkaline west coast waters to acid, peaty blanket bog lakes in the centre and east of the island. In summer red and black-throated divers fish the lochs while, if you are very lucky, you may hear the characteristic clicking call of corncrakes which still survive amongst the traditional farmsteads on the north west of the island. One evening, I made my way to a small loch under the hill of Uneval and was fishing away when an enormous bird hove into view, causing me to put down my rod and fumble through my creel for my binoculars. A magnificent golden eagle was spiralling up on thermals in the evening light, scanning for carrion on the hillsides. So captivated was I by this sight that I clean forgot about my fishing tackle and wandered off along the shoreline, bird watching as I went. After some minutes the eagle soared away over the hill tops and I turned to retrace my steps. Where my rod had been, there now stood a small herd of cattle. I chased them off and had to disinter my precious carbon wand from under about six inches of gravel and shingle. It seemed certain that the blanks must have been split by the experience, but a trial cast confirmed that, miraculously, the rod had survived intact. I have it still.

If you have the chance to visit the Scottish Outer Isles, I suggest that you take it. The fishing covers salmon, sea trout, brown trout, ferox and Arctic char and the people, scenery and wildlife leave you with cherished happy memories. There are no nicer people than island folk. Scotland offers a myriad of varied waters to the visiting trout angler; I recommend Bruce Sandison's excellent 'Trout Lochs of Scotland' (Unwin Hyman, 1987) for a mouth-watering introduction.

Pitsford

We lived in Buckingham for twelve years through the 1980s and, when the opportunity arose, I whizzed up to Pitsford reservoir, north of Northampton for an evening's fishing on that much under-rated water with friends Dave and Pat. Many happy memories spring to mind, here are just a few.

A public road crosses the reservoir on a causeway just below the fishing lodge and the steep concrete banks shelve down into relatively deep water. A tunnel goes through the centre, linking the boat bay below the lodge to the main body of the reservoir. Early in the season, when the water was clear, you could scan the depths from the causeway and watch trout cruise by. These fish taught us a good deal about still water trout behaviour. Typically, the rainbows moved quickly through mid-water in small shoals, following a circuitous route which they repeated every so often. They would cruise along, picking off mid-water prey (probably midge pupae, water boatmen, *Daphnia*, etc), always keeping on the move. Later in the year, they would use a similar tactic when hunting shoals of fry. Sometimes, more than one fish would go for an item of food, introducing a degree of competition. This was often the case where a big fly, perhaps a daddy long-legs, had got stuck in the surface film, prompting a hurried, splashy rise. We could catch these rainbows on mid-water nymphs (pheasant tails, gold-ribbed hares ear, corixids or small Montanas), fished back briskly on floating or slow sink lines. By keeping an eye open for surface movements, it was possible to keep track of the pods of foraging rainbows and to lay out a cast to intercept them, as they went past. What did prove frustrating, however, was their common behaviour of keeping well out from the shore when a clumsy wading angler made too much noise. As with all fishing, one noisy individual and you might as well move pitches or go down to the pub.

Whilst the rainbows were, to a degree, social, the browns behaved differently. They would tend to keep well down towards the reservoir bed, cruising along singly, picking-off snails, water lice, caddis larvae, various nymphs, etc. It was rare to see more than one brown trout at a time or to see one moving at any speed (they should work for the Government). The browns may have been defending home ranges and these cautious fish could be caught on leaded, long-shanked stick flies with an orange or green tag on the butt which may have been passable imitations of caddis larvae. In spring, as the water warmed, a small black spider or green buzzer would be added to a dropper, about four feet above the point fly. Last knockings, just as the sun was disappearing over the horizon, quietly wading out to the very tops of our thigh waders and putting out a long, straight cast towards the causeway, you could provoke really quite savage takes, but had to get your fly right down amongst the leaf litter to stand much of a chance of success. Usually, you ended-up with a lump of weed on the point fly, but just occasionally you got a big, irate brown trout which burned off into the middle distance. Many of those browns were three pounds-plus and in perfect condition, having overwintered and gained splendid fins and body condition from the past several months of feeding in the rich Pitsford waters.

We often wondered whether the orange tag, which seemed such a successful addition to the stick fly, may have picked up the last red rays of late evening sunlight as they penetrated the clear reservoir margins. I remember an occasion when a visiting American angler strolled along the bank, paused to chat with locals and politely asked if he could have a cast near to where they were fishing. Unused to such courtesy, they agreed and watched him effortlessly fire out a big bucktail lure with a crimson body on the end of a light, sinking shooting head. That chap was a champion caster and he used his skill to good effect. By working his lure along the base of the causeway, he latched into the finest Pitsford brown trout I ever saw caught. We will never know what it weighed because he sportingly released it without even bothering to net it. As he waded back out he quietly mentioned that it might have gone five pounds, then strolled-off into the sunset, rod over his shoulder. We just looked at each other and shook our heads in a mixture of admiration and disbelief.

One day, whilst boat fishing along the main dam at the far end of the reservoir, I saw a much bigger Pitsford brown trout, but it wasn't even hooked. I had resorted to using a fast-sink line and monster yellow muddler minnow, cast out as far as possible and then allowed to settle on the bottom. The buoyant muddler would flit along above the silt in the gloomy depths, down where the big fish lived, or so I hoped. This technique proved to be manifestly hopeless, except for one retrieve when I looked down over the side of the boat, idly wondering whether anything was happening. Immediately behind my muddler was an absolutely massive brownie which followed each pull of the fly and then stopped when the fly stopped; very close inspection, but no take. As the fly got closer to the boat, the trout kept on coming. I was fast running out of line and so I stopped the retrieve and let the fly dangle, just giving it the odd twitch. The brown hovered motionless, seemingly fascinated by this yellow apparition which had invaded its space. After a tense 30 seconds or so I gave the line another pull but, instead of provoking the hoped-for take from what was certainly a double-figure fish, I just saw a huge swirl as the trout departed back down to its shady lair. Despite re-casting many times, I never saw that fish again.

A similar thing had happened to me as a youngster in Somerset. In the absence of anything more productive to do, I was fishing a big yellow jointed plug on the Wellow Brook and that, too, was followed nose-to-tail by a big brownie which didn't attack the lure but which seemed fascinated by it. I never did catch a trout on that plug although it worked well on pike in local lakes. Perhaps brown trout escort large underwater invaders out of their personal space, not bothering to attack them if they don't pose any particular threat. However, this may endow trout with a capacity for reasoning which they really don't have! Pike, on the other hand are more than happy to attack something potentially edible even if it is big and brightly coloured. Pike, I'm sure, have pretty low I.Qs.

The cream of our Pitsford fly-fishing was with a light floating line, using small imitative nymphs, emergers and buzzers which copied hatching lake olives, chironomid midges or caddis flies. In common with most reservoir fishing, it was usually very difficult to work out whether trout were taking buzzers or sedges. If you were unlucky, things turned even more difficult and you got plastered all evening with little white, broadwinged *Caenis* mayflies. Trout would be rising everywhere but, in our experience, were completely uncatchable under these conditions. So disgusted did we become with these hatches of 'The Curse', that we usually packed up and went home as soon as we saw them hatching off.

At the back end of each season, Pitsford rainbows switch diet to roach fry and they then feed hard, well into the frosty weeks of autumn. Fry shoal-up and hide around anything that provides cover. One such spot at Pitsford was the boat landing jetty and an early morning stealthy stalk in its vicinity, just after first light, would usually reveal trout charging into the shoals, stunning fry and then coming back upwind to pick off wounded stragglers. We found that a long-shanked, foam-bodied floating fry pattern could be fished singly on a long, strong leader right in and around the fry killing zone. Prime rainbows of three to four pounds would sidle up to the lure and, if convinced, sip it down like a grasshopper. Setting the hook into one of those fish saw your spool empty like there was no tomorrow – what fighters they were!

You do, however, need a sharp hook for this game. One early morning, after seeing me lose a couple of fish, a visiting Yorkshireman wandered over to commiserate, looking at my fly he said 'Eh lad, no wonder they're gettin off, you could ride to York on that hook and not puncture yer arse'. I nodded and dug the sharpening stone out of my tackle bag. An alternative tactic, if the fry-feeders weren't so evident, was to strip a big white muddler back in around weedy shorelines and especially through a decent wave if it was breezy. Seeing a bow wave home-in on your surface lure was heart-stopping stuff, and it still is. There is no doubt that reservoir trout fishing can provide sport of the highest quality.

The west of Ireland: Lough Corrib

I was in the West of Ireland with an old friend Ian collecting historical sea trout catch records from various estates for subsequent analysis. On occasional days off, we drifted around on Lough Corrib, chasing trout. At over 30 miles long, stretching from Galway City in the South to Cong in the North, around 44,000 acres in surface area and with many, varied islands, the lough takes a bit of getting to know. The Corrib, as it is known by the locals, is an awesome trout water by any standards and it is worth doing a bit of research before you go. The Western Regional Fisheries Board map and information leaflet is well worth studying and you can contact this helpful band of fisheries biologists via the web site: www.wrfb.ie.

The productivity of the Corrib is immense. In May 2001, for instance, over 9,000 brown trout were reported caught at an average weight of a pound and a quarter. Many of these fish would have been returned. Whilst a little stocking of juvenile trout is carried out by the Fisheries Federation from their hatchery, the vast majority of Corrib trout are as wild as the wind and there is plenty of wind around most of the time in Connemara. There are four traditional methods of catching these fish: legering worms, trolling spoons or natural baits, such as minnows, dapping natural flies (mayflies, grasshoppers, daddy long-legs) or bushy artificials and standard fly fishing. We opted for the last approach, preferring to venture out on the late summer waters with ten foot, weight 6 rods, floating lines, long leaders and teams of bushy dry flies. My favourites at that time were G&H sedges, although now I would probably go for elk hair sedges.

Talking to Roy Peirce of Cornamona, a small village on the Doorus peninsula at the northern end of the Lough, Ian and I learnt the importance of concentrating drifts over the most productive waters. Roy, who runs a very comfortable fishing lodge (Grasshopper Cottage), is an expert Corrib angler with many years experience of both fishing and gillieing. We were told by Roy that, 'If you are keen to fish on top with dry flies in the evening, then drifting island shorelines is a good bet'. This advice we heeded. Out with the drogue to slow the drift and out with teams of flies, cast carefully over limestone boulder-strewn shallows of 1-2 metres depth and then twitched smartly back, the degreased leaders keeping the presentation as lifelike as possible. Many species of caddis fly pupae swim strongly for the surface, popping out of their skins pretty quickly and then skating along on their newly-dried wings, heading for the sanctuary of the shoreline. Much of this activity happens towards dusk and into the gloaming.

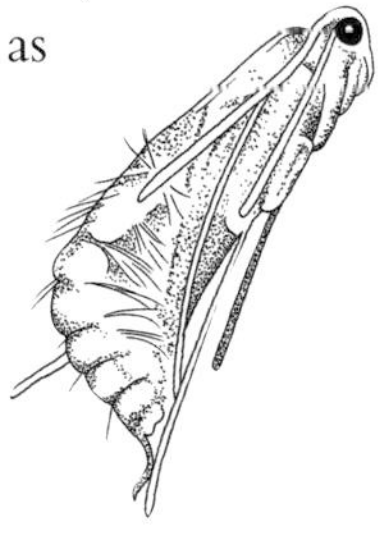

Twitching a dry fly back across the surface is an electrifying experience, especially when a trout materialises right behind it. Many of these wary fish inspect the fly and then leave it well alone, others give it a hard nip and miss the point, but just sometimes, one hangs on.

We had been told by another old Corrib hand (Ned) that these wild brownies fight at 'ten minutes to the pound'. This figure caused me to wonder – could this really be true? Ten minutes is a long time. As I sat musing, casting and retrieving, putting my flies right in amongst large wave-washed boulders, the rod was almost wrenched from by grip as a powerful fish raced for freedom. Ian back-paddled the boat to keep it away from the rocks, guiding it along the edge of the island. I just hung on as the trout first decided to explore shallows some 25 metres away and then changed its mind and powered back to circle the boat. This must have been worth watching as I first braked the edge of the spool, keeping my fingers away from the whirring reel handles, reeled back in like a dervish, then leapt unsteadily to my feet to try and stop the leader (and dropper flies) fouling the drougue rope. Ian, getting over his laughter, took pity on me and retrieved the drogue, the boat speeded-up on the breeze and off went the trout again on another high speed sight-seeing trip. What really impressed me was the rock-solid power of that fish. Making the best use of its broad fins and muscular body, it really went for it. The battle waged long and hard. At one point, I actually said to Ian that I didn't think we would ever see the fish in the boat – he replied, in his usual succinct way, with a one word answer, with two ll's in the middle. Finally, a combination of sustained pressure and good fortune paid-off and a three pound six ounce crimson and black spotted gillaroo graced the net. The fight had taken thirty five minutes; ten minutes to the pound.

Although I have only been lucky enough to fish it on a handful of occasions, Lough Corrib is my favourite wild brown trout water. Fine quality wild trout are caught right through the season from the chironomid (duck fly) hatches of early springtime (March – April), the olives of April-May, the Mayfly of May-June and the caddis flies (sedges) daddy long-legs and grasshoppers of early summer to the back end. Wild trout, having spawned in winter start to regain condition in early spring when they feed avidly on thick hatches of big, fat chironomids, also exploited by mallard and other ducks. Medium depth, weedy bays with silty beds produce the best duck fly hatches and trout gently fin along up-wind, head-and-tailing as they take pupae, emergers and adult midges sitting on the surface. This is testing fishing as the weather can be freezing cold, the trout choosy and fly choice tricky. If you get it right, however, this is a fine time to catch that glass case lunker which you have always dreamed of. Roy Peirce has just such a fish set-up in his lounge and it's a beauty.

Dapper days

Sitting in Grasshopper Cottage one afternoon, Ian and I looked out over the lough when Roy pointed out a flock of excited gulls hovering close over the water in the middle distance – 'Mayflies are hatching out there' was his verdict. We had collected mayfly duns and a few early daddy long legs from lakeside hedgerows the evening before and they lay safely tucked away in an old wooden box with a sprung, perforated lid. Not long afterwards, we were spinning along in a well-found boat, dapping rods bundled in the back and the box of flies stowed under a seat. We slowed right down as we reached the area with the gull activity, motoring gently upwind, stopping the engine and setting up the rods. An oar was slid into the rowlock behind so that the boat could be kept fairly square to the breeze and steered downwind towards areas of activity. Hooks were baited with two mayflies and a daddy long legs on the point. The waxy skins of the mayfly duns make them very buoyant and water-repellent. The daddy is thought to help represent the trailing shuck (nymphal skin) of the mayfly and its addition can make a big difference to catches on the dap. As we drifted, we noticed swirling takes in the ripple as hatching mayflies, a little slow off the mark, were engulfed by eager brownies. The breeze billowed the dapping floss out in a smooth curve so that the flies skittered and danced lightly across the surface. Long, light rods enabled us to vary the presentation from still in the surface tension, moving along at a slow drag on the breeze or hopping and skipping from wave top to top. Trout were immediately interested, but often swirled and missed the fly or neatly removed them, avoiding the hook. Sometimes, however, the take was followed by a confident draw on the leader as the trout moved away with the hook and a gentle tightening made contact with a Corrib torpedo. We both caught two or three trout between one and two pounds before the hatch subsided, the crying gulls dispersed and the trout swam off in various directions in search of their next meal. On the boards of the boat lay a brace of fish for supper, the others being released to fight another day. One of the trout was a spotty gillaroo whilst the other was slimmer, more silvery with dark fins and with just a smattering of small black spots. Natural variability; both were in superb condition. On a previous occasion, Ian rose, hooked and successfully landed a fine grilse on the dapped mayfly. I'm told that this isn't a rare event when fishing over rocky salmon lies in certain areas of the lough. A nice bonus during a days trouting.

By now it was mid-afternoon and the islands close-by beckoned, so we motored slowly through the rocky shoals and pulled the boat up onto a gravel beach. The ritual of Irish tea by the waterside began. From the bowels of the boat we retrieved the battered aluminium Kelly Kettle and collected dry twigs to arrange as a wigwam in the base with a crumpled bit of dry paper snuggled in below. One match sufficed to ignite the mini-bonfire and the water-filled kettle was lowered over the base, smoke and flames licking up through the central chimney. Larger twigs were dropped down this central tube to keep the embers burning as a pint or two of crystal lough water came gently to the boil. There is nothing to beat a hot brew of tea in the fresh Irish air, shared amongst friends after a successful fishing session. A piece of fruit cake adds luxury to the moment. We relaxed, lying back on the beach and idly scanned the water with binoculars for signs of action. Broods of mallard secretively searched sheltered bays for flies, wagtails gleaned pickings from the shoreline, gulls wheeled on the breeze, ever vigilant for new patches of emerging flies; it was Heaven just to be there.

Eager for action, a fellow angler further down the shore had drunk his tea, eaten his cake and strung-up a nymphing rod which he was flexing over the gravel shallows, propelling a single Walker mayfly nymph out toward trout cruising along the top of the breeze. The nymph looked perfect to us, darting through the crystal waters, but the trout had a different opinion, viewing it with such contempt that the angler switched to a traditional orange bumble on the dropper and a gosling on the point. These straggly local gosling patterns, tied with long, soft yellow hen hackles and which look so un-nymph-like in the hand, sleek down in the water into skinny, stream-lined life forms with 'legs' and 'tails' which splay out between the long smooth pulls of the retrieve. As is so often the case, local flies did the trick and two further fine browns were caught and released in the shallows whilst less assiduous fellow anglers finished-off the fruit cake. The trout weren't netted, but were brought to hand, finger nails sliding down the leader to the bend of the hook and the fish simply turned off the barbless restraint. This involved minimal hassle for the fish, no air in the gills, no handling of the delicate mucus layer on the skin and is truly sustainable angling.

Fry up

We were back on the Corrib in September, a fisheries conference in Galway allowing other priceless opportunities to commune with Irish

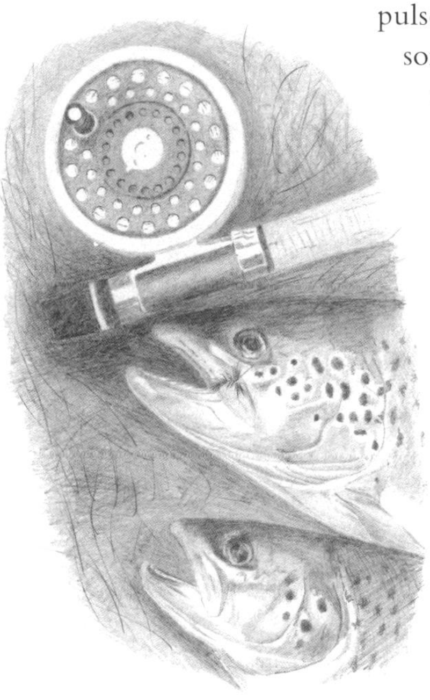

Nature. The weather, however, was not of kindly disposition and all self-respecting flies were hiding in the hedgerows away from the 45 degree heavy rainfall which battered them every half hour or so. We were out from Oughterard on the western shore amid a series of islands which provided some degree of shelter from the driving westerly wind. Seven weight rods were matched with sinking lines and six pound leaders straight through to single small minkie lures. Skues may be spinning in his grave at this affront to genteel tactics, but necessity is the mother of invention and we wanted to catch some fish. Amongst the rocky shoals and weeded gravel patches, some ten to fifteen feet below us, were hoards of perch fry which had hatched in May, then spent five months gobbling down *Daphnia*, duckflies, a host of nymphs, shrimps and tiny pin head roach fry. These little perch are themselves a potential prey for the bigger perch, pike and predatory trout which are never far away in this lough. Our minkie lures flexed and pulsed along close to the lake bed, sometimes stopping and fluttering down, then accelerating towards the surface or left to dangle for a few moments before lift-off and re-casting. September trout, packing on fat and muscle for the forthcoming rigours of winter spawning, were on the hunt. This may not have been 'matching the hatch', but it was matching the prevailing feeding conditions. Under these conditions, when your arm tires, a long line can be left to trail out of the back of the boat, fishing a curve of water where interception by a lusty trout is always on the cards. I don't spend much time lure fishing these days as I much prefer the floating line approach but, you have to admit, it does work!

We caught several prime trout, ranging from half pounders with eyes bigger than their bellies, through to sleek fish pushing three pounds. Make no mistake, a trout is an effective fish predator; a fast, nimble and precise tail-nipper, ambushing and chasing prey to devastating effect. All of our trout were bulging with perchlets whose spiny fins and gill covers provided insufficient defence against needle teeth and grasping jaws. Once trout get a taste for fish, they can specialise in a predatory way of life and go down the fast-growth road to feroxhood.

Ferox

At pretty much any time of the Corrib season, should you so wish, you can troll certain deep water spots for ferox. Much of this fishing is done in mid-summer when standard fly-fishing approaches can prove disappointing. Maybe, by then most of the ordinary-sized trout are bloated on their rich duck fly, olive and mayfly feast or, maybe, there is just a lull in the main fly hatches. Much as I would love to catch a ferox, the tedium of trolling (when I could be fly fishing) has always stopped me from spending a precious Corrib day in their pursuit. However, I do have friends who give it a go. Dead roach of several ounces are mounted on a flight of trebles, weighted down and trolled slowly over deep-lying boulder fields. These big rocks may act as cover for these wary fish which tend to be contacted in the same areas, trip after trip. The wrenching take of a ferox as it attacks a natural bait is, I am told, well worth the hours of trolling.

Traditionally on the Corrib, the natural trolling bait was a minnow (brigheen) which was deeply fished on stout gear until the rod-tip nodded down and battle commenced. An occasional tactic was to let the heavy, but buoyant, rod drop into the water to be towed around by the fish until exhaustion allowed its retrieval. Whether this is true, I don't know – it sounds remarkably like whaling to me - but some of these fish really are of whaleish proportions. Mighty ferox trout can weigh up to twenty pounds and, in their prime, are simply magnificent specimens. Whilst some are taken for the table or for the taxidermist, very many are returned alive to fight another day, a fine gesture of sportsmanship. We have no idea how abundant the Corrib ferox stock really is. These fish may be commonplace throughout much of the lough or they may be localised and readily catchable, giving an overly-optimistic impression of their numbers. When faced with such a lack of knowledge upon which to base management policy, it is best to be cautious. Catch-and-release trout fishing is commonplace amongst both keen locals and visitors who would have difficulty in keeping a catch in good condition for the home trip, anyway. When you have a natural resource as valuable and enjoyable as the wild trout of the West of Ireland, the last thing that you could want to do, it seems to me, would be to kill them all. The locals, with typical Irish perspicacity, agree. I recommend Peter O'Reilly's books of 1987 and 1991 for a great review of the wealth of game fishing available in the splendid Emerald Isle.

Carp fishing for trout

It was early July, the heat was on and my younger son, Will and I were fishing just after dawn in the early cool of the day. We were awoken in our little tent by a deafening dawn chorus of dozens of songbirds announcing their territories in deepest Wiltshire. Damned wildlife, we couldn't get back to sleep! A mole had burrowed along under our groundsheet the evening before and, as the light levels dropped, glow worms sparkled in the long grass around the woodland which borders each side of the Wiltshire valley. The lake, formed over a hundred years ago by the building of a substantial dam, covers many acres and is generally clear, with jade-tinted water. It's a superb place to spend a day or two just chilling-out. The chalk influence on the water chemistry makes for a productive piece of water and there are extensive milfoil weed beds on the shallows and marginal pondweed, lily, rush and reed beds. A survey with a pond net revealed dense populations of midge and caddis larvae, corixids, beetles, snails, mussels and tiny worms. The estate has mixed areas of sheep grazing meadows and woodlands, wild flowers abound and several species of bats live in old, overgrown stone caves and follies built around the lake. Early morning fishermen often see deer, badgers and foxes. Water voles paddle along reedy margins, grass snakes slither after frogs and varied dragonflies buzz around on the summer breeze. It's the sort of place which makes you light-hearted and happy.

We were fishing with freshly-cooked cockles, hoping for a tench or carp. The line on one rod started slowly to peel off the spool as a fish took off on a trundling run. The strike was met with dogged resistance, soon turning into rapid dashes for freedom, but the bamboo Mark IV Avon rod was more than a match for this fish. After a couple of minutes we were surprised to see a spotted snout slide over the rim of the landing net and a beautiful wild brown trout glaring up from the meshes. The size 10 barbless hook was soon slipped from the scissors and the fish duly admired, especially by Will who is developing a fine regard for wild trout. He slipped him back and our trout rested in the shallows, regaining its wind. This gave us a chance to have a close look at him and to ponder on the trout population living in this carp lake. How did they get here?

The fish was about three pounds in weight and probably four or five years old. The lake regularly turns up brownies of several pounds, including, this spring, a monster of over ten pounds. They all tend to be in fine fettle and, believe it or not, are hardly fished for as the syndicate which leases the fishing from the owners is a happy band of carp fishers.

The carp run very big and are hard to catch with any regularity. This is a challenge willingly accepted by the rods who cherish the tranquil fishery as if it were their own.
Trout living in the lake run up the principal chalk tributary to spawn each winter. This clear, clean spring-fed stream is full of Ranunculus, gravel-bedded and stuffed to bursting point with invertebrates and trout parr. The parr live in the stream for their first months, gradually dropping down to the lake where they hide amongst stones and under weed beds, trying to avoid the bigger predatory trout. There are no pike, but there are perch and big eels, both of which may also take unwary young trout. A couple of autumns ago, a good friend Chris and I watched an osprey fishing this lake. The bird would have been on passage south, visiting the lake on a refuelling stop-over en route to Africa. With such varied predators around, life for wild trout isn't guaranteed.

Those brownies which survive the various dangers which lake life presents, mature at two or three years of age and begin their annual spawning migration from the lake up into the small spawning stream. It must be quite a sight to see all those hefty trout vying for redd space on the gravel shallows in early winter. There must be intense competition for spawning habitat, given the large size of the lake and the tiny size of the stream. It is probably this bottleneck in habitat availability which limits the size of the lake's brown trout stock. After spawning, surviving kelts have only a half mile run back downstream to regain the sanctuary of the lake. With its burgeoning invertebrate fauna, plus perch and roach fry, kelts rapidly pack weight back on and regain condition. These big browns aren't ferox, but are big, well-fed chalk/greensand country brown trout, lucky enough to live somewhere where they are left largely to their own devices.

The lake used to be stocked with rainbows, but that fizzled out and the carpers took it over from the trout fishermen. The last of the rainbows have died out now, leaving the lake to the wild brownies, eels and bullheads which lived in the stream long before the big dam was built. The dam created the lake and along with it a new range of habitats, supporting much bigger trout and new populations of tench, perch, roach and carp. With typical adaptability, the wild trout carried on spawning in the headwater stream but took up residence in the newly-flooded valley. After more than a hundred years, they are there still and thriving.

Wild trout and grayling on the River Wylye

I took Will and his friend James out for a day on the Wiltshire River Wylye – they were keen to see what dry fly fishing is all about. The stretch we were fishing is unstocked, with fair numbers of wild brown trout and grayling plus some stockie browns which filter down from upstream. I have done quite a bit of habitat improvement work here over the years and the stream now has a lovely sequence of pools, gravel riffles and glides with abundant woody cover, water crowfoot and starwort beds. Trout and salmon spawn in winter and grayling, dace, bullheads and lampreys in the spring on the stony gravel riffles which are de-silted each autumn. The river throngs with wildlife from flag iris, goat willows and mayflies to kingfishers, water voles and otters. It's a beautiful fishery.

Our chosen spot was a sluice pool which used to serve as a take-off point for water meadow irrigation, but which has fallen onto disrepair. The pool has a central fast-water run where trout and grayling hold close to the bed beneath the turbulent main flow. Here, they are hard to reach with anything other than a heavily-leaded nymph and we left them alone as leaded flies are difficult for youngsters to cast. Towards the tail of the pool and along the side eddies, however, the current is steady and even and undisturbed fish were rising gently for the varied flies brought to them on the current. Casting was hampered by overhanging willows, but the cover which they afford holds the fish and so it's a necessary complication.

It was late summer and sedges were on the wing. I tied on a small, straw-coloured elk hair caddis on a barbless size 16, coupled with a 3lb fluorocarbon point and rolled out a couple of short casts to test the conditions. The boys looked on with interest, there were plenty of fish there and it was just a matter of time – right? Well, yes, actually – I caught a couple of browns in quite quick succession and the boys were mightily impressed. They both had a go and caught a trout each, too. All the fish were quickly released and we reviewed progress. How could it be that we caught so many fish, relatively easily, without spooking the whole pool in double-quick time? You guessed it; our fish were some of the stocked brownies which had dropped downstream. These trout are just not the full shilling when it comes to wariness. They are great for teaching youngsters but, ultimately, rather routine compared with the challenge of catching wild trout. I showed the youngsters the fins on the next fish we caught – they were well mended, but still had the tell-tale curly rays which betrayed their ragged stew pond history. These trout were also markedly lean, life in the wild had been a tough transition for them and few, if any, would have made it through the winter. Maybe it

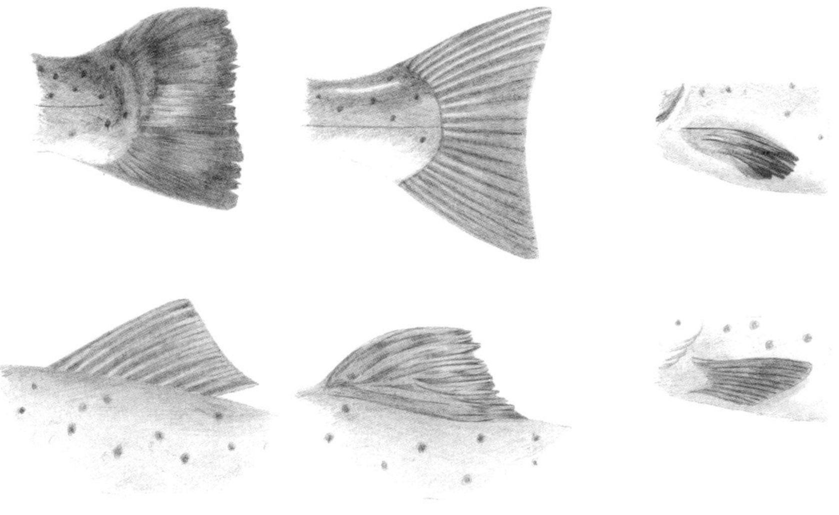

would have been best to take them home to eat, but C&R rules are rules, and they would probably help to feed the local otters which need a square meal more than we do, especially when the seasons click around to winter.

We moved on from the relatively easy 'stockie pool' to a series of medium-depth and medium-paced glides where we waded very slowly upstream, trying desperately not to spook fish. Here, there weren't any big stocked trout, just a sprinkling of smaller wild ones, interspersed with shoals of grayling. Whilst the trout stayed close to cover, the grayling lay out in the open in shallow scoops and pools, relying on their perfect camouflage to blend in with the gravel bed. The boys marvelled at their ability to disappear before our very eyes. Of most interest, however, was their reaction to nymphs. We switched to a pale grey, leaded shrimp selected deliberately so that we could see it. Fish can see everything. The grayling inspected it and then simply moved aside and let it trundle by. Either we had scared them or they were suspicious of the fly. The wild browns had made themselves scarce and were hiding under their logs, waiting for us to go away and so we moved on, but more quietly this time. We managed, eventually, to tempt out some medium-sized grayling with ragged hare's ear nymphs, dead-drifted along the bottom of a scour pool. Their magnificent red and purple dorsal fins shone bright in the afternoon sunlight as they finned back to freedom.

Deep nymph fishing for grayling can be even more effective if you are gently wading upstream, searching scoops and glides, fishing a team of nymphs on a short line – the so-called 'Czech nymphing' technique. The method involves flicking a short line of leaded nymphs (often caddis larva imitations) upstream, and following them back towards you, raising your rod until the flies are around your feet. Grayling can be caught literally right in front of you, if you have been stealthy in your approach. Takes can be induced by twitching the nymphs as they pass in front of fish. When using this technique, consider connecting-up your cast by blood-knotting tippet material from the bend of one hook to the eye of the next. No droppers, just two or three flies in-line, New Zealand style. This works well, but does tend to pick up weed and algae from the river bed. Whilst it is frustrating to have to clean your flies and occasionally to lose tackle on the bottom, you will potentially catch a lot of fish because the nymphs are behaving quite naturally and are right in the feeding zone next to the river bed.

It had been a great trip to the Wylye and much had been learnt by the youngsters. Stocked trout and wild trout are different propositions. Grayling hang deep but will suck in a nymph or wet spider, if correctly presented and if you haven't scared the fish with a clumsy approach. I hope to be able to go back sometime to have a go at the grayling with little black dry flies on fine tippets, the next stage in the boys fishing adventure.

Longleat

I was on the Wylye again, but this time working for the Longleat Estate, improving habitats over more than a mile of river. I wrote this book in the evenings and worked on the river through the day: no rest for the wicked! The project included extensive gravel cleaning, cutting back over-shading marginal goat willows, using woven live willow stakes to revet banks, creating series of new small pools with upstream-V current deflectors and narrowing over-wide sections of channel with low-level chestnut-staked bundles of hazel branches. This latter technique builds a new bank line at summer water levels, facilitating silt-trapping during high winter flows. Gradually, the accumulated silt is colonised by reeds and grasses, consolidating a new shallowly-shelving bank which contains low summer flows but which allows winter flood flows to rise gently over the top. There is a future plan to restore a large former water meadow along the lower end of the fishery which will help to retain floodwaters during the winter and early spring time, for the benefit of native wetland plants, wading birds such as redshank and snipe and a range of wintering wildfowl. The re-worked low-flow channel is deliberately sinuous and the current fast, encouraging the growth and spread of water crowfoot (*Ranunculus*) beds and other associated plants. Many species thrive in the mosaic of aquatic and wetland habitats produced; biodiversity is high and rising.

The Estate is very conservation-conscious and there is no stocking so all the brown trout are wild. This means that habitat quality must be kept good, otherwise there isn't any fishing. The fishing income helps to justify the money spent on keeping the river in good shape, fishing is catch-and-release and the syndicate is kept at a modest number of members many of whom seldom fish, but certainly enjoy it when they do. As we worked along the banks we saw water vole burrows and a diverse natural flora as there was no close-mowing of the bank edges, just some judicious strimming of pathways set back from the stream edge. Buzzards mewed and wheeled overhead, circling high on the thermals. In the wet ditches herons were joined by a rapidly growing population of white egrets, evidence of climatic warming as they extend their European distribution northward each year. Swallows and martins flocked along the valley, fuelling-up on a rich banquet of flies prior to their long migratory flight southward for the winter. Some of the flies never reached these birds, however, as they were intercepted by the brown trout, finning cautiously in the clear, chalky waters.

Although we were driving chestnut stakes securely into the gravel bed (it's damned hard work getting through that lime concretion!), the trout still held their lies not far upstream, continuing to rise for tiny midges and aphids, seemingly oblivious to our presence. However, as soon as we waded toward them, they raced for cover. Pleasingly, soon after we staked in the hazel bundles or built a new pool, trout moved in to take advantage of the new wealth of natural cover. Cleaner spawning gravels will produce more fry each spring, stronger weed growth in faster currents will support better fly populations and more year-round cover will promote better survival of wild trout of all sizes. The cherry on the cake at the end of a long, hot day, was to have three kingfishers arrow by and for one of them to dip a wing-tip into the water as it made a hard turn to the right, alighting precisely on the end of a newly-positioned chestnut stake. As the azure wings and vivid orange breast feathers shone bright in the late afternoon sun, Dave and I commented once again on the astonishing ability of wildlife to seize the advantage of new habitat opportunities. The kingfisher scanned the shallows for sticklebacks and bullheads while cautious trout continued to sip in flies along the stream edges, ever-vigilent for the threat of predation.

The king of the pool

A little way downstream from where we were working there is a big mill pool fed by an undershoot sluice. The powerful flow generates a big, fast back-eddy which circles the pool, rejoining the inflowing current in a steady stream. Riding in this back eddy lay the biggest brownie we had seen during the project. It must have weighed three and a half pounds, a big fish for a medium-sized chalk stream. This cock fish had a large head, a hooked kype of a lower jaw, a thin body and was probably approaching the end of its days at five or six years old. It would have spawned that winter, but was unlikely to see the following spring. In the meantime it was the king of the pool and aggressively defended the best lie. Directly above the fish, the fast inflowing water created a continuous heavy surface ripple providing ideal overhead cover. To the fish's right, there was an over-hanging shrubby willow providing additional sanctuary and underneath him was a dense waving crowfoot bed. The current speed on the nose of the fish was probably around a foot per second - just right. The lie was close to the brick wall of the sluice where frictional resistance slowed the current to comfortable cruising speed so that flies and other invertebrates swept in on the flow circled in a continuous supply of food. The trout switched between picking off drifting nymphs and rising for the juiciest of surface flies. Anything which he missed floated by to lesser trout eagerly waiting downstream.

An angler was sitting on the old timber seat to the side of the pool. He had a vintage Hardy bamboo brook rod with a slight set in the top section, a fine tippet and a carefully-chosen dry fly. The tippet was grease-free, the fly well-oiled. He was in no hurry, puffing away at his pipe, only too aware that time spent on reconnaisance is seldom wasted. A pod of half pound trout was spread out over the tail of the pool, singleton adult browns of a pound-plus holding station here and there over the pool bed and, at the head, the big, old trout, lying secure in his impenetrable lair by the sluice. A smile spread across the angler's face as he weighed up the challenge of the situation. A short cast would probably catch a short fish, with few problems, a longer cast might tempt up a middling trout from the pool, but even the longest cast would only just reach the leviathan and would scatter everything in the rest of the pool in the process. The smaller trout acted as sentinels for their big brother. Even if he could reach that fish without creating mayhem, the rapid surface current would skate the dry fly within a very few seconds. He might get him on a nymph, but would be much more likely to hang the fly up either on the willow above or the crowfoot bed below. In short, the king of the pool was safe. That's why he had survived for so long and grown so big. When he reached the end of his road, the next fittest fish moved on up the trout social hierarchy and those jostling for position below adjusted positions to take up the new slack. It's like a game of aquatic chess: the king is dead, long live the king.

Christchurch Harbour

The nearest piece of coast to me is where the Hampshire Avon and Dorset Stour join the English Channel at Christchurch, Dorset. The estuary has a commercial sea trout net fishery for a few weeks each summer and, currently, in view of the parlous state of Avon and Stour stocks, operates under an agreement to release all salmon caught. The sea trout, on the other hand, seem to be doing pretty well and the netsmen catch good numbers of fine fish each season, including double figure specimens. These sea trout interest me a good deal. Talking to the anglers who fish for them often, I find that very few even try to catch trout in the lower harbour where they have just run in from the sea. Bass, eels and flounders are caught there, together with both thin and thick-lipped grey mullet, but not many sea trout. Further up the harbour you reach the Clay Pool, fished by the Christchurch Angling Club of which I am a member. People fly-fishing this pool do catch some trout, but not what you would call baskets-full. Many believe that the pool has filled-in to some extent in recent years and may now hold fewer trout than it used to, most locals that I have spoken to reckon that it used to be better in the old days. Mind you, when talking to fishermen, most fishing seems to have been better in seasons past.

Christchurch harbour is a special place where otters live in reed beds and warbler's nests deep in the reeds are parasitized by cuckoos which call loudly in early summer in search of mates. Wading birds probe the mud for worms and shellfish, geese graze the marshes and cormorants fish the channels for the many small flatfish, eels, bass and mullet. Salmon and sea trout smolts have to get past these efficient predators each spring. Sea trout making a move upstream in summer are very wary, hugging the banks and deeper harbour channels. A clumsily presented fly has no chance. After dark, those night owls who persevere with light gear, small flies and a very stealthy approach should achieve success. Classic patterns like silver butchers and black pennels are reckoned to be the right medicine.

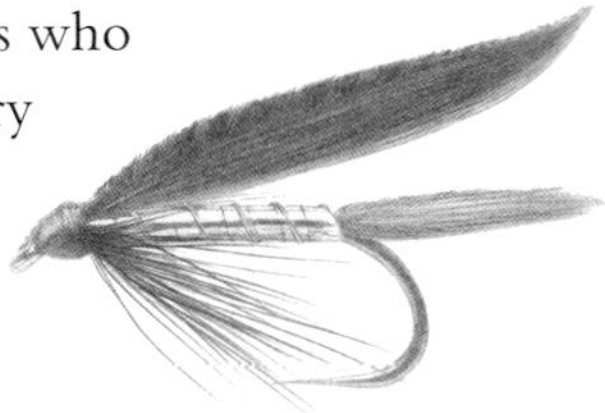

Just upstream from the Clay Pool, the performance of the sea trout fishery rises very markedly in the famous Bridge Pool situated next to Christchurch Priory. This little piece of fishing is situated right in town with holiday-makers wandering over the bridge next to the pool. It's not everybody's idea of a quiet fishing spot, but all fish migrating up the Avon must pass either through here or through the Waterloo Pool on the parallel arm of the river. On the Bridge Pool, anglers fishing from a moored punt, either trotting worms or maggots or fly-fishing, catch many fresh-run trout each summer. There is strong competition for tickets. Whilst much of the catch is comprised of small finnock, many of the sea trout are rather larger.

A particular story which springs to mind is of a visiting angler who popped into Davis Tackle in Christchurch for some advice from the then proprietor, Graham. The chap wanted to catch a big sea trout and the advice was to fish a tandem black lure on a sunk line, cast to the base of a small willow which sticks out from the left hand bank towards the tail of the Bridge Pool. This the fisherman did, persevering for hours until, around dusk, he finally got his trophy fish. Good advice plus dogged determination brought success. Why is the Bridge Pool fishing relatively predictable whilst the sea trouting in the rest of the harbour apparently so hit or miss? Well, I guess that the standard story of sea trout on the move upstream through the open, clear waters of a harbour not being free-takers really may hold true here. Also, the chance of putting your fly across the nose of a potential taker in such a large area of water is likely to be rather low. I am told that trout caught by the netsmen rarely have food in their stomachs and so, perhaps, they have more or less stopped feeding by the time they reach the estuary. On reaching the Bridge Pool, many fish will probably pause in their migration and may, in true Hugh Falkus style, become takers soon after occupying a new lie (see Falkus, 1977).

Teifi lessons

A few years ago I was invited by an old friend, Pat, to have a look at the River Teifi in west Wales, produce a short report and, after giving an evening lecture, go sea trout fishing on the river around Llandysul. A long day, but an eventful one! The river survey was fun and challenging, the company for the evening talk was typically Welsh - thoughtful and deeply interested in the fishing. The overall quality of the river was a revelation to me, with its mix of brown trout, sewin and salmon fishing: what a splendid fishery the Teifi is (see O'Reilly, 2005).

I was taken fishing by Pat and local photographer Melvin. Both explained the importance of remaining quiet and not getting into the water until it is really dark as sewin are very easily scared and, once frightened, are uncatchable. The time was right (mid-summer) and spring rainfall had brought plenty of fresh fish migrating upstream. As we waited until after sundown, trout which had been lying quiet through the day started to swirl and move around the pool under cover of darkness. Amid the hooting of tawny owls and the whir of the wings of numerous bats hunting over the river, we waded quietly into the margins of a deep glide with dense alder tree cover on the opposite bank. Pat recommended a size 10 silver butcher which he tied on for me by feel in the darkness. Although Pat and Melvin carry torches, they use them as little as possible.

We stood quietly in the afterglow of sunset, assessing the situation when Pat quietly said 'there's a fish – under the alders'. With the best will in the world and peering myopically into the gloom, I said 'where?' Pat has the ability to see sewin shimmer underwater as over many seasons he has honed his fish-spotting ability to become osprey-like. All that I could do was to believe him and try to get my fly in under the right tree. Extending line carefully, I aimed to land my silver butcher a few feet upstream of the fish and let it sink down to nose level by the time it reached him. To my surprise, this worked and a bright trout of two to three pounds hit the fly like a ton of bricks, surging off across the pool in a strong bid for freedom. After a spirited fight, he was slipped from the hook and released to continue his upstream migration, maybe a little wiser for the experience. I wouldn't have caught that fish without Pat's observational ability. Keeping your eyes open is a large part of being a good angler. If you want to benefit from this knowledge and experience and to attend one of Pat's well known flyfishing courses, have a look at www.dreamstreams.net.

Make hay while the sun shines

Sea trouting, perhaps more than any other form of trout fly fishing, requires an intimate knowledge of traditional fish lies: the shapes of pools, glides and shallows and the whereabouts of safe cover. On natural lakes, sea trout tend to shoal over rocky lies in quite shallow water and over ledges or sandy points off river mouths. Ghillies on big wild waters really earn their fee when positioning boats in just the right places for visiting anglers to cover these lies without scaring fish. This requires both detailed local knowledge and good boat handling skills. Shoaling is usual and so it follows that, if you spook one sea trout, you will probably spook the lot, but if you catch one carefully, there will probably be another one to fish for. Fishing from downstream is often a good move – a hooked fish can be played away from the shoal, leaving you with the possibility of catching a bag of fish from a good pool over the course of a well planned night's fishing.

A team of quite small (sizes 12 to 8) dark, slimly-tied wet flies incorporating some flash (silver or gold) is the order of the day, often fished on a slow sinker or intermediate line to avoid wake. By casting first onto the pool tail and then progressively further up the far bank, you approach the shoal from behind. Takes tend to come in purple patches of activity when the trout suddenly switch on their curiosity or aggression responses. You have to make hay while the sun shines with sea trout, going fishing when river and weather conditions seem just right. Keen anglers do a days work, go home for an evening with their family and then venture back out for a night's fishing on the river – a tiring and demanding way of life. No wonder keen sea trouters can look a bit worn around the edges during the summer. The rewards, however, are worth all the effort, being out there with the badgers, owls and bats, listening to the sea trout crashing about in pools, seeing them bow-wave across gravel shallows to rest on pool tails, maybe to nip at your carefully cast flies - wonderful. Remember that sea trout in peaty waters seem much more willing to accept flies during the day than sea trout in clear waters. I guess that this is mostly about underwater light levels and the ability of the fish to see you on the bank. Night time fishing isn't necessary under these conditions.

A few pointers on night sea trouting may be welcome:

- Wear sombre clothing.
- Use a strong leader – sea trout can really pull your string.
- Fish barbless, unhook fish in the water and kill only what you need. Remember that sea trout often recover from spawning and a fish returned today may be your fish of a lifetime next season.

- If you intend to wade, avoid fishing soon after or during really heavy rain. Up to your chest in a shingle-bedded river is not the place to be when a sudden spate rolls down river. Be careful, this really can happen.
- Don't wade until it is really dark and only wade where you know the lie of the river bed.
- Try to fish into the moonlight, rather than being silhoueted by it.
- Minimise the use of a torch.
- Choose a warmish night. Mist rising from the water under a crisp, clear, chilly starlit sky is a bad sign, in my experience Mild, windy low pressure fronts rolling-in from the Atlantic are a much better prospect.

The Dorset Allen

Close to where I live lies the valley of the River Allen, a lovely chalk stream which, despite a history of water abstraction and occasional serious pollution, still has otters, abundant fly life, native crayfish, lampreys, wild brown trout, grayling and a sprinkling of spawning salmon and sea trout in winter. The migratory fish head up from Christchurch Harbour, make their way up the Dorset Stour to Wimborne, and then turn right up the Allen. A fish pass is currently being built to overcome an obstruction to migration at an old papermill and so migrants should have more spawning and nursery habitat available in future.

The river runs clear and fast, the brown trout are wary and smart and the grayling are no mugs, either. So productive is the Allen that record-sized grayling are on the cards. I have only just started fishing this section of the river and, partly in return for syndicate fees, we are carrying out some habitat improvements – additional dead wood for cover, de-silting of spawning gravels, coppicing willows, fixing bank erosion problems and helping to manage the pike population, etc. The aim is to have a catch-and-release wild brown trout and grayling fishery with no stocking, at least for the time being. Just recently Dave Wettner and I worked through the middle beat, de-silting spawning riffles with our high-powered water jetter. Despite a clean-looking river bed there was plenty of silt just below the surface, probably with little or no through-flow for successful egg incubation. The systematic application of a water jet in the right areas has made a big difference to the spawning gravels. This work gave us the opportunity to wade slowly through pools and glides, seeing pods of fat grayling, literally around our feet, startled brownies and occasional languid chub. In the margins, under logs and flat stones hide native crayfish and on one big rock we found a neat pile of chewed-up claws and legs which were the remains of an otter or mink crayfish feast. Along the banks, just below summer water level, are many holes excavated by generations of crays. I guess that, as dusk falls, out come the crayfish to trundle around the river bed cleaning up detritus and hunting out prey. Just at that time, the otters come out too and a deadly game of hide-and-seek takes place.

One bright winter's afternoon, I took a guest, Trevor (the illustrator of this book) down to the river. Trevor wanted to catch a two pound Allen grayling and we forsook the fly and went trotting with our trusty centre pin reels. There is something especially nice about watching a float running down through a swim, hence the famous H.T.Sherringham quote along the lines of a float being pleasing in its appearance and even more pleasing in its disappearance! We fished double maggot on 3lb line, using a weighty float, bulk-shotted around a foot from the hook to keep the bait close to the river bed. A free-running centre pin reel can be checked slightly by thumb pressure on the edge of the spool and this holding-back of the float causes the shot to rise in the water and the tackle to swim up and over weed beds or gravel bars. In this way, by careful manipulation of the reel, all of the undulations along the bed of a swim can be searched systematically and grayling shoals located.

Over a couple of hours, we explored a fair stretch of this interesting little river, concentrating mainly on the deeper water, trotting our floats through long glides, gulleys and corner pools. On this bright afternoon we thought it likely that the fish would be avoiding the riffles, waiting until evening before venturing out onto shallows for the fly hatch. As we walked downstream, we noted spots which looked worth a second visit on our return journey. One particular glide and pool, completely enclosed by alders on our bank, looked a very inviting piece of grayling habitat. Because of its inaccessibility, we thought it may well hold the two pound grayling which we were looking for. By fording the river downstream and quietly making our way back up the far bank, we found a gap in the trees big enough to allow a cast into the top of the glide. Holding the float back hard, we could trot the double maggot down over the shallows, easing-off the pressure as the float entered the deeper pool.

Despite our caution, the sight of the rod scared a big sea trout which roared off downstream from the riffle and into the pool. Would this have disturbed any grayling present? Trevor soon showed that we needn't have worried by expertly extracting a brace of pristine two pounders, the best weighing two pounds five ounces. An excellent result, especially as the fish swam off strongly, none the worse for their experience. I aim to return this summer with a 4 weight fly rod and leaded shrimp to see if there is a two and a half pounder in that pool. It might be possible to get up there under those alders in a pair of chest waders, but will my casting be up to the challenge?

Our pleasant winter afternoon carried on as we ambled back upstream, with the catching of several smaller grayling and a few wild brown trout. It struck me just how easy it is to catch graying and trout on bait and how fly fishing really is a 'gentleman's handicap' which limits the potential impact of angling on wild game fish stocks. We could have emptied the river if we had wished. In fact, of course, we returned all of our fish and by keeping an eagle eye on the float and tightening immediately into takes, we made sure that all were hooked around the lips and could easily be slipped free with minimal fuss. Any hesitation with a take and the gullible grayling and trout would have swallowed the hook, I'm afraid.

Summer fly fishing on this stream is comprised of a lightweight rod, a floating line, a short, fine, clear, degreased leader and a fly which looks quite like what the trout are feasting on at the time. On a clean-watered chalk stream, this leaves a bit of room for observation and experimentation. There are plenty of pale watery and olive mayflies, Green Drake Ephemera mayflies, a whole host of caddis fly species, myriads of midges and reed smuts. The bed of the stream is crawling with shrimps, the bank side vegetation has caterpillars, beetles, spiders and grasshoppers. Hawthorn flies, alder flies, damsel flies and dragonflies are on the wing, too. If a trout has a real appetite, it could always try tackling a crayfish or one of the multitude of minnows which throng the shallows. No wonder wild Allen trout do so well and fishing friends have caught them to over five pounds from various stretches – very big fish in such a small stream. Amid this plenty, the trout can afford to be choosy, making them hard to catch and that's just fine with me.

This, I guess, is probably my final phase of trout fishing. I don't mind if I don't catch many and that's just as well where the trout are so wily. I am as pleased to find a half-eaten eel discarded by an otter, as I did just the other evening, or to watch wagtails catching hatching mayflies, as I am to cast a fly. The hunting instinct hasn't left me though, and I look forward to catching the big old trout I've marked down in the corner pool upstream of the bridge. If I do manage to catch him, I know that he will race back to the safety of cover on release. Come to think of it, the cover will probably have been provided by us in the form of a strategically-staked marginal oak log, and that seems appropriate, too. If the fish has to suffer the indignity of being caught, at least we can offer it safe sanctuary in return. That trout won't be an easy proposition, the pool is hard to approach and a back-eddy means that the fish may be facing up or downstream, but it's a challenge to look forward to, it will be fun and that, after all, is what fishing is all about.

REFERENCES & BIBLIOGRAPHY

Ade, R (1989) The trout and salmon handbook: a guide to the wild fish. Croom Helm.

Allen, K.R. (1938) Observations on the biology of trout in Windermere. Journal of Animal Ecology, 7, 333-349.

Aprahamian,M.W, Martin Smith,K, McGinnity,P, McKelvey,S, & Taylor,J (2003) Restocking of salmonids – opportunities and limitations. The Scientific basis for management of salmonid stocks in the British Isles. Guest Editor, David Solomon. Fisheries Research 62(2) 211-227 (2003).

Atlantic Salmon Trust (1984) The biology of the sea trout. AST, Moulin, Pitlochry, Perthshire, PH16 5JQ.

Atlantic Salmon Trust (1993) Problems with sea trout and salmon in the Western Highlands. AST, Moulin, Pitlochry, Perthshire, PH16 5JQ.

Bachman, R.A (1984) Foraging behaviour of free ranging wild and hatchery brown trout in a stream. Transactions of the American Fisheries Society, 113, 1-32.

Bagliniere, J-L, & Maise, G. (1999) Biology and ecology of the brown and sea trout. Praxis Publishing, Chichester, UK.

Ball,J.N. (1961) On the food of the brown trout in Llyn Tegid. Proceedings of the Zoological Society of London, 137, 599-622.

Buktenica, M.W, Mahoney, B.D, Girdner, S.F & Larson, G.L (2000) Response of a resident bull trout population to nine years of brook trout removal, Crater Lake National Park, Oregon. Wild Trout VII. Management in the new Millenium. Are we ready?

Centre for Ecology & Hydrology, Environment Agency, Joint Nature Conservation Committee (2004) Freshwater fishes in Britain: the species and their distribution. Harley Books, Colchester, Essex.

Champigneulle,A, Buttiker,B, Durand,P & Melhaoui,M (1999) Main characteristics of the biology of the trout in Lake Leman (Lake Geneva) and some of its tributaries. In Bagliniere & Maisse (1999) Biology and Ecology of the brown and sea trout. Springer & Praxis Publishers.

Clarke, B. (1975) The pursuit of still water trout. A&C Black Ltd, London.

Clarke, B (2000) The Stream. Swan Hill Press.

Cove, A (1991) My way with trout. The Crowwood Press.

Dawkins, R (1989) The Selfish Gene. Oxford University Press.

Dillon,J, Schill,D, Teuscher,D, & Megargle,D (2000) Triploid hatchery trout programs in Idaho – meeting public demand for consumptive angling while protecting genetic integrity of native trout. Wild Trout VII.

Old Faithful Inn, Yellowstone National Park.
Elliott, J.M (1989) Wild brown trout: the scientific basis for their conservation and management. Freshwater Biology, 21, 1, February, 1989.

Elliott, J.M (1994) Quantitative ecology and the brown trout. Oxford University Press.

Environment Agency (Annual) Reel Life (a magazine for anglers).

Environment Agency (2002) Inventory of trout stocks and fisheries in England and Wales.

Environment Agency (2003) Fisheries Statistics 2002.

Environment Agency (2004) National Trout and Grayling Fisheries Strategy.

Environment Agency (2004) Our Nation's Fisheries.

Environment Agency & English Nature (2004) The state of England's chalk rivers.

Euzenat, G, Fournel, F & Richard, A (1999) Sea trout in Normandy and Picardy. In Bagliniere & Maisse (1999) Biology and Ecology of the brown and sea trout. Springer & Praxis Publishers.

Fahy, E (1985) Child of the tides: a sea trout handbook. Glendale Press.

Falkus, H (1977) Sea trout fishing. H.F. & G. Witherby Ltd, London.

Fallon, N (1986) Fly fishing for Irish trout. Poolbeg Press, Dublin.

Ferguson, A (2004) Gene pool. Salmo trutta (Wild Trout Trust) Vol. 7, 2004, 48-51.

Fisheries Ireland News – fin. Quarterly newsletter of the Central and Regional Fisheries Boards of Ireland. Contact info@cfb.ie

Fitzmaurice, P (1979) Selective predation on Cladocera by brown trout, Salmo trutta. Journal of Fish Biology, 15, 521-525.

Frost, W.E & Brown, M.E. (1967) The Trout. Collins New Naturalist Series.

Fryer, G (1991) A natural history of the lakes, tarns and streams of the English Lake District. Freshwater Biological Association.

Gargan, P.G, Tully, P & Poole, W.R (2002) The relationship between sea lice infestation, sea lice production and sea trout survival in Ireland, 1992-2001.

Gathercole, P (2003) The Fly-tying Bible. Aurum Press.

Gamblin, M, Dillon, J, & Powell, M (2000) Recovery and conservation of the Henrys Lake Yellowstone cutthroat trout population. Wild Trout VII, Old Faithful Inn, Yellowstone National Park, October, 2000.

Gierach, J (1991) Where the trout are all as long as your leg. Lyons & Burford, New York.

Gierach, J (1993) Trout Bum. Pruett Publishing Co. Boulder, Colorado, USA.

Gierach, J (1997) Fishing Bamboo. The Lyons Press, New York, USA.

Giles, N (1989) Assessing the status of British wild brown trout, *Salmo trutta*, stocks: a pilot study utilising data from game fisheries. Freshwater Biology 21, 125-133.

Giles N. (1992) Status of wild trout populations in the British Isles. In "Freshwater Quality", the 16th Report of The Royal Commission on Environmental Pollution.

Giles, N & Summers, D.W. (1996) Helping fish in lowland streams. Game Conservancy Trust, Fordingbridge, Hampshire.

Giles, N & Summers D.W. (2001) Habitat restoration in lowland rivers for sustainable game and coarse fish stocks. IFM Annual Study Course Proceedings, Sparsholt 1999.

Giles, N, Westgarth, J & Hewlett, N (2004) Management advice for trout, grayling and Arctic char fisheries. Environment Agency Technical Report W2-045/TR.

Goddard J & Clarke, B (1980) The trout and the fly. Ernest Benn Ltd, London.

Goddard, J (1988) John Goddard's Waterside Guide. Unwin Hyman.

Greenhalgh, M & Ovenden, D (1998) The Complete Fly-Fishers Handbook. Dorling Kindersley, London.

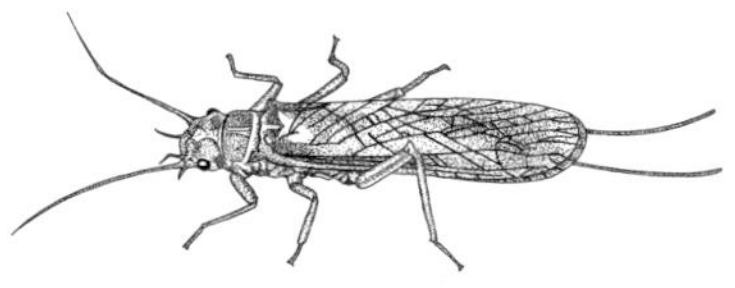

Guffey, S (2000) Persistence of native brook trout in Great Smoky Mountains National Park after 35 years of stocking with northern derived hatchery strains. Wild Trout VII, Old Faithful Inn, Yellowstone National Park, October, 2000.

Guyomard, R (1999) Genetic diversity and the management of natural populations of brown trout. In Baliniere & Maisse - Biology and ecology of the brown and sea trout. Praxis Publishing, Chichester, UK.

Harris, G & Morgan, M (1989) Successful sea trout angling. Blandford Press.

Harris,G (2000) Sea trout stock descriptions. Environment Agency R&D Report W224.

Hayter, A (2002) F.M. Halford and the dry fly revolution. Robert Hale, London.

Hunt, P.C & Jones, J.W. (1972) The food of brown trout in Llyn Alaw, Anglesey, North Wales. Journal of Fish Biology, 4, 1994-1998.

Hunt, R.L (1987) Characteristics of three catch-and-release fisheries and six normal regulation trout fisheries for brown trout in Wisconsin. Catch and Release Fishing – a decade of experience. Symposium proceedings, Humboldt State University, Arcata, California.

Hunt,R.L (1988) A compendium of 45 trout stream habitat development evaluations in Wisconsin during 1953 – 1985. Technical Bulletin No. 162, Department Natural Resources, Madison, Wisconsin.

Hunt, R.L. (1993) Trout stream therapy. University of Wisconsin Press.

Hunter, C (1991) Better trout habitat. Montana Land Reliance.

IFM (Institute of Fisheries Management) FISH magazine (published quarterly).

Jonsson,B (1989) Norwegian brown trout. In Wild Brown Trout, the scientific basis for their conservation and management, Freshwater Biology 21, 71-86.

Kreh, L (2003) Ultimate guide to fly fishing. The Lyons Press, Guilford, CT, USA.

Lapsley, P (2003) River Fly Fishing; the Complete Guide. Robert Hale, London.

Laikre, L, editor (1999) Conservation genetic management of brown trout (*Salmo trutta*) in Europe. See current web site http://www.qub.ac.uk/bb/prodoh/TroutConcert/TroutConcert.htm

Lucas M.C. (1993) Food interrelationships between brown trout and rainbow trout in a small still water fishery. Aquacultre & Fisheries Management, 24, 355-364.

MAFF (2000) Salmon & Freshwater Fisheries Review.

MAFF (2001) Review of Salmon and Freshwater Fisheries: Government Response.

Mahoney,D & Ruzycki, J.R (2000) Protection of native cutthroat trout using a removal program for a non-native predator: Lake trout reduction in Yellowstone Lake. Wild Trout VII proceedings, October, 2000.

Maitland, P.S (1966) Studies on Loch Lomond 2: The fauna of the River Endrick, University of Glasgow.

Maitland, P.S (1972) Key to the freshwater fishes of the British Isles. FBA, Cumbria.

Mann, R.H.K, Blackburn, J.H & Beaumont, W.R.C. (1989) Trout in chalk streams. In Wild Brown Trout, the scientific basis for their conservation and management, Freshwater Biology 21, 57-70.

McDowall, R (1968) Interactions of the native and alien faunas of New Zealand and the problem of fish introductions. Transactions of the American Fisheries Society 97: 1-11.

McDowall, R. (2001) Conserving and managing the Falkland Islands' freshwater fishes. Falklands Islands Journal, 2001, Volume 7, Part 5.

McGuane, T. (1999) The Longest Silence : a life of fishing. Yellow Jersey Press, London.

McGinnity, P, Prodohl, P, Ferguson, A, Hynes, R, O'Maoileidigh, N, Baker, N, Cotter, D, O'Hea, B, Cooke, D, Rogan, G, Taggart, J & Cross, T. (2003) Fitness reduction and potential extinction of wild populations of Atlantic salmon *Salmo salar* as a result of interactions with escaped farm salmon. Proceedings Royal society London B (2003).

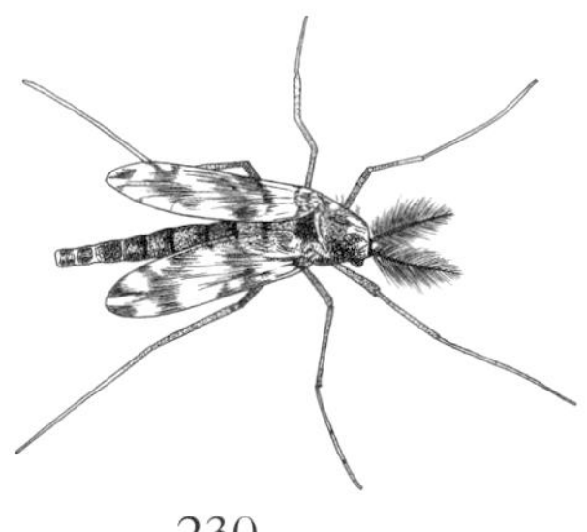

Nall, G.H. (1930) The life of the sea trout. Seeley Service, London.

North, E (1983) Relationship between stocking and anglers' catches in Draycote Water trout fishery. Fisheries Management 14, 4, 187-198.

O'Reilly, Peter (1987) Trout and salmon loughs of Ireland: a fisherman's guide. Unwin Hyman, London.

O'Reilly, Peter (1991) Trout and salmon rivers of Ireland: an angler's guide. Merlin Unwin Books.

O'Reilly, Pat (1997) Matching the hatch. Swan Hill Press.

O'Reilly, Pat (2004) Llandysul Angling Association, Current Affairs, February 2004.

O'Reilly, Pat (2005) A Flyfisher's guide to the Teifi valley. First Nature, Llandysul, Wales.

Plunket Greene, H (1924) Where bright waters meet. Philip Allan & Co. London.

Potter,E.C.E, MacLean,J.C, Wyatt,R.J, & Campbell,R.N.B. (2003) Managing the exploitation of migratory salmonids. The Scientific basis for management of salmonid stocks in the British Isles. Guest Editor, David Solomon. Fisheries Research 62(2) 127-142 (2003).

Salmo Trutta (Annual) Magazine of the Wild Trout Trust.

Sandison, B (1987) Trout lochs of Scotland: a fisherman's guide, 2nd Edition. Unwin Hyman, London.

Shelton, R (2002) The Longshoreman. A life at the water's edge. Atlantic Books, London.

Shields, B.A. (1996) Aspects of the ecology of the brown trout, *Salmo trutta* in relation to management of the fishery on the River Don, Aberdeenshire. PhD thesis, Department of Zoology, University of Aberdeen.

Slack, H.D (1957) Studies on Loch Lomond 1. University of Glasgow.

Stark,J, Todd, S, & Rider, L. (2000) Biological and socio-economic aspects of natural state catch and release regulations. Wild Trout VII, Old Faithful Inn, Yellowstone National Park, October, 2000.

Solomon,D.J. (1994) Sea trout investigations. Phase 1 final report. NRA R&D Note 318.

Summers, D.W., Giles, N. & Willis, D (1996) Restoration of riverine trout fisheries. Environment Agency Fisheries Technical Manual 1.

Thuember,T (1975) Fish and the blue ribbon streams. Wisconsin conservation Bulletin 40, 16-17.

TROUT Quarterly magazine of Trout Unlimited.

Turrell, W.R (1993) Oceanographic influences on Scottish west coast salmon and sea trout. Problems with sea trout and salmon in the western highlands. Atlantic Salmon Trust Blue Book, 1993.

Vincent, E.R (1984) Effect of stocking hatchery rainbow trout on wild stream dwelling trout. Wild Trout III, Yellowstone National Park.

Walker, A.F. (1994) Sea trout and salmon stocks in the western highlands. Report of one day conference: Problems with sea trout and salmon in the western highlands. Atlantic Salmon Trust, Pitlochry, Perthshire, Scotland.

Weaver, M (1991) The pursuit of wild trout. Merlin Unwin Books, Ludlow.

Wells, J (1987) Catch-and-release fishing, the Montana experience. Catch and Release Fishing – a decade of experience. Symposium proceedings, Humboldt State University, Arcata, California.

White, R. J & Brynildson, O (1967) Guideleines for management of trout stream habitat in Wisconsin. Dept. Natural Resources, Madison, Wisconsin, USA.

Williams, W.D & Aladin, N.V (1991) The Aral Sea: recent limnological changes and their conservation significance. Aquatic conservation: Marine and Freshwater ecosystems, Vol. 1, 3-23.

Wyatt, R (2004) Trout hunting: the pursuit of happiness. Swan Hill Press, Shrewsbury, UK.

Youngson, A.F, Jordan, W.C, Verspoor, E, McGinnity, P, Cross, T & Ferguson, A (2003) The Scientific basis for management of salmonid stocks in the British Isles. Guest Editor, David Solomon. Fisheries Research 62(2) 193-209 (2003).